Jon E. Lewis is the author of numerous books in the Autobiography series, including *England: The Autobiography*, *London: The Autobiography* and *Spitfire: The Autobiography*. His books have been published in languages as diverse as Japanese and Portuguese Brazilian, and have sold more than a million copies.

Praise for his previous books:

England: The Autobiography:
'A triumph' Saul David, author of *Victoria's Army*

The British Soldier: The Autobiography:
'This thoughtful compilation … almost unbearably moving'
Guardian

'Compelling Tommy's eye view of war' *Daily Telegraph*

'What a book. Five stars' *Daily Express*

Other books by Jon E. Lewis

World War II: The Autobiography
London: The Autobiography
Rome: The Autobiography
Survivor: The Autobiography
SAS: The Autobiography
The Mammoth Book of Native Americans
The Mammoth Book of The Edge

VOICES
FROM THE
HOLOCAUST

EDITED BY JON E. LEWIS

ROBINSON

Constable & Robinson Ltd
55–56 Russell Square
London WC1B 4HP
www.constablerobinson.com

First published in the UK by Robinson,
an imprint of Constable & Robinson Ltd, 2012

A copy of the British Library Cataloguing-in-Publication Data is
available from the British Library

ISBN: 978-1-84901-723-7

Printed and bound in the UK

1 3 5 7 9 10 8 6 4 2

MIX
Paper from
responsible sources
FSC
www.fsc.org   FSC® C018072

CONTENTS

INTRODUCTION

This is a history of the Holocaust against the Jews. The term 'Holocaust' is sometimes extended to other victims of the Nazis – Roma, homosexuals, political opponents – but the Jews held a special place in the demonology of the Third Reich. The Nazis' motive for the mass murder of Socialists – or even the Roma – was not the same, in type or extent, as for their destruction of European Jewry. This war against the Jews began in earnest in 1941, after nearly a decade of preliminaries, when Germany invaded the Soviet Union, bringing millions of Jews within the borders of the Third Reich. For four years SS 'special groups' and camp guards, aided and abetted by Wehrmacht soldiers and local sympathizers, waged war on the Jews; at the height of the persecutions, between 1942 and 1944, Jews were daily being murdered by the thousand. By the time of Germany's defeat in May 1945 six million European Jews had died; it was only invasion by the Allies that put a stop to the genocide, and saved the lives of Europe's remaining two million Semites.

During the Holocaust as many as two million Jews were shot in the open air, in streets and forest clearings; perhaps two and three-quarter million were gassed in the extermination camps; the remainder of those who perished did so from disease or malnutrition in the camps and ghettos, or were worked to death, or succumbed in the 'death marches' of the winter of 1944–5.

There are many who deny the scale of the Holocaust, or even the fact of its existence. The testaments of those who survived the genocide of the Jews comprise the prime evidence of the Holocaust, and it is some of these 'voices' that are gathered in this book to show the tragedy that befell both individuals and a whole race of people. I have also included the voices of the perpetrators – not for 'balance', but because the greatest indictment – and the most incontrovertible proof – of the Holocaust is the records kept by the SS themselves. Few of these records are as chilling as the dry, statistical report from the Commanding Officer of Einsatzkommando 3 in December 1941 in which he records the execution of 137,346 East European Jews, listed by place and number killed.

The Holocaust did not spring fully formed from the monstrous, collective head of Adolf Hitler, Himmler, Heydrich and other senior Nazis. Anti-Semitism in Germany and Eastern Europe had deep roots; the Nazis found it bewilderingly easy to turn ancient prejudice into modern mass murder. In dark corners of Europe, Christians had believed for centuries that the Jews killed Christ and that the blood of Christian babes was used in the making of Passover bread. Had Martin Luther himself not stated in 1543 that in payback for these 'crimes', synagogues 'should be set on fire' and the Jews driven from the land? Numerous European political entities took him and his fellow anti-Semites at their word. Throughout the medieval and early-modern eras Jews were expelled from one land after another, or confined to ghettos. On the surface, the nineteenth century seemed, at last, to bring enlightenment to the racial politics of Europe, and Jews were 'assimilated' into mainstream society and politics. Britain even had a Jewish prime minister, Benjamin Disraeli. Yet the integration was never universal; in whole swathes of Eastern Europe peasant pogroms against Jews continued unabated. These same areas – the Ukraine, Poland, Volhnyia – would offer enthusiastic support for the Holocaust once they were incorporated into the Third Reich. But supposedly assimilated Jews in urban, 'sophisticated', nineteenth-century society also found themselves on the receiving end of racism, constantly being vilified as grasping usurers and political Machiavellis. And aliens.

Such was the case in Germany, the most modern of major European countries. In 1881, a mere decade after unification, a quarter of a million Germans signed the so-called 'Anti-Semites Petition' which declared:

In all regions of Germany the conviction has prevailed that the rank growth of the Jewish element bears within it the most serious dangers to our nationhood. Wherever Christian and Jew enter into social relations, we see the Jew as master, the indigenous Christian population in a subservient position ...

After railing against the concentration of capital in Jewish hands and the baleful influence of Jews in the press and public offices, the petition called upon the Reich Chancellor to, *inter alia*, exclude Jews from all governmental positions, restrict their numbers in the judiciary, and expel them as teachers from the classroom.

Anti-Semitism was part of the fabric of German society from the outset. There was something else stitched into the weave: German nationalism was early defined by the sense of *Volk* and the primacy of the Aryan race. How toxic was the racist nationalism of Germany was demonstrated in a far-off corner of another continent, when the Aryan rulers of German South West Africa caused the deaths of 100,000 of the Herero and Nama peoples between 1904–7. Germany committed the first genocide of the twentieth century, as well as the largest one.

Among those who applauded the ethnic cleansing of South West Africa were the myriad *Volkisch* clubs and societies in Germany, which added a strand of occultism to the country's hyper-racist nationalism. One such society was the obscure Order of Teutons, founded in 1912. Those who wished to join the Order were required to sign an oath by which:

The signer hereby swears to the best of his knowledge and belief that no Jewish or coloured blood flows in either his or in his wife's veins, and that among their ancestors are no members of the coloured races.

Once branch of the Order of Teutons (symbol: the swastika) developed into the Thule Society which then became the German Workers' Party, later organized by Hitler into the National Socialist German Workers' Party (NSDAP), or Nazi Party. Fascism was not inherently anti-Semitic; Mussolini generally considered persecution of the Jews to be ludicrous, and the Spanish dictator Franco positively protected Spanish nationals from the Holocaust. But the German preoccupation with blood purity – rather than politics – meant that German fascism was irrevocably anti-Semitic. This was further exacerbated by Germany's defeat in the Great War. Loud and insistent voices were raised, blaming 'the Jews' for the country's shame – either because they were 'Bolshevik' traitors, or because they were arch-capitalist manipulators who put profit before country. In all likelihood Adolf Hitler was genuinely convinced that the Jews were responsible for Germany's woes, but he was not above opportunistic scapegoating to gain mass support. Whatever the root cause, it became his unshakable conviction that Germany's Jews should be removed from the face of the country in a race war. Hitler told an NSDAP meeting on 12 April 1922:

> ... there can be no compromise – there are only two possibilities: either victory of the Aryan or annihilation of the Aryan and the victory of the Jew.

In case anyone outside the beer halls of Munich and the NSDAP's 3,000-strong membership failed to heed his anti-Semitic message, he made it the motif of his political testimony, *Mein Kampf* (My Battle), written in prison following the failed Putsch of 1923:

> It is the inexorable Jew who struggles for his domination over the nations. No nation can remove this hand from its throat except by the sword. Only the assembled and concentrated might of a national passion rearing up its strength can defy the international enslavement of peoples. Such a process is and remains a bloody one.

In another passage he declared:

> The fight against Jewish world Bolshevization requires a clear attitude towards Soviet Russia. You cannot drive out the Devil with Beelzebub.

After meeting Jews in Vienna in his youth, Hitler wrote, he came to wonder:

Was there any shady undertaking, any form of foulness, especially in cultural life, in which at least one Jew did not participate? On putting the proving knife carefully to that kind of abscess one immediately discovered, like a maggot in a putrescent body, a little Jew who was often blinded by the sudden light.

And most ominously, in light of later events, he wrote:

If at the beginning of the War and during the War, twelve or fifteen thousand of these Hebrew corrupters of the people had been held under a poison gas, as happened to hundreds of thousands of our very best German workers in the field, the sacrifice of millions at the front would not have been in vain.

Only by destroying the Jews, Hitler argued, could Germany become great again.

His attack on the Jews was not confined to paper. He had already set up the brown-shirted Sturmabteilung, or 'Stormtroopers', in the Nazi Party, whose duties were divided between defending NSDAP meetings from the 'Reds' and beating up Jews on the streets.

Despite the high sales of *Mein Kampf* and the street antics of the Sturmabteilung, the Nazis were nothing but a strident right-wing sect until 1929, when the Weimar Republic began splitting asunder. Inflation began to rise, as did unemployment – the latter reaching three million by the end of 1929. Amongst the political benefactors was the German Communist Party (KPD), whose gains in membership and electoral seats created panic in middle Germany. Almost overnight, Hitler's NSDAP, a presumed bulwark against 'Jewish Bolshevism', became a serious contender for political power. In the Reichstag election of 1928, the Nazi Party had secured twelve seats; when Germans went to vote on 14 September 1930 they returned 107 Nazi deputies; in the elections of July 1932 the Nazis won 230 seats in the Reichstag. Hitler had enough deputies to form a government in coalition with other parties, but refused to accept any arrangement in which he was not Chancellor. The political crisis rumbled on, and fresh elections were called for 6 November 1932.

To the dismay of Hitler, Nazi votes and seats fell (the latter to 196). He need not have worried. In the end, to borrow Alan Bullock's famous maxim, Hitler was 'jobbed into power by a backstairs intrigue'. Faced with the prospect of a KPD-Socialist government, the parties of the right and centre struck a deal in which Hitler would head a coalition. He grabbed his chance: on 30 January 1933 the forty-three-year-old Austrian former corporal was appointed Chancellor.

The Holocaust had already begun, with the murder of eight Jews by the Sturmabteilung in Berlin on 1 January 1930. With the Nazis' seizing of power the eradication of Jewry became official policy; for the first time in history a state would dedicate itself to the genocide of a people. Six million more Jews would follow the victims of Berlin into the grave.

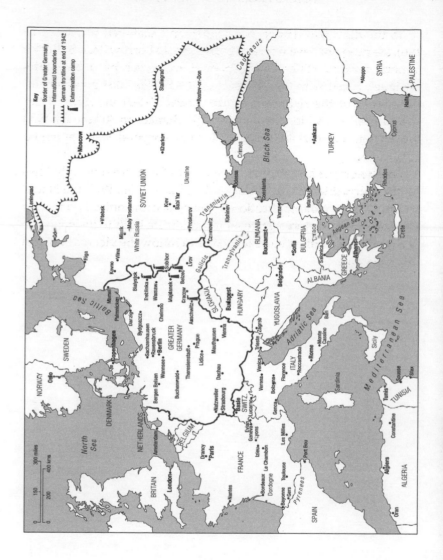

Key

Border of Greater Germany

International boundaries

German frontline at end of 1942

Extermination camp

Moscow

Leningrad

Stalingrad

Caucasus

Rostov-on-Don

Kharkov

Crimea

Black Sea

SOVIET UNION

White Russia

Vitebsk

Minsk

Maly Trostanets

Ukraine

Kiev

Babi Yar

Proskurov

Czernowitz

Kishinev

Odessa

Constanta

Varna

Ankara

TURKEY

Aleppo

SYRIA

PALESTINE

Haifa

Cyprus

Riga

Kovno

Vilna

Memel

Palmnicken

Danzig

Bialystok

Treblinka

Warsaw

Majdanek

Sobibor

Belzec

Lwow

Galicia

Transnistria

Transylvania

RUMANIA

Bucharest

BULGARIA

Sofia

Rhodes

Crete

Aegean Sea

GREECE

Athens

Salonica

Thrace

ALBANIA

Belgrade

YUGOSLAVIA

Zagreb

Trieste

Venice

ITALY

Rome

Monte Cassino

Roccastrada

Florence

Bologna

Genoa

Verona

Vienna

Bari

Adriatic Sea

Mediterranean Sea

Sardinia

Sicily

Tunis

TUNISIA

Sousse

Sfax

Constantine

ALGERIA

Algiers

Oran

Port Bou

Pyrenees

Gers

Bayonne

Toulouse

Bordeaux

Dordogne

Nantes

FRANCE

Paris

Drancy

Izieu

Le Chambon

Lyons

Evian

Geneva

Lucerne

SWITZ.

Basle

Natzweiler

Strasbourg

Les Milles

SPAIN

BRITAIN

London

North Sea

Amsterdam

NETHERLANDS

BELGIUM

Bergen Belsen

Buchenwald

Theresienstadt

Lidice

Dachau

Mauthausen

GREATER GERMANY

Prague

Ravensbruck

Sachsenhausen

Berlin

Wannsee

Bydgoszcz

Chelmno

Cracow

Auschwitz

SLOVAKIA

Budapest

HUNGARY

Copenhagen

DENMARK

NORWAY

Oslo

SWEDEN

Baltic Sea

0   150   300 miles

0   200   400 kms

PART I: SPARK

The Nazis and the Jews
in Germany, 1933–1938

On the bleak winter's day of 30 January 1933, shortly before noon, Adolf Hitler took office as Chancellor of Germany. He swore the following oath:

> *I will employ my strength for the welfare of the German people, protect the Constitution and laws of the German people, conscientiously discharge the duties imposed on me and conduct my affairs of office impartially and with justice to everyone.*

Not a word of this oath would Hitler go on to observe, except in the breaching of it. Within four days he had persuaded Paul von Hindenburg, President of Germany, to sign a decree banning public meetings and publications likely to endanger public security. In other words, meetings by and newspapers of the organizations opposed to Hitler. On 27 February the Reichstag building was set afire. The arson was allegedly the work of a deranged Communist Dutchman, Marinus van der Lubbe; more likely the Nazis set the building alight themselves. Whatever the true facts were, the incident gave Hitler the opportunity to issue more decrees undermining both the constitution and basic liberties, including free speech and right of assembly. House searches no longer required warrants, while a rule regarding 'protective custody' legalized arbitrary incarceration. Germany had taken the first decisive steps towards dictatorship; henceforth the heavy banging on the door at night, the stamp of the goose-step, and pop-pop-pop of the *Maschinenpostole* would become the soundtrack of the Third Reich.

The Reichstag is Set Alight, Berlin, 27 February 1933
D. SEFTON DELMER

Sefton Delmer was a journalist working for the British *Daily Express*.

> 'This is a God-given signal! If this fire, as I believe, turns out to be the handiwork of Communists, then there is nothing that shall stop us now crushing out this murderous pest with an iron fist.'

Adolf Hitler, Fascist Chancellor of Germany, made this dramatic declaration in my presence tonight in the hall of the burning Reichstag building.

The fire broke out at 9.45 tonight in the Assembly Hall of the Reichstag.

It had been laid in five different corners and there is no doubt whatever that it was the handiwork of incendiaries.

One of the incendiaries, a man aged thirty, was arrested by the police as he came rushing out of the building, clad only in shoes and trousers, without shirt or coat, despite the icy cold in Berlin tonight.

Five minutes after the fire had broken out I was outside the Reichstag watching the flames licking their way up the great dome into the tower.

A cordon had been flung round the building and no one was allowed to pass it.

After about twenty minutes of fascinated watching I suddenly saw the famous black motor car of Adolf Hitler slide past, followed by another car containing his personal bodyguard.

I rushed after them and was just in time to attach myself to the fringe of Hitler's party as they entered the Reichstag.

Never have I seen Hitler with such a grim and determined expression. His eyes, always a little protuberant, were almost bulging out of his head.

Captain Göring, his right-hand man, who is the Prussian Minister of the Interior, and responsible for all police affairs, joined us in the lobby. He had a very flushed and excited face.

'This is undoubtedly the work of Communists, Herr Chancellor,' he said.

'A number of Communist deputies were present here in the Reichstag twenty minutes before the fire broke out. We have succeeded in arresting one of the incendiaries.'

'Who is he?' Dr Goebbels, the propaganda chief of the Nazi Party, threw in.

'We do not know yet,' Captain Göring answered, with an ominously determined look around his thin, sensitive mouth. 'But we shall squeeze it out of him, have no doubt, doctor.'

We went into a room. 'Here you can see for yourself, Herr Chancellor, the way they started the fire,' said Captain Göring, pointing out the charred remains of some beautiful oak panelling.

'They've hung cloths soaked in petrol over the furniture here and set it alight.'

We strode across another lobby filled with smoke. The police barred the way. 'The candelabra may crash any moment, Herr Chancellor,' said a captain of the police, with his arms outstretched.

By a detour we next reached a part of the building which was actually in flames. Firemen were pouring water into the red mass.

Hitler watched them for a few moments, a savage fury blazing from his pale blue eyes.

Then we came upon Herr von Papen, urbane and debonair as ever.

Hitler stretched out his hand and uttered the threat against the Communists which I have already quoted. He then turned to Captain Göring. 'Are all the other public buildings safe?' he questioned.

'I have taken every precaution,' answered Captain Göring. 'The police are in the highest state of alarm, and every public building has been specially garrisoned. We are waiting for anything.'

It was then that Hitler turned to me. 'God grant,' he said, 'that this is the work of the Communists. You are witnessing the beginning of a great new epoch in German history. This fire is the beginning.'

And then something touched the rhetorical spring in his brain.

'You see this flaming building,' he said, sweeping his hand dramatically around him. 'If this Communist spirit got hold of Europe for but two months it would be all aflame like this building.'

By 12.30 the fire had been got under control. Two Press rooms were still alight, but there was no danger of the fire spreading.

Although the glass of the dome has burst and crashed to the ground the dome still stands.

So far it has not been possible to disentangle the charred debris and see whether the bodies of any incendiaries, who may have been trapped in the building, are among it.

At the Prussian Ministry of the Interior a special meeting was called late tonight by Captain Göring to discuss measures to be taken as a consequence of the fire.

The entire district from the Brandenburg Gate, on the west, to the River Spree, on the east, is isolated tonight by numerous cordons of police.

There would be many victims of Nazi injustice, but no one would suffer more than the Jews of Germany and Europe. With the *Machtergreifung* – the seizure of power – Hitler's long-cherished dreams of purging the Jews from Germany could be put into effect. After bullying and cajoling the Reichstag to support his Enabling Act of 23 March, which gave a pseudo-legal basis to the dictatorship of the National Socialist Germany Workers' Party, Hitler turned immediately to the 'Jewish Question', summoning Joseph Goebbels, Minister of Public Enlightenment and Propaganda, to his holiday retreat at Berchtesgaden. Goebbels noted in his diary that Hitler's view was:

> *We shall only be able to combat the falsehoods abroad if we get at those who originated them or at those Jews living in Germany who have thus far remained unmolested. We must, therefore, proceed to a large-scale boycott of all Jewish business in Germany. Perhaps the foreign Jews will think better of the matter when their racial comrades in Germany begin to get it in the neck.*

The NSDAP leadership called for a one-day boycott of Jewish businesses on Saturday, 1 April 1933. Windows were daubed with anti-Jewish slogans, chiefly: *Deutsche, kauft nicht bei Juden! Die Juden sind unser Unglück!* (Germans, don't buy from Jews! The Jews are our misfortune!). Pairs of armed SA guards stood outside and prevented 'German' customers from entering the emporia.

Jewish doctors and professionals were also boycotted. Or worse. Members of the 400,000-strong Sturmabteilung – the Nazis' private army – were well versed in terror tactics, and in March 1933 began the systematic physical intimidation of Jewish judges and lawyers. The SA objected not only to the 'defiling' of the German justice system by Jewish blood; they also feared that Jewish lawyers, and the courts as a whole, might halt the Nazi Revolution.

The Brown Shirts Throw Out Jewish Judges, Berlin, 31 March 1933
SEBASTIAN HAFFNER

Sebastian Haffner was an articled clerk in the Berlin *Kammergericht*, the highest court in Prussia. Although himself an 'Aryan', Haffner's best friend and girlfiend were Jewish:

I went to the *Kammergericht*. It stood there, cool and grey as always, set back from the street in a distinguished setting of lawns and trees. Its halls were filled with the hushed fluttering of barristers in their bat-like, black silk gowns, carrying briefcases under their arms, with concentrated, serious expressions on their faces. Jewish barristers were pleading in court as though this day were a day like any other

Not being due in court, I went to the library (as though this were a day like any other), settled down at one of the long work tables, and started reading a document about which I had to give an opinion. Some complicated affair with intricate points of law. I carried the heavy legal tomes to my place and surrounded myself with them. I looked up decisions of the high courts of the Reich and made notes. As always, the high-ceilinged, spacious room was filled with the inaudible electricity of many minds hard at work. In making pencil marks on paper, I was setting the instruments of the law to work on the details of my case, summarising, comparing, weighing the importance of this or that word in a contract, investigating what bearing this or that clause would have on the matter, according to the precedents. When I scribbled a few words something happened, like the first cut in a surgical operation: a question was clarified, a component of a judicial decision put in place. Not the final decision, naturally: 'It is thus irrelevant whether the plaintiff ... so it remains to investigate whether ...' Careful, precise, silent work. Everybody in the room was similarly immersed in their own cases. Even the ushers, somewhere between beadles and policemen, moved more quietly here in the library, and seemed to try and make themselves invisible. The room was full of extreme silence, a silence filled with the high tension of deeply concentrated work. It was like a silent concert. I loved this atmosphere. At home I would have been unable to work; today, here it was perfectly easy. Your thoughts just could not stray. It was like being in a fortress, or better, a test-tube. No breath came in from the outside world; here there was no revolution.

What was the first noticeable noise? A door banging? A distant sound like an order being given? Suddenly everybody raised their heads, and strained to hear what it was. The room was still utterly quiet: but the quality of the silence had changed. It was no longer the silence of concentrated work. It was filled with alarm and agitation. There was a clatter of footsteps outside in the corridor, the sound of rough boots on the stairs, then a distant indistinct din, shouts, doors banging. A few people got up and went to the door, looked out, and came back. One or two approached the ushers and spoke quietly with them – in here no one ever raised their voice. The noise from outside grew stronger. Somebody spoke into the silence: 'SA.' Then, not particularly loudly, somebody else said, 'They're throwing out the Jews,' and a few others laughed. At that moment this laughter alarmed me more than what was actually happening. With a start I realized that there were Nazis working in this room. How strange.

Gradually the disturbance took shape – at first it had been intangible. Readers got up, tried to say something to one another, paced about slowly to no great purpose. One man, obviously a Jew, closed his books, packed his documents and left. Shortly afterwards somebody, perhaps a superintendent, appeared in the doorway and announced clearly but calmly, 'The SA are in the building. The Jewish gentlemen would do well to leave.' Almost at once we heard shouts from outside: 'Out with the Jews!' A voice answered, 'They've already gone,' and again I heard two or three merry giggles, just as before. I could see them now. They were *Referendars* just like me …

The scouts later explained what had happened in the main part of the building. No atrocities, why, certainly not! Everything went extremely smoothly. The courts had, for the most part, adjourned. The judges had removed their robes and left the building quietly and civilly, going down the staircase lined with SA men. The only place where there had been trouble was the barristers' room. A Jewish barrister had 'caused a fuss' and been beaten up. Later I heard who it was. He had been wounded five times in the last war, had lost an eye, and even been promoted to captain. It had probably been his misfortune that he still remembered the tone to use with mutineers.

In the meantime, the intruders had arrived at the library. The door was thrust open and a flood of brown uniforms surged in. In a booming voice, one of them, clearly the leader, shouted, 'Non-Aryans must leave the premises immediately.' It struck me that he used the careful expression 'non-Aryans', but also a rather colloquial expression for 'premises'. Someone, probably the same person as before, answered, 'They've already left.' Our ushers stood there as though they were about to salute. My heart beat heavily. What should I do, how keep my poise? Just ignore them, do not let them disturb me. I put my head down over my work. I read a few sentences mechanically: 'The defendant's claim that ... is untrue, but irrelevant ...' Just take no notice!

Meanwhile a Brown Shirt approached me and took up position in front of my work table. 'Are you Aryan?' Before I had a chance to think, I had said, 'Yes.' He took a close look at my nose – and retired. The blood shot to my face. A moment too late I felt the shame, the defeat. I had said, 'Yes'! Well, in God's name, I was indeed an 'Aryan'. I had not lied, I had allowed something much worse to happen. What a humiliation, to have answered the unjustified question as to whether I was 'Aryan' so easily, even if the fact was of no importance to me! What a disgrace to buy, with a reply, the right to stay with my documents in peace! I had been caught unawares, even now. I had failed my very first test. I could have slapped myself.

Haffner eventually left Germany for Britain, where he worked for the *Observer*.

In these early days of the Third Reich the boycotts and street hooliganism of the Nazis caused anxiety, even among those sympathetic to the swastika. Hindenburg himself complained to Hitler on 4 April 1933:

In the last few days a whole series of cases has been reported to me in which war-wounded judges, lawyers and civil servants in the judiciary, with unblemished records of service, have been forcibly furloughed and will later be dismissed simply because they are of Jewish origin. For me personally, revering those who died in the war and grateful to those who survived and to the wounded who suffered, such treatment of Jewish war veterans in the civil service is altogether intolerable ... If they were worthy to fight and bleed for Germany, then they should also be considered worthy to continue serving the fatherland in their professions.

Hitler replied that the solution to the Jewish problem 'will be carried out legally, and not by capricious acts'. It was a half-truth, because 'capricious acts', cheered on by Julius Streicher's racist *Der Stürmer*, were by now daily events.

Throughout March and April gangs of SA and SS – the Schutzstaffel, the Nazis' elite paramilitary guard – wandered the streets of Germany beating up Jews. Behind closed doors, the SA were getting away with murder. Among the dead was a young Jewish sportsman, Siegbert Kindermann, beaten to death in the SA barracks in Berlin and his corpse thrown out of the window. A large swastika had been cut into his chest. More ominous still, in March the regime had opened its first concentration camp, on the site of a former gunpowder factory at Dachau, outside Munich. By the last day of March more than 15,000 'enemies' of the Reich had been rounded up in Prussia and put in 'protective custody' in Dachau and Oranienburg. They included Communists, Socialists, homosexuals and Jews.

A year later a central command structure for Dachau and its imitations was formalized: all prison guards were organized into the Totenkopfverbände, the 'Death's Head' units of the SS. By March of 1934 there were seven concentration camps in Germany.

The Nazi terror was not confined to boycotts and beatings of adults. Jewish children found themselves having to endure bullying almost daily.

'It was bullying all down the line': A Jewish Childhood in Berlin, 1933
JOHN SILBERMANN

I was only seven years of age in 1933 and I had just started school a year before. There were warnings from parents and others not to get mixed up in fights with the *Hitler Jugend* (Hitler Youth). The *Hitler Jugend*, if you want to give it its kindest interpretation, was a sort of Boy Scouts. Of course the Jews were not wanted, Jews were to be chased and beaten up. After 1933 it was just accepted that if you were a Jewish child you were liable to be beaten up, bullied or whatever else they chose to do with you. It was no use appealing to policemen or teachers because they're not supposed to interfere or even be interested in helping you because you are perceived as an enemy of the state. That was fed into my mind as a matter of self-preservation. One took care; travelling to the Jewish school on the public trains, we used to travel in groups of twos and threes together, which gave a certain amount of protection. However, one stayed clear of travelling large groups as that would be seen as provocative, and as we didn't wear swastika badges or *Hitler Jugend* uniforms, we were clearly identifiable. The bullying and verbal assault was not confined to German children: it was quite common if some adult, who was nothing more than an ignorant thug, called you names, or kicked you. It was bullying all down the line and that was totally accepted.

The one grain of truth in Hitler's reply to Hindenburg of April 1933 was that, for all the beatings and baitings of Germany's 500,000 Jews, the main thrust of Nazi anti-Semitism *was* initially channelled into legal sanctions. For the first five years of the Reich, the Nazi government concentrated on restricting the professional and economic activity of Jews through legislative means, beginning on 7 April 1933 with the Law for the Restoration of the Professional Civil Service. Article 3, section 1, specified that:

> *Civil servants who are not of Aryan descent are to be retired; if they are honorary officials, they are to be dismissed from their official status.*

Due to the insistence of Hindenburg, war veterans were exempt. In case there was any confusion as to who was 'non-Aryan', an implementing decree appeared four days later defining the term:

> *It is enough for one parent or grandparent to be non-Aryan. This is to be assumed especially if one parent or one grandparent was of the Jewish faith.*

A further battery of more than fifty discriminatory laws prevented Jews from entering government and the professions, as well as restricting the educational opportunities open to Jewish children, by firstly limiting their numbers in state schools (under the Law Against the Overcrowding of German Schools), then by segregating them in Jewish-only schools.

On 15 September 1935 a special sitting of the Reichstag, held during the Nazi Party congress in Nuremberg, passed two new laws which sent a cold shudder through European Jewry and civilized society collectively: the Law for the Protection of German Blood and German Honour, and the Reich Citizenship Law, which was further expanded by the First Decree to the Reich Citizenship Law.

Law for the Protection of German Blood and Honour, 15 September 1935
THE FÜHRER AND REICH CHANCELLOR, THE REICH MINISTER OF THE INTERIOR, THE REICH MINISTER OF JUSTICE, THE DEPUTY OF THE FÜHRER

Imbued with the insight that the purity of German blood is prerequisite for the continued existence of the German people and inspired by the inflexible will to ensure the existence of the German nation for all times, the Reichstag has unanimously adopted the following law, which is hereby promulgated:

§ 1   (1) Marriages between Jews and subjects of German or kindred blood are forbidden. Marriages nevertheless concluded are invalid, even if concluded abroad to circumvent this law.

(2) Only the State Attorney may initiate the annulment suit.

§ 2   Extramarital intercourse between Jews and subjects of German or kindred blood is forbidden.

§ 3   Jews must not employ in their households female subjects of German or kindred blood who are under 45 years old.

§ 4   (1) Jews are forbidden to fly the Reich and national flag and to display the Reich colours.

(2) They are, on the other hand, allowed to display the Jewish colours. The exercise of this right enjoys the protection of the state.

§ 5 (1) Whoever violates the prohibition in § 1 will be punished by penal servitude.

(2) A male who violates the prohibition in § 2 will be punished either by imprisonment or penal servitude.

(3) Whoever violates the provision of §§ 3 or 4 will be punished by imprisonment up to one year and by a fine, or by either of these penalties.

§ 6 The Reich Minister of the Interior, in agreement with the Deputy of the Führer and the Reich Minister of Justice, will issue the legal and administrative orders required to implement and supplement this law.

First Decree to the Reich Citizenship Law, 14 November 1935
THE FÜHRER AND REICH CHANCELLOR, THE REICH MINISTER OF THE INTERIOR, THE DEPUTY OF THE FÜHRER

Pursuant to § 3 of the Reich Citizenship Law of 15 September 1935 (*Reichsgesetzblatt* I, p. 1146), the following is decreed:

§ 1 (1) Until further regulations concerning the certificate of Reich citizenship are issued, subjects of German or kindred blood who on the effective date of the Reich Citizenship Law possessed the right to vote in Reichstag elections, or to whom the Reich Minister of the Interior, in agreement with the Deputy of the Führer, granted provisional Reich citizenship, will be provisionally deemed Reich citizens.

(2) The Reich Minister of the Interior, in agreement with the Deputy of the Führer, may revoke provisional Reich citizenship.

§ 2 (1) The provisions of § 1 also apply to subjects who are Jewish *Mischlinge*.

(2) A Jewish *Mischling* is anyone who is descended from one or two grandparents who are fully Jewish as regards race, unless he is deemed a Jew under § 5, Paragraph 2. A grandparent is deemed fully Jewish without further ado, if he has belonged to the Jewish religious community.

§ 3 Only a Reich citizen, as bearer of full political rights, can exercise the right to vote on political matters, or hold public office. The Reich Minister of the Interior or an agency designated by him may, in the transition period, permit exceptions with regard to admission to public office. The affairs of religious associations are not affected.

§ 4 (1) A Jew cannot be a Reich citizen. He is not entitled to the right to vote on political matters; he cannot hold public office.

(2) Jewish civil servants will retire by 31 December 1935. If these civil servants fought at the front during the World War for the German Reich or its allies, they will receive the full pension according to the salary scale for the last position held, until they reach retirement age; they will not, however, be promoted according to seniority. After they reach retirement age, their pension will be newly calculated according to the prevailing salary scales.

(3) The affairs of religious associations are not affected.

(4) The conditions of service of teachers in Jewish public schools remain unchanged until the issuance of new regulations for the Jewish school system.

§ 5 (1) A Jew is anyone descended from at least three grandparents who are fully Jewish as regards race. § 2, Paragraph 2, Sentence 2 applies.

(2) Also deemed a Jew is a Jewish *Mischling* subject who is descended from two fully Jewish grandparents and

a. who belonged to the Jewish religious community when the law was issued or has subsequently been admitted to it;

b. who was married to a Jew when the law was issued or has subsequently married one;

c. who is the offspring of a marriage concluded by a Jew, within the meaning of Paragraph 1, after the Law for the Protection of German Blood and German Honour of 15 September 1935 (*RGBI.* I, p.1146) took effect;

d. who is the offspring of extramarital intercourse with a Jew, within the meaning of Paragraph 1, and will have been born out of wedlock after 31 July 1936.

§ 6 (1) Requirements regarding purity of blood exceeding those in § 5 that are set in Reich laws or in directives of the National Socialist German Workers Party and its units remain unaffected.

(2) Other requirements regarding purity of blood that exceed those in § 5 may be set only with the consent of the Reich Minister of the Interior and the Deputy of the Führer. Insofar as

requirements of this kind already exist, they will become void as of 1 January 1936, unless approved by the Reich Minister of the Interior in agreement with the Deputy of the Führer. Application for approval is to be made to the Reich Minister of the Interior.

§ 7 The Führer and Reich Chancellor may grant exemptions from provisions of the implementation decree.

These Nuremberg Laws legitimized anti-Semitism, defined Jewishness with a pedantic exactitude – including the status of *Mischling*, or part-Jews – and made 'Aryan blood' a legal concept. What tattered and few legal rights the Jews had retained were formally at an end.

Effectively, Jews were now isolated from the general population of Germany. As if to underline the point, placards appeared at the entrance to hundreds of towns and villages, declaring 'Jews not wanted'. Thousands of Jews emigrated from Germany. Meanwhile, the anti-Semitic successes of the Nazis in Germany emboldened their fellow-travellers in neighbouring countries.

'Litigious politics entered the classroom': A Jewish Childhood in Vienna, 1933–8
GEORGE WEIDENFELD

Born in 1919, George Weidenfeld belonged to Vienna's large upper class. His 'sunny youth' was rudely interrupted by the growing confidence of Austria's Nazis following Hitler's accession to power in Germany in 1933.

From our windows overlooking the main road leading from the centre of Vienna to the suburbs, we were able to gauge any political demonstration – Left, Right or centre – as there were assembly points on little squares near our house. On that particular day I suddenly heard unfamiliar staccato noises and well-rehearsed choruses. Leaning from the balcony, I saw serried ranks of brown-shirted youths in tight black trousers and jackboots, led by officers. No military band, just choruses: *'Germany awake, Judah perish.'* The leader of each platoon would cup his hands to his mouth and shout *'Heil Adolf'* in a long drawl, and the followers would complete the slogan with a clipped *'Hit-ler'*. The leader would continue, legato, with *'Germany'*, and the crowd would answer: *'Awake'*. The leader would resume with *'Judah'*, the crowd with *'Perish'*. And so it went on, slogan after slogan.

After the first thousand or so uniformed and disciplined crack formations had passed our house, an even more frightening sensation was in store. Huge bands of white-shirted and white-stockinged novices of the Nazi Party, who clearly had neither the money nor, as yet, the status to wear the appropriate uniforms and insignia, marched in seemingly endless rows, shaking their fists at passers-by, stopping at corners, jostling and nudging stunned onlookers and singing in growling tones the early songs of the 'Heroic Age' of the Hitler movement: the Horst-Wessel song, *'Volk ans Gewehr'* ('People to the Rifle') and others. Their performance was not as well rehearsed as that of the Brown Shirts, but its effect was all the more menacing and primeval. Later, as a specialist in German propaganda at the BBC during the war, I made a closer study of Nazi Party music, but even then I was intuitively aware of the two radically different strands of music that reflected the two poles of the Hitler movement: the nihilistic, destructive, expressionist beat of metal heels on urban pavements, and the romantic, lilting, folkloristic sounds of the countryside, the melancholy ballad, the green forest, the wind, the snow and the sea.

By the time the last few thousand white shirts with the swastika armlets had marched by, dusk had fallen, torches had been lit, voices, hoarse from all the shouting, had become even more threatening until at last, as I stretched my neck to the left in the direction of the suburbs, the crowds seemed to be thinning out. The rearguard was a regiment, again, of uniformed, well-disciplined Brown Shirts and four rows of drummers wearing black jackets over their brown shirts – the SS, the newly created elite formation of Hitler's bodyguard regiment ...

During these years, litigious politics entered the classroom. The fifty or so boys of my class in the Piaristen-Gymnasium were neatly divided into three camps. Nazis and Catholics were equal in number and accounted for 90 per cent. The rest were Socialists, but since my fellow pupils' background was largely professional and upper-middle-class, practically all the remaining five to seven boys who had Socialist sympathies were Jews. We had a class parliament, an obligatory institution in all Viennese schools, and I represented the

Socialist Jewish minority, which held the balance between the Nazis and the Catholic patriots. I was spokesman for my group, so from an early age I learned, often the hard way, how to operate between two evils – by playing off the Blacks against the Browns I was able to get concessions for my diminutive flock. We had a voice in determining the programmes of the twice-yearly concerts, which were politically charged. Nationalist marches or Verdi choruses predominated, whilst *The Magic Flute* was vetoed by the Nazis as Freemason propaganda.

Even skiing or other excursions arranged by the school during the holidays had subtle political undertones. The winter outings have for ever dampened my enthusiasm for skiing. I remember one ordeal which started on the endless train journey to a Tyrolean mountain resort. Ten of us were crammed into one compartment: eight Nazis, another Jewish boy and myself. Feeling free and unfettered, our eight companions played with a miniature football which intermittently landed on my face. They sang nursery songs with improvised texts, of which the most harmless went: 'Jew, Jew, spit in your hat and tell your mummy I like that.' As the journey progressed, the verses became less innocent. References to knifing, shooting, the gallows and the guillotine crept in. Once we had arrived at our godforsaken destination, hardly had the Nazi contingent gulped down a supper consisting of hot lard, potatoes and coarse black bread than they rushed off parading swastikas and singing raucous songs. The Catholic Conservative element imitated these displays with a rather feeble 'patriotic' camp fire, singing old regimental songs and lewd barrack-room ditties from Habsburg days. Our little band of Jews and Socialists, which was one and the same thing, huddled together, praying for the time to pass more swiftly.

I had my revenge when it came to nominating the First Eleven for the school soccer cup. The Nazi head boy came up to me and declared, 'We won't have a Jew in the team this year.' At the same time he insisted that we refrain from voting for a Catholic majority, warning, 'There'll be trouble for you if you do.'

I stood my ground. 'You won't only have to have one, you'll have to have two Jews on the team, or there'll be trouble for you.'

'Lick my arse. Take it or leave it, you can only have one Jew!'

'Have it your way, but we'll vote for an all-Catholic team and give up our place to the loyal supporters of the Government.'

Silence.

'All right, two Jews it will be.'

We ended up with a 'grand coalition' of Nazis, Catholics and two Jews, one of whom – not myself, I need hardly say – scored the decisive goal in the final ...

The Austrian Nazi Party gathered self-confidence, the Nazis in my school scented victory, and the school masters began to profess colour more overtly. More than half of them sided with Hitler. Quite a few of them, my favourite history teacher among them, were genuinely anti-Nazi, but the majority vacillated. There is a typically Austrian verb of Gallic provenance – '*lavieren*' – which means moving in an undulating way, avoiding commitment, bending to the wind. Well, there was plenty of *lavieren* among the Piarist masters. Yet the attitude to Jews was complex. For instance, a Nazi master who taught German literature continued to treat me as his favourite up to the end. On the other hand, a semi-fascist, anti-Nazi Catholic persecuted me for my alien influence on the spirit of the class. I fell into a trap when, in a mood of reckless impudence, I once exposed him to derision. Professor H. liked to play a game. He used to challenge the class to offer famous quotations for which he would then give us the source – and vice versa. When my turn came, I recited a two-line verse in the style of a classical elegiac distich:

Just as the rosy dawn appeared on the distant horizon,
Xerxes reached for his luminous chalice.

Professor H. hesitated and frowned, uncertain as to what to say. Stunned silence reigned in the class. The tension grew until an embarrassed Professor H. finally declared himself defeated, muttering, 'I fear I don't know.'

I replied demurely, 'Weidenfeld's *Collected Works*.'

He fulminated, 'This is not just an impertinence, it's typical of your race. You will leave the classroom and spend the rest of the day in the "dungeon"' – a form of solitary confinement in an outhouse of the school building.

Weidenfeld's reaction to Nazism had been to become 'more pronouncedly and consciously Jewish', and as a teenager he joined the Zionist cause. By one of the contradictions of Nazism, Zionist Jews were preferred to assimilationist Jews, because the former generally wanted to leave Germany for Palestine and so accorded with the Nazi desire for *Entjudung* (de-Jewification) and *Judenrein* (a society and economy 'cleansed of Jews').

* * *

1938 was the year of the watershed, or perhaps more accurately the bloodshed, in Germany's treatment of the Jews. Scenting the opportunity for an expansionist war, the Nazi regime ramped up its economic measures against them, obliging Jewish businesses to be 'voluntarily' transferred to 'Aryan' owners at the rate of more than 200 a month. In addition, tens of thousands of Jewish actors, musicians and journalists were removed from their jobs. The result was widespread impoverishment: by 1938 about 20 per cent of Germany's Jews were in need. On 23 July all Jews were brought under the complete control of the police by a decree forcing them to carry identification cards. Three weeks later all male Jews were required to add the name of Israel to their given name on all legal documents, and all female Jews the name of Sarah. Ominously, the concentration camps at Dachau, Buchenwald and Sachsenhausen were enlarged and arrangements made to exploit inmates' labour. At Dachau prisoners were ordered to sew the Star of David on to uniforms; mass incarceration of Jews duly followed throughout the summer.

This was also the year in which Austria was annexed by Germany – the *Anschluss* as it became known. Jews there were immediately deprived of civil rights and subjected to public humiliation. Jews in Germany proper had been subjected to Nazi anti-Semitic measures piecemeal; Jews in Austria had no chance for gradual acclimatization. Under Obersturmführer Adolf Eichmann, the SS Security Forces in Vienna operated so brutally – with arbitrary incarcerations in Mauthausen, beatings, the forced cleaning of public latrines and so on – that 500 Jews committed suicide in the four weeks following *Anschluss*. Within six months of Anschluss 45,000 Austrian Jews – mostly from Vienna, where they formed one-sixth of the population – chose to emigrate. George Weidenfeld was among them.

Departure: A Young Student Leaves Vienna, July 1938
GEORGE WEIDENFELD

A group of friends and I banded together 'consulate-hopping' in search of a final safe haven. The United States had a rigid quota system and Austria could only lay claim to a tiny share. Britain was highly selective and Palestine was virtually closed to Jewish immigrants. Adolf Eichmann had taken up his post at the Rossauerlaender police station, seat of the Vienna Gestapo, and the first Zionist transports of illegal emigrants began to form. Many of my friends applied. The official Zionist organization in Jerusalem sent emissaries to make arrangements, among them the young, blue-eyed, blond Teddy Kollek, and the chubby, suave Ehud Avriel, both Viennese by birth and both kibbutz youth leaders in Palestine who were later to become commanding figures in the State of Israel, and intimate friends. The revisionist Zionists (one of whose underground leaders was the young Menachem Begin) organized their own transport. With the tacit help of the Gestapo, these illegal emigrants would assemble at dawn at the Danube quay and travel all the way down to the Black Sea and thence by unseaworthy boats to the shores of Palestine. My mother would not let me join any of these transports. She wanted me to hang on until my father's release, and never gave up hope that we would depart as one family – uncles, grandmothers and all.

My friends and I worked ceaselessly in search of an immigration target, exchanging news and information. Shanghai was a popular destination because it was fairly easy to get a visa, and the same was said to apply to various South American countries. But before long it became clear that some of the visas were ineffective, and we heard reports of immigrants being turned away at the border.

I had a distant relative in London – the newly married wife of a doctor in Battersea. She had already done her best to bring her closest relations over and reluctantly sent me a carefully phrased letter stating that, once in England, she and her husband would look after me for a while so that I would not be a burden on the country. The letter was not strong enough to get me a British entry visa. We needed more British-born referees. I thought a few heavyweight names would help, so with two friends I went to the reading room of the British legation to consult *Who's Who*. From there we copied addresses of those we thought to be eminent British Jews. There was no point, we agreed, in writing to legendary names like Rothschild,

Montefiore, Bearsted, Reading or Samuel – we assumed that they must be flooded with requests – so we resolved instead to find less obvious candidates. We fell on the letter G and found the name of Viscount Greenwood. Feeling sure that this must be an Anglicized version of Gruenwald, I wrote him a long letter asking for support. He replied by return of post, coolly stating that he was unable to help and that, incidentally, he was a churchgoing Anglican. I also wrote to Lord Robert Cecil, because he was renowned for his humanitarian and staunch anti-Nazi views, and received a charming letter back in which he offered his support with the British passport authorities as well as help with my studies in England.

Even this was not enough. But through the intervention of the Diplomatic Academy's English tutor, the eccentric Welshman who wore summer suits throughout the year and looked like Ronald Colman in the role of a Foreign Legion officer, my mother and I obtained an interview with Captain Kendrick, the passport officer. Just as he was about to end the interview with a lugubrious mien and a shrug of his shoulders, my mother broke down and sobbed. Captain Kendrick relented and gave me the flimsiest of all visas – the right to enter England for a period of three months in transit to a final destination.

I had a month to prepare for my departure. First I finished my exams, and then I embarked on a round of farewell visits. Those of us who were preparing to leave plunged into a febrile social season. Threatened with severance, old friendships and budding romances, deep love affairs and callous flirtations accelerated in pace, and marriages were impulsively arranged. There was a mood of intensity and reckless abandon in which conventional inhibitions suddenly disappeared. Countless bottle parties helped to drown the sense of sadness and despair whilst lubricating a sense of adventure enhanced by the lure of the unknown. The farewells were filled with black humour, 'humour of the gallows', as the German saying goes. We danced to the latest tunes and, when it was thought to be safe, sang biting parodies of the current Nazi anthems. The party given for me by one of my cousins and two female students at the academy ended to the strains of the hit of the moment, 'The Lady is a Tramp'.

A week before my departure I was allowed to see my father in prison. He shuffled to the interview grille, looking haggard and ashen-faced, his clothes smelling of prison detergents. The law prescribed that he sign a document 'releasing me from parental authority' to allow me to make proper business decisions. We spoke very little. On parting he held up his right hand, waving and bending it in some vague gesture of benediction. At that moment in the prison I felt I had formally come of age.

One evening after a hot day at the end of July I left for the Western Railway Station with one suitcase, a postal order for sixteen shillings and sixpence in English money, an exam certificate from the Diplomatic Academy, a sheaf of curricula vitae of hapless friends wishing to join me in England and the blessings of many relatives and friends. My mother and grandmother, Uncle Kleinmann, the inveterate optimist, his wife and her spinster sister, my father's secretary and two of his faithful card partners came to see me off. Even that little assembly was risky because the Gestapo especially discouraged Jewish farewell groups at railway stations.

We passed the Swiss border in the morning. Fact and fiction about refugees being hounded out of the train and sent to concentration camps abounded, but my train went through unscathed. After the self-important, bellowing Nazi guards the phlegmatism of the Swiss border police came as a relief.

When I arrived in Zurich after breakfast, my first task was to visit the Jewish refugee centre. All I remember is an endless queue stretching along the four walls of a courtyard and two female secretaries checking the names and documents before disappearing behind shuttered doors. They would come back, call out names, and people would either leave the queue and go in through the door or go to the exit, dejected. It all seemed quite mysterious. After an hour's waiting, a bearded man with a black hat suddenly came out of the office, called out my name and ushered me into the office with great courtesy. This sudden preferment caused great dismay in the queue. Someone behind me hissed, '*Luxusemigrant*' – deluxe refugee.

The bearded old man introduced me to the presiding officer of the committee. He knew my family. 'They've been generous to many good causes,' he said, apologizing that his organization was short of money and could not reciprocate in the same way, but telling me they would pay for board and lodging and give me a little pocket money.

I spent my first day of freedom at a lakeside café listening to Swiss military music. It sounded heavenly after the harsh, syncopated tones of the SS anthems or the Prussian military marches played by Austrian bands with exaggerated zeal.

Weidenfeld was later joined in London by both his parents.

Hitler Speaks, Nuremberg, September 1938
VIRGINIA COWLES

The Nazi Party held annual rallies (*Parteitage*) in Nuremberg from 1933 onwards; the 1938 rally was the last, because from 1939 onwards the Reich was at war. Virginia Cowles, a British journalist observed it.

One night I went to the stadium with Jules Sauerwein to hear an address Hitler was making to Nazi political leaders gathered from all over Germany. The stadium was packed with nearly 200,000 spectators. As the time for the Führer's arrival drew near, the crowd grew restless. The minutes passed and the wait seemed interminable. Suddenly the beat of the drums increased and three motor-cycles with yellow standards fluttering from their windshields raced through the gates. A few minutes later a fleet of black cars rolled swiftly into the arena: in one of them, standing in the front seat, his hand outstretched in the Nazi salute, was Hitler.

The demonstration that followed was one of the most extraordinary I have ever witnessed. Hitler climbed to his box in the Grand Stand amid a deafening ovation, then gave a signal for the political leaders to enter. They came, a hundred thousand strong, through an opening in the far end of the arena. In the silver light they seemed to pour into the bowl like a flood of water. Each of them carried a Nazi flag and when they were assembled in mass formation, the bowl looked like a shimmering sea of swastikas.

Then Hitler began to speak. The crowd hushed into silence, but the drums continued their steady beat. Hitler's voice rasped into the night and every now and then the multitude broke into a roar of cheers. Some of the audience began swaying back and forth, chanting '*Sieg Heil*' over and over again in a frenzy of delirium. I looked at the faces around me and saw tears streaming down people's cheeks. The drums had grown louder and I suddenly felt frightened. For a moment I wondered if it wasn't a dream; perhaps we were really in the heart of the African jungle. I had a sudden feeling of claustrophobia and whispered to Jules Sauerwein, asking if we couldn't leave. It was a silly question, for we were hemmed in on all sides, and there was nothing to do but sit there until the bitter end.

At last it was over. Hitler left the box and got back in the car. As soon as he stopped speaking the spell seemed to break and the magic vanish. That was the most extraordinary thing of all: for when he left the stand and climbed back into his car, his small figure suddenly became drab and unimpressive. You had to pinch yourself to realize that this was the man on whom the eyes of the world were riveted; that he alone held the lightning in his hands.

In 1938, no doubt inspired by the example of its Nazi neighbour, Poland passed legislation whereby passports held by its citizens were revoked if the holder had lived abroad for five years. The law was a not-so-subtle attempt to prevent the repatriation of the 50,000 Polish Jews living in Germany and Austria. The answer of Berlin to the 'problem' of the stateless Polish Jews stranded within Germany was quick and brutal: it herded them into railway carriages with a piece of luggage each and dispatched them to the German-Polish border.

Expulsion of Polish Jews from Germany, 31 October 1938
ANONYMOUS

A letter sent to a friend:

On Friday morning about 5.30 a policeman came to our house, got my father and myself out of bed and told us we would have to go immediately to the police station. He stated that it was simply for the important question of revising our Polish passports. He declared: 'Dress warmly and take food with you for twenty-four hours.' I asked why we should take food for twenty-four hours when there was nothing more involved than the revision of passports. He replied: 'Oh, there are so very many Poles.' He even refused us enough time to make a few sandwiches. We were obliged to leave immediately, being allowed to take with us only a pencil, and a comb, as well as four marks – though later he changed this to ten marks in order to buy food.

As soon as we reached the street, he handed me the expulsion order, which bore a time limit of 24 hours. In order to prevent our escaping we were first taken to the Hitler Youth building, then in police cars to the Maikafer Barracks on the Chausseestrasse. Other Jews, I learned later, were taken to other barracks. Here we were abused, ordered about without reason, and told we were 'international crooks' etc. Then we were taken, again in police cars, by an indirect route to the Treptow Station and put on a train whose length seemed endless. Everywhere we were escorted by police with fixed bayonets. We were threatened with shooting should anyone try to escape. Some of the police were very decent and even talked to us, but they said, 'Service is Service.' Others were swine, and others like machines. The Berlin population, as far as I could see, behaved very well. Near the Schlesesche Station many Aryan Berliners were gathered to watch us. I myself saw some of them crying.

In the train we were crowded together like cattle – literally one on top of the other like cattle, so one could neither breathe nor move. It was so full it was impossible to move from one seat to another. We were locked into the carriages. We had neither bread nor water. When we told the guards we had not been allowed to take any food with us, they said, 'Our Sudeten Germans were treated just like this.' After forty hours like this in the train other Jews who had arrived in Bentschen from other parts of Germany gave us some dry bread. Some of the younger men climbed through the windows to get water for the rest of us in Bentschen, whereupon the Polish station police beat a fifteen-year-old boy over the head and shoulders with their truncheons.

When at last we were allowed to leave the train the great majority of us were forced to sleep all on the ground in the open air, though it was raining. About 1,400 Jews who had to leave their train on the German side of the frontier were chased by 300 SS armed with machine guns, and were told they would be shot if they came back. Only because of this, and after long hesitation, would the Poles let them cross the border.

It is untrue, as I have read in the papers, that only a few thousand were expelled in this way. Only yesterday not less than 18,000 people arrived in Bentschen, and many were sent to other frontier stations.

As far I know, all male Polish Jews were expelled from Berlin. Even men older than eighty-five and very small boys. I believe that the number expelled from Berlin alone must total about 40,000. One man in my train wept all the way like a baby. He showed me a photograph of his three-month-old girl, whose mother died when [the child] was born. On Friday morning this man was just feeding his baby when the police arrived. The baby was snatched away from him, given to a neighbour, and he was led away.

In other cities, whole families were expelled. In Cologne the police behaved well. The Jewish community was allowed to give large amounts of food to those expelled. However, owners of stores and shops were forced to turn them over either to [a] landlord or [to] police. A girl from Cologne told me that the policeman who came to get her carried away her heavy suitcase through the streets. SA in the streets called him a 'lackey of the Jews' but he paid no attention and kept [hold of] the suitcase. Elsewhere I was told police were kind, except in Vienna, where all the expelled were given certificates of health without even seeing a doctor. They were also forced to sign a promise never to return. From Southern Germany a woman in her ninth month of pregnancy was put on the train. Yesterday three people died in Bentschen, and a young girl went mad. Today, I hear typhus has broken out.

The Polish police claim to have no instructions to help us, though several empty trains were standing in the station. Of course, there was no possibility of sleep. I slept last night for the first time, on the floor.

None of us has a pfennig, but this is important only in so far as it prevents our buying tickets to go further into Poland. The Jews here are giving us superhuman help. What they are doing for us cannot be described in words. Unfortunately, they are starving themselves. The few marks we did have are almost all spent now. In the Bentschen station Poles asked one mark for four cigarettes and for one sausage I had to pay ninety pfennig.

Seventeen thousand of the German-Jewish citizens of Polish origin were dumped in the no-man's town of Zbąszyń (Bentschen) on the German-Polish border. One of the stranded was Berta Grynszpan. She sent the following message on a postcard to her young brother

26

Herschel, who was living in Paris, after she and their parents had been deported from Hanover to Zbąszyń.

A Postcard from Zbąszyń, circa 1 November 1938
BERTA GRYNSZPAN

Dear Herschel,

You must have heard about the disaster. I shall tell you what has happened. On Thursday evening, rumours were circulating that Polish Jews in our city were being expelled. None of us believed it. At nine o'clock that evening a policeman came to our house to tell us to report to the police station with our passports. We all trooped off as we were to the police station. Practically the whole neighbourhood was already there. Almost immediately we were taken to the town hall in a police car; so was everyone else. No one told us what was up, but we realized that this was going to be the end. They shoved an expulsion order into our hands, saying we had to leave Germany before 29 October. We were not allowed to go home. I pleaded to be allowed to fetch a few things and a policeman accompanied me. I packed a case with the most important clothes, but that was all we could salvage. We haven't a penny. Could you send us something at Łódź? Love from all of us.

Berta

Incensed by the treatment of his family, Herschel Grynszpan bought a gun and entered the German Embassy in Paris under the pretext of delivering an important document. On being shown into the office of Third Secretary Ernst vom Rath, Grynszpan pulled out his 6.35 calibre pistol and cried, 'You are a filthy boche and here, in the name of twelve thousand persecuted Jews, is your document.'

Grynszpan fired five shots at vom Rath, mortally wounding him.

The assassination provided Goebbels with the opportunity to whip up a wave of anti-Semitic attacks throughout Germany, Austria and the Sudetenland on the night of 9–10 November. The pogrom became known as *Kristallnacht*, 'night of broken glass'.

Kristallnacht: *Shopwreckers in Berlin, 10 November 1938*
GUARDIAN CORRESPONDENT

The operations of the wreckers of Jewish shops and places of business were in two parts. First small wrecking squads, who began their work as early as two in the morning in some cases, smashed the windows and showcases of Jewish-owned premises, whether the proprietors were foreign Jews or German Jews. All Jewish shops are marked with special signs, which facilitated their work. The first squads, working quickly and in darkness, only dealt, however, with the Jewish premises on main streets. When Berlin went to work this morning it experienced the extraordinary sight of wholesale smashed windows with dummy figures and the like leaning out on to the streets; nothing, however, was then plundered.

But about midday the work of the original squads was supplemented by the wreckers proper. They operated too in small bands and were followed by crowds of supporters who proceeded to smash the interiors of the Jewish shops to pieces and in many cases to throw the goods in them out into the streets. These wreckers in their turn were supplemented by others, including many youngish boys. They seized whatever implements they could find and absolutely broke up everything to hand. A small page boy sent out from an hotel was seen to interrupt his commission for a few minutes smashing with the rest of the crowd.

In some part of Berlin foodstuffs, clothes, underclothing, and even furs were thrown out to the crowds. In other shops none of the contents, apart from the windows and fittings, were touched until this evening. Plundering did not seem to be the purpose of the wreckers themselves. Where there was plundering they threw out the contents of the shops to the crowds standing outside.

Kristallnacht: *'A Planned Action', Berlin, 9–10 November 1938*
ANONYMOUS

At exactly three in the morning the house in which I lived, in which there was a small Jewish business, started to shake. Both window-panes were shattered and the contents of the shop-windows ruined. Naturally I cannot tell whether this had happened the first time. I lived in the Kurfürstendamm district. As I am in the habit of sleeping with the window open, I heard the noise of breaking windows from this area. In the house where I lived, a second bombardment of the undamaged parts had been organized. From my window I saw a small car pass by; two men in civilian clothes got out and smashed the windows. Evidently it had all been carefully planned, because they got back into the car in order to repeat their action nearby. At about six in the morning another convoy arrived, who likewise destroyed anything that was left to be destroyed. At intervals during these three hours fire engines could be heard rushing through the streets, and the smoke from Fasanenstraße was an omen of what was likely to have occurred. In any case it was a planned action carried out by SA, SS and Hitler Youth in civilian clothes. In a barber's shop, one of those involved related in my presence that they had been drinking till three in the morning to prepare themselves for the action. The next morning a terrible sight was to be seen, and the smouldering synagogue in Fasanenstraße was like a signal. As far as I could observe, people looked at the devastation in silence, and perhaps with some inner emotion. Indeed, some people openly expressed indignation. While I was crossing the Kurfürstendamm in the morning, an old gentleman with snow-white hair addressed me impulsively and expressed his outrage, calling the event a crime against civilization for which the Germans would one day have to atone.

Kristallnacht: *The Confidential Report of the American Consul in Leipzig, Saxony, November 1938*
DAVID H. BUFFUM

Sent by Consul Buffum to the Consul General in Berlin.

The macabre circumstances that form the subject matter of this report had a fittingly gruesome prelude in Leipzig a few hours before they occurred in the form of rites held on one of the principal squares of the city on the night of 9 November 1938, in commemoration of fallen martyrs to the Nazi cause prior to the political takeover in 1933. To such end apparently anything in the corpse category that could be remotely associated with Nazi martyrdom, had been exhumed. At least five-year-old remains of those who had been considered rowdyish violators of law and order at the time, had been placed in extravagant coffins; arranged around a colossal, flaming urn on the *Altermarkt* [Old Market] for purposes of display, and ultimately conveyed amid marching troops, flaring torches and funeral music to the *Ehrenhain*, Leipzig's National Socialistic burial plot. For this propagandistic ceremony the entire market place had been surrounded with wooden lattice work about ten yards high. This was covered with white cloth to form the background for black swastikas at least five yards high and broad. Flame-spurting urns and gigantic banners completed a Wagnerian ensemble as to pomposity of stage setting; but it cannot be truthfully reported that the ceremony aroused anything akin to awe among the crowds who witnessed it. Judging from a few very guardedly whispered comments, the populace was far more concerned over the wanton waste of materials in these days when textiles of any kind are exceedingly scarce and expensive, rather than being actuated by any particularly reverent emotions. On the other hand for obvious reasons, there were no open manifestations of disapproval. The populace was destined to be much more perturbed the following morning during the course of the most violent debacle the city had probably ever witnessed.

The shattering of shop windows, looting of stores and dwellings of Jews which began in the early hours of 10 November 1938, was hailed subsequently in the Nazi press as 'a spontaneous wave of righteous indignation throughout Germany, as a result of the cowardly Jewish murder of Third Secretary von [*sic*] Rath in the German Embassy at Paris.' So far as a very high percentage of the German populace is concerned, a state of popular indignation that would spontaneously lead to such excesses, can be considered as non-existent. On the contrary, in viewing the ruins and attendant measures employed, all of the local crowds observed were obviously benumbed over what had happened and aghast over the unprecedented fury of Nazi acts that had been or were taking place with bewildering rapidity throughout their city. The whole lamentable affair was organized in such a sinister fashion, as to lend credence to the theory that the execution of it had involved studied preparation. It has been ascertained by this office that the plan of 'spontaneous indignation' leaked out in Leipzig several hours before news of the death of Third Secretary von Rath had been broadcast at 10 p.m. 10 November 1938. It is stated upon authority believed to be reliable, that most of the evening was employed in drawing up lists of fated victims. Several persons known to this office were aware at 9 p.m. on the evening of 9 November 1938 that the 'spontaneous' outrage was scheduled for that night sometime after midnight and several of such persons interviewed, stayed up purposely in order to witness it.

At 3 a.m. on 10 November 1938 was unleashed a barrage of Nazi ferocity as had had no equal hitherto in Germany, or very likely anywhere else in the world since savagery, if ever. Jewish dwellings were smashed into and contents demolished or looted. In one of the Jewish sections an eighteen-year-old boy was hurled from a three-storey window to land with both legs broken on a street littered with burning beds and other household furniture and effects from his family's and other apartments. This information was supplied by an attending physician. It is reported from another quarter that among domestic effects thrown out of a Jewish dwelling, a small dog descended four flights to a broken spine on a cluttered street. Although apparently centred in poor districts, the raid was not confined to the humble classes. One apartment of exceptionally refined occupants known to this office, was violently ransacked, presumably in a search for valuables that was not in vain, and one of the marauders thrust a cane through a priceless medieval painting portraying a biblical scene. Another apartment of the same category is known to have been turned upside down in the frenzied course of whatever the invaders were after. Reported looting of cash, silver, jewellery, and otherwise easily convertible articles, have been frequent.

Jewish shop windows by the hundreds were systematically and wantonly smashed throughout the entire city at a loss estimated at several millions of marks. There are reports that substantial losses have been sustained on the famous Leipzig 'Bruhl', as many of the shop windows at the time of the demolition were filled with costly furs that were seized before the windows could be boarded up. In proportion to the general destruction of real estate, however, losses of goods are felt to have been relatively small. The spectators who viewed the wreckage when daylight had arrived were mostly in such a bewildered mood, that there was no danger of impulsive acts, and the perpetrators probably were too busy in carrying out their schedule to take off a whole lot of time for personal profit. At all events, the main streets of the city were a positive litter of shattered plate glass. According to reliable testimony, the debacle was executed by SS men and Storm Troopers not in uniform, each group having been provided with hammers, axes, crowbars and incendiary bombs.

Three synagogues in Leipzig were fired simultaneously by incendiary bombs and all sacred objects and records desecrated or destroyed, in most instances hurled through the windows and burned in the streets. No attempts whatsoever were made to quench the fires, functions of the fire brigade having been confined to playing water on adjoining buildings. All of the synagogues were irreparably gutted by flames, and the walls of the two that are in the close proximity of the consulate are not being razed. The blackened frames have been centres of attraction during the past week of terror for eloquently silent and bewildered crowds. One of the largest clothing stores in the heart of the city was destroyed by flames from incendiary bombs, only the charred walls and gutted roof having been left standing. As was the case with the synagogues, no attempts on the part of the fire brigade were made to extinguish the fire, although apparently there was a certain amount of apprehension for adjacent property, for the walls of a coffee house next door were covered with asbestos and sprayed by the doughty firemen. It is extremely difficult to believe, but the owners of the clothing store were actually charged with setting the fire and on that basis were dragged from their beds at 6 a.m. and clapped into prison.

Tactics which closely approached the ghoulish took place at the Jewish cemetery where the temple was fired together with a building occupied by caretakers, tombstones uprooted and graves violated. Eye-witnesses considered reliable reports that ten corpses were left unburied at this cemetery for a week's time because all grave-diggers and cemetery attendants had been arrested.

Ferocious as was the violation of property, the most hideous phase of the so-called 'spontaneous' action, has been the wholesale arrest and transportation to concentration camps of male German Jews between the ages of sixteen and sixty, as well as Jewish men without citizenship. This has been taking place daily since the night of horror. This office has no way of accurately checking the numbers of such arrests, but there is very little question that they have gone into several thousands in Leipzig alone. Having demolished dwellings and hurled most of the movable effects to the streets, the insatiably sadistic perpetrators threw many of the trembling inmates into a small stream that flows through the Zoological Park, commanding horrified spectators to spit at them, defile them with mud and jeer at their plight. The latter incident has been repeatedly corroborated by German witnesses who were nauseated in telling the tale. The slightest manifestation of sympathy evoked a positive fury on the part of the perpetrators, and the crowd was powerless to do anything but turn horror-stricken eyes from the scene of abuse, or leave the vicinity. These tactics were carried out the entire morning of 10 November without police intervention and they were applied to men, women and children.

There is much evidence of physical violence, including several deaths. At least half a dozen cases have been personally observed, victims with bloody, badly bruised faces having fled to this office, believing that as refugees their desire to emigrate could be expedited here. As a matter of fact this consulate has been a bedlam of humanity for the past ten days, most of these visitors being desperate women, as their husbands and sons had been taken off to concentration camps.

Kristallnacht: *Synagogues Fired, Vienna, 10 November 1938*
REUTERS CORRESPONDENT

All Vienna synagogues were destroyed today with the exception of one in the centre of the city.

Police, assisted by Nazi black-uniformed guards, went from house to house arresting all male Jews under sixty years of age. Jews were also taken up in the streets and trams. A number were arrested as they were waiting in a queue outside the British Consulate for visas. Those arrested were taken to police headquarters, but were not told what their fate would be. It is understood, however, they are to be sent to the new Austrian concentration camp in the quarries of Mauthausen. No official number of arrests has been issued, but it is estimated to be at least 10,000.

Some of the arrested men were supplied with spades and taken to the destroyed synagogues, where they were made to clear away the ruins.

A number of Jews are reported to have fled to Vienna Woods, hoping to escape arrest.

Twenty-two suicides of Jews have been reported in Vienna since the beginning of the demonstrations.

The synagogue at Linz was set on fire this morning by a crowd of 500 persons and completely burned down.

Around 7,500 Jewish shops and synagogues were destroyed in Germany on 'Crystal Night'. Nearly 100 Jews were killed.

Kristallnacht: *'everything devastated and destroyed'*, Vienna, 9–10 November 1938
GISA, VIENNESE TEENAGER

A letter to a relative:

You cannot imagine how things have been with us. Papa with a head-wound, bandaged, myself in bed with severe fits, everything devastated and destroyed. And the poor child had to look after us, cook, and run errands, although still in a state of serious exhaustion. It has already been nearly fourteen days, and I still can't take it in – I have already told you that we had a similar visit on Yom Kippur, and it had a similar bloody and tragic ending. At first I was just glad that we had survived, but when I realized that I had no dresses, no coat, and to cap it all not even a stitch of underwear any more, then I thought again that my heart would break. So that you don't think I'm exaggerating, let me tell you that when the doctor came to bandage Papa, Rosa and Herta, all three of them bleeding copiously from head wounds, we couldn't give him a towel or any piece of cloth to wipe the blood off his hands, so he had to leave. My poor heart had to take in the fact that the place was so full of fragments and splinters, because all the glasses, windows and mirrors had been smashed, that we didn't know where to turn. The day after, we were sent two shirts to put on, one for me and one for Papa. I can't tell you how many tears I shed, we are destitute, we don't even have the most basic clothing, we can't even go out into the street; in any case I have no desire to do so! But even that was not enough; two days later we were told that I had to make room at once and accommodate two more families in my flat; furthermore, I was to be ready within three hours. What could I do but get up and take everything from the bedroom into the dining room, and the two families, Frau Kramer with two children

and Frau Terner with one child and a sick mother, moved in with me.
You cannot imagine what things look like here.
With lots of love,
Your unhappy Gisa

Kristallnacht: *'A Jew is Taken to Oranienburg Concentration Camp'*, November 1938
ANONYMOUS

Following *Kristallnacht* about 30,000 Jewish men were arrested and taken to concentration camps.

When we arrived at the camp, first of all our names were called and entered in a register, then we were made to line up in the courtyard from about five in the morning till about two in the afternoon. Anyone who moved was kicked or punched in the face. Our requests to be allowed to relieve ourselves were denied, and the guards responded with the most coarse abuse. Finally at about midday a senior officer agreed that we could be taken together to the latrine The first food was not distributed until twenty-four hours after our arrest. The food was good.

We had to hand over all our clothes, and received in return ragged concentration camp clothing, consisting of threadbare army uniforms, overalls and the like. Jews are completely forbidden to smoke in Oranienburg and are not allowed to cater for themselves, or buy anything in the canteen.

The next day we had to do drill. It was bearable for the younger ones, as many of us had been front-line soldiers. The older men collapsed, and were kicked, punched, slapped in the face and hit with rifle-butts, always accompanied by the most vulgar and obscene insults. Among the prisoners in my section was H., a businessman from H., over seventy years old, and former lawyer J., also over seventy. Both were mistreated in the manner described above. When people returned to the line after individual drill, they were kicked so that they fell flat on their faces, and then without provocation the guards trampled on their backs and buttocks with their hobnailed boots.

The camp Commandant inspected the ranks at roll-call. Sometimes he stopped and insulted one of the prisoners in a very coarse manner, which cannot be repeated. He said without provocation to a man next to me, 'Now I've got to take my glove off especially for you, you filthy Jewish swine,' and after he had calmly done this, he struck the unfortunate victim several times in the face and on the chin.

A Rabbi is Incarcerated in Buchenwald, November 1938
RABBI WILDE

Buchenwald (German for 'beech forest') concentration camp was situated outside Weimar, the city of Goethe and Schiller. Between April 1938 and April 1945 approximately 240,000 were incarcerated in the camp, of whom one-fifth are thought to have died from ill treatment.

We were made to hurry down some steps that descended from the [railway station] platform. In their first exhibition of sadism our new guards had coated these with soap, and the many who slipped were mauled with rifle-butts. Two thousand five hundred members of the Adolf Hitler Guard in grey uniforms continued pummelling us with their rifle-butts all the way to a tunnel. Here we were lined up facing the wall and told, 'Don't turn round. Throw down your knives and razors.'

After we had stood in the darkness for an hour and a half they ordered us to move on. We had to trot over to some armoured trucks which then carried us to the camp. No notice was taken of any who dropped from exhaustion; they stayed where they dropped. Older people had to struggle to hoist themselves into the trucks, which were a good four feet off the ground. The SS lined the running boards and watched us through chinks between the planks. They distracted themselves during the long journey by grabbing prisoners' heads and slamming them to unconsciousness.

Upon our arrival we had to run with hats or skull-caps in hand to a square not far from the main gate. On our way we had to pass between two rows of SS troopers armed with whips, some of which seemed to be fitted with barbed wire or pieces of lead. One trooper, perched on a platform to one side of the gate, swung a great whip down on the heads of passers-by beneath.

One man slumped to the ground at my feet. I managed to side-step him but then lost my footing on the gravel and fell flat on my face.

My head was bleeding. I leaped up to hurry on, but an SS trooper was already descending on me. I realized that he was going to hit me in the jaw. More by reflex than by intention I halted in my tracks, so that the blow he landed lost some of its force. He walked away without a word. I was so shocked that I did not feel the pain.

We stood on our feet from morning until evening to be trained in camp 'discipline'. Three men were flogged twenty-five times each as public punishment for some 'infringement' or other. When the victims cried out they received twenty-five more blows. I was too far from them to hear more than the swish of the stick and the yells of the prisoners. I realized that they were trying to unnerve us, to sap our will and our dignity. An SS officer began screaming, 'None of you will leave this camp alive.' And from that moment I vowed that no matter the cost and no matter how brutal the spectacle I was made to endure, I would not allow my will or my dignity to be belittled. The SS seemed little more than a bunch of maniacs and sadists or the petty henchmen of a criminal gang. I realized that these eighteen-year-old or twenty-three-year-old boys were being systematically trained to display brutality towards everyone in the execution of their orders, whether young or old, innocent or guilty. They were gathering strength for a war against foreign enemies and even against their own people. Whenever I saw the camp Commandant I reminded myself that we were civilized people, but that he was dirt.

The following morning I saw the corpses of two suicides. One of them had thrown himself against the electrified barbed wire; the other had died from a guard's bullet. The idea of committing suicide never entered my head while I was in detention, even though I was surrounded by large numbers of men who had lost their sense. Later, mental cases were locked in a washroom behind our barracks, and one of my friends, a neurologist, was told to look after them.

Kindertransport: *A Boy Leaves Berlin, December 1939*
JOHN SILBERMANN

By 1938 Nazi persecution had reached such levels that an increasing number of Jews desperately tried to leave Germany. In order to address the refugee problem US President Roosevelt called a conference in the French town of Evian. This achieved little because in a climate of recession most major countries, including the US and Great Britain, refused to take more refugees. In the aftermath of *Kristallnacht* the British parliament, however, had a change of heart and agreed to take in an unspecified number of Jewish children under the age of eighteen. By the so-called *Kindertransport* 10,000 Jewish children left Germany and Austria for Britain.

Over the years since 1933, my parents were changing from hoping that the Nazi era would only be short-lived, that life was going to be hard and we needed to lower our standards and our sights for a while, withdrawing to the inner family and survive as best we can economically. But with the Nuremberg Laws it became quite evident that there was no future for Jews in Germany and that's when people seriously started to consider emigration. But even then it was half-hearted.

Putting it in today's comparable terms: if you're in your forties or fifties age group, with children at school, with a home and no serious economic difficulty, and if somebody says to you: Look, there's a threat on the horizon and you may not be able to carry on this lifestyle, why don't you emigrate to Uruguay, or Iceland? You say: Yes, that sounds sensible, I'll think about it. That was just about the atmosphere: Jews realized that it wasn't sensible to stay where they were but the likely points of immigration were not attractive; added to which there was a language problem and an economic problem because already the Nazis had laws in place forbidding Jews to take assets and capital out. So if you left you were going to be poor in a world which was just clawing its way out of the 1929–30 recession.

So wherever you went from 1935 to 1938, you were going to be fighting the local population for an income, for work or setting up business. Everyone understood that they *ought* to be emigrating, but it was only when the watershed of *Kristallnacht* occurred in November 1938 that my parents, in common with 90 per cent of other German Jews, thought: It's no good staying, they're going to kill us. Survival in the life-threatening sense was the only thing that mattered ...

I remember in my carriage there was a baby of two or three years old, and this child was given to a teenage girl who was told, 'Look after her until you get to England.' What courage that took for those parents! We travelled from Berlin for several hours until we came to the Dutch border. It made a *huge* impression on me: here I'd been in an ever-deepening situation of bad treatment, bullying, vulnerability, victimization, and here comes the Dutch border. Trains used to stop on one side of the border while the German officials did their stuff, then the train shunted over to the Dutch side and the same thing happened all over again. But, with one difference: accompanying the Dutch officials came a load of ladies in grey uniforms and I think it was the first time for years that non-Jewish people said something kind to us. They brought chocolate, soft drinks; they gave us postcards to mail home to our parents [to say] that we had crossed the border. Somebody had gone to a lot of trouble there to understand what kids would need. We hadn't expected it and to this day I have a great fondness for the Dutch.

Kindertransport: *A Boy Leaves Vienna, 1939*
JOHN RICHARDS

I went up to my father before I got on the train and put my arms around him and I said, 'I'm sorry about the [torn] trousers, I don't want to go, I love you so much.' He kissed me and said, 'I forgive you, try and behave and be a good boy.' I went up to my mother and she kissed me; although she was my stepmother I could see tears in her eyes and she told me she loved me. I then went to my stepbrother Heini and he came into my arms and we kneeled down, we had those long socks on, you don't see them in England, and he kissed me and hugged me and *begged* me not to go. Little Zilla was there, I kissed her and said my farewells and we got on the train.

I held my sister's hand. We found a compartment. As we got on the train they shut the door, we tried to open the windows and all of a sudden these black uniforms appeared and they pushed our parents back, they weren't allowed to come near us. Father tried to shout something, but with all the commotion, we couldn't hear. The younger children started to cry then. I had a sense of relief; I felt a sense of sadness; I felt a sense of anger. I thought: Was I such a bad lad to be torn away from my father and mother? Will I ever be lucky enough to see them again? The emotions that were going through me! For some reason, I don't know what, my sister didn't cry. Later on in life, she told me that from the day we left Nordbahnhof in Vienna, she cut the past out of her life.

Kindertransport: *A Girl Arrives in Britain, 1939*
ANONYMOUS

The first thing I remember about being in England is Aunt Helen trying to put me on her lap. We are on a train taking us from London to Swansea, and since I speak no English it is difficult to resolve my urgent need to get off the lap of this woman I have never seen before. Not, at least, without becoming impolite about it. I have been warned of dire consequences if I fail to be polite when I get to England.

Luckily, my sister Ruth is along. Ruth speaks English. 'I have to go to the bathroom,' I tell her in German. She translates this for the woman with the lap, who threatens to get up and take me there. 'Not her. *You* have to take me,' I say to Ruth. My poor sister – she is thirteen, an awkward age at best, and the Basic English she has learned at school has never been tested on a native speaker. I have admired and adored her from afar for years – my handsome, scornful, heroic sister, six years older than I am and good at sports – but at that point she must be loathing me. 'If you don't make that woman put me down,' I tell her when we are finally alone in the corridor heading towards the toilet, which in fact I do not need, 'I will start screaming.'

But by the time we get back to the compartment, nothing needs to be explained after all: the woman's lap has been magically withdrawn from combat and is no longer a menace. It is filled with egg salad sandwiches, and I can settle down in my own and distant corner to eat one without fear of further interference.

I do not remember the journey before that, though I know it was a journey of children: children of every age and size and condition. I vaguely recall weeping adults, my mother presumably among them, although I do not remember her. They stood, blocked by wooden barriers, as we were taken along the platform and put into railway compartments, which I seem to remember had hard, slatted seats. There was a boy, a country boy I suppose, with a huge basket of strawberries that he handed around to us all. The guard came by now and then and made jokes, and the officer in uniform and with a swastika armband who collected our papers at the border looked upon me with what I took to be parental concern as he handed back my passport, which under my name – augmented by the Jewish 'Sarah' mandated by the Third Reich – had been stamped STATELESS. I remember feeling a shy affection for him, a sense of safety in travelling in this carriage under his care.

I know that to cross to England we boarded the boat at Rotterdam. I know this because I had thought we would go through Amsterdam, which I had read about in the *Bibi* books of Karen Michaëlis; Rotterdam, unsung in literature, was a great disappointment, which I resented enough to file firmly in memory. But the crossing itself is a blank. Probably we were all asleep. The next day comes to mind as the revelation of a huge London station with massive steel arches overhead. Liverpool Street Station. There were, I think, people at tables who shuffled through papers and who spoke an incomprehensible language that I knew must be English. I was wearing a brown hat with a rolled-up brim, and there were labels pinned to my collar and dangling from the various buttons of my new brown coat.

And then a tall, thin, aquiline woman, encased in a tweed suit that looked as if it would cause severe abrasions to any skin with which it came in contact, emerged from the crowd to lay claim to this refugee package from Germany, and she led us away.

That point of my life is where my real memory begins. My earlier recollections are not much more than mental snapshots of discrete moments, deprived of emotional content and effect. Or if there is any emotion, it tends towards shame, which I have somehow breathed in during my last year there, from the air of Karlsruhe. I understand, for instance, when my best friend Ursula no longer comes to my house, that shame must be the element that most properly belongs to me. When I go to visit her, her mother will not open the gate, and when on my way home three children call out names at me which I completely fail to comprehend, I nevertheless know them to be shameful.

One day, coming home from school, I see a quartet of *Hitler Jugend* knocking on the door; they are rattling coins in round tins marked with swastikas in which they are collecting money for some worthy Nazi cause. I have been told that we never give money to the *Hitler Jugend*'s worthy causes and that we regard swastikas as hostile emblems. I shrink against the privet hedge, trying to be invisible, and am preparing myself to run away when, to my embarrassment, I find that terror has just made me pee in my pants. Luckily, however, the *Jugendbund* has given up knocking and is running down the path, going right past me on their way out. They are chatting and still rattling their tins and seem totally unaware of my shame: my twin shames, actually – of being Jewish and being incontinent. But even when they are gone, I am so overwhelmed by humiliation that for several minutes I can't move.

Shame is there in abundance. Other emotions, other moods, seem to have evaporated from the scenes I call up for myself.

My father's death, for instance, is encapsulated in a single image of a featureless figure wrapped head to toe in bandages, looking, I have lately come to think, more like the Michelin man or the Pilsbury Doughboy than a human being – though unlike the Michelin man and the Doughboy this creature does not have a face. I suppose I am extrapolating from the bandages around my father's head at the time he died – of uremic poisoning from a carbuncle at the base of his neck. In my waking life there were never any particular feelings associated with this apparition – no fear or affection or yearning – though throughout my childhood it consistently invaded my dreams and led them into nightmare. Up to that moment when Aunt Helen collected us it is as though I had flattened everything out for easy storage, and to make things simpler I seem to have removed the sound track as well. But in that second-class compartment, halfway between London and Swansea, my memory springs into three dimensions – becomes, I suppose, normal. It decorates itself with words and sounds and feelings; it attaches itself to things like regret and pleasure. None of this is entirely reliable, of course – over the years the landscape of memory shifts and its details rearrange themselves; or it fails to shift and one knows that what is being remembered is not a memory any more at all – that it has petrified into myth. But, as I say, all that is normal, more or less. And in some way impossible to define, my life begins when I am seven going on eight – when I have just set foot in England. It is 1939 – the end of April or perhaps the beginning of May. By the time the train has arrived in Swansea and the taxi has driven us to Aunt Helen's house, it is early evening.

The house is huge, much grander than anything we have ever lived in in Karlsruhe. A young woman wearing a black dress and a little white apron opens the door for us and takes our bags; she is wearing a starched white cotton tiara thing on her head like the women who served *Mandeltorte* and *Schillerlocken* in the *Konditorei* on Kaiserstrasse. Aunt Helen has taken my reluctant hand and is leading me upstairs, followed by two of our suitcases under the care of the young woman in black. Ruth trails behind; the rucksack containing our papers and disposable treasure (two Swiss watches and some gold and platinum jewellery in case there should be an emergency need for ready cash) is clutched to her heart. Aunt Helen did try at the door to separate Ruth from the rucksack, a move that established an even firmer bond between them. Ruth and rucksack are now inseparable.

But when we get to the room where we are to sleep, she loosens her clutch a little; the two beds are turned down and there are two bowls of steaming, creamy mushroom soup on the bedside table. There is a fire in the fireplace too, and the curtains breathing at the slightly opened window frame a twilight view of a walled spring garden beyond which there is a distant glimmer of sea.

There were four Harveys. Aunt Helen you have already met, but at her introduction she was wearing a Harris tweed suit – topped by a sprightly fedora that I did not mention, with a rakish little feather in it announcing its readiness for battle. But that was a different Aunt Helen from the one who floated in through the firelight an hour later to kiss us goodnight – our soup finished, our cup of Horlicks drunk, our pyjamas already on. This white-gowned woman, the new Aunt Helen, had about her the aroma of something wonderful: roses, perhaps, and lavender.

I had never eaten mushroom soup in bed before or drunk Horlicks; I had never walked down two miles of corridor before to go to the bathroom. I had certainly never been kissed before by someone wearing an evening gown. Kissed, more or less, by two people in evening clothes, because right behind Aunt Helen came Uncle Bourke, and he was wearing what I know now beyond a reasonable doubt to have been a dinner jacket. Not that it was exactly me he kissed. It was the air three inches above my right ear and three inches to the right of the spot on my scalp that still held the memory of Aunt Helen's goodnight on it.

It was a ritual, an unfaltering expression of affection balanced exquisitely with reticence, which was conducted every night for the seven years we were in England.

Part II: FLAME

The Holocaust,
1939–19 January 1942

Hitler had decided, even before going to war on 1 September 1939, that Jews in areas occupied by the expanded Third Reich would be exterminated. In the mind of the Führer, war for greater living space (*lebensraum*) was synonymous with war against the Jews. As he stated in 1939:

> *Today I will be a prophet again: if international finance Jewry within Europe and abroad should succeed once more in plunging the peoples into a world war, then the consequence will be not the Bolshevization of the world and therewith a victory of Jewry, but on the contrary, the destruction of the Jewish race in Europe.*

On the destruction of the Jews, Hitler for once kept his word. By 1939 the Führer had also convinced Germany that race war and imperialist expansion were synonymous; German trains carrying troops to the front had daubed on them the slogan: *Wir fahren nach Polen, um Juden zu versohlen.* We're off to Poland, to thrash the Jews.

'All Necessary Measures': Heydrich's Instructions to the Einsatzgruppen, 21 September 1939
REINHARD HEYDRICH, CHIEF OF THE SECURITY POLICE

As Chief of the Security Police and Security Service, Heydrich had primary responsibility for implementing the Final Solution. The preliminary to extermination was the removal of Jews from those areas of Poland which would be incorporated into Germany, and their concentration in large settlements, preferably near railways, 'so as to facilitate subsequent measures'. The clock was now ticking for Poland's Jewry.

The Einsatzgruppen (*Einsatzgruppen der Sicherheitspolizei und des SD*) were SS paramilitary special-duty groups under Heydrich's direct control; before using them to hunt Jews, Heydrich had employed them in the capture and killing of political opponents of the Nazis in Austria and Czechoslovakia.

His directive, fashioned after a lunch with his cohorts (including Adolf Eichmann), is a landmark along the road to the Final

Solution because it acknowledges a pre-existing master plan for the extermination of Europe's Jews – the 'planned overall measures' which are to be kept 'strictly secret'. When faced with the document at his trial in Israel in 1961, Eichmann agreed that 'planned overall measures' meant genocide.

The Chief of the Security Police

SECRET   Berlin: 2 September 1939

To: *Chiefs of all Einsatzgruppen of the Security Police*
Subject   Jewish question in the occupied territory

I refer to the conference held in Berlin today and once more point out that the *planned overall measures* (i.e., the final aim) are to be kept *strictly secret*.

Distinction must be made between:
(1) The final aim (which will require extended periods of time), and
(2) The stages leading to the fulfilment of this final aim (which will be carried out in short terms).

The planning measures demand the most thorough preparation in their technical as well as economic aspects.

It is obvious that the tasks that lie ahead cannot be laid down in full detail here. The instructions and guidelines below will at the same time serve the purpose of urging the chiefs of the Einsatzgruppen to give the matter their practical thought.

I

For the time being, the first pre-requisite for the final aim is the concentration of the Jews from the countryside into the larger cities.

This is to be carried out with all speed.

In doing so, distinction must be made:
(1) between the areas of Danzig and West Prussia, Posen, Eastern Upper Silesia, and
(2) the rest of the occupied territories.

As far as possible, the area mentioned (in *item* 1) is to be cleared of Jews; at least the aim should be to establish only a few cities of concentration.

In the areas mentioned in *item* 2, as few concentration points as possible are to be set up, so as to facilitate subsequent measures.

In this connection, it is to be borne in mind that only cities which are rail junctions, or at least are located along railway lines, are to be designated as concentration points.

On principle, Jewish communities of *fewer* than 500 persons are to be dissolved and to be transferred to the nearest city of concentration.

This decree does not apply to the area of Einsatzgruppe 1, which is situated east of Kraków and is bounded roughly by *Polanico, Jaroslaw*, the new line of demarcation, and the former Slovak-Polish border. Within this area, only an improvised census of Jews is to be carried out. Furthermore, Councils of Jewish Elders, as discussed below, are to be set up.

II
Councils of Jewish Elders [Jüdische Ältestenräte]

(1) In each Jewish community, a Council of Jewish Elders is to be set up, to be composed, as far as possible, of the remaining influential personalities and rabbis. The council is to comprise up to twenty-four Jews (depending on the size of the Jewish community).

The council is to be made *fully responsible*, in the literal sense of the word, for the exact and punctual execution of all directives issued or yet to be issued.

(2) In case of sabotage of such instructions, the councils are to be warned of the severest measures.

(3) The Jewish councils are to take an improvised census of the Jews in their local areas – broken down if possible by sex (age groups): a) up to sixteen years of age, b) from sixteen to twenty years of age, and c) over, as well as by principal occupational groups – and are to report the results in the shortest possible time.

(4) The Councils of Elders are to be informed of the dates and deadlines for departure, departure facilities, and finally departure routes. They are then to be made personally responsible for the departure of the Jews from the countryside.

The reason to be given for the concentration of the Jews into the cities is that Jews have most influentially participated in guerrilla attacks and plundering actions.

(5) The Councils of Elders in the cities of concentration are to be made responsible for appropriately housing the Jews moving in from the countryside.

For general reasons of security, the concentration of Jews in the cities will probably necessitate orders altogether barring Jews from certain sections of cities, or, for example, forbidding them to leave the ghetto or go out after a designated evening hour, etc. However, economic necessities are always to be considered in this connection.

(6) The Councils of Elders are also to be made responsible for appropriate provisioning of the Jews during the transport to the cities.

No objections are to be voiced in the event that migrating Jews take their movable possessions with them, to the extent that this is technically possible.

(7) Jews who do not comply with the order to move into the cities are to be allowed a short additional period of grace where circumstances warrant. They are to be warned of strictest punishment if they should fail to comply with this latter deadline.

III

On principle, all necessary measures are always to be taken in closest accord and cooperation with the German civil administration agencies and locally competent military authorities.

In carrying them out, care must be taken that the economic security of the occupied territories not be impaired.

(1) Above all, the needs of the army must be considered.

For example, for the time being it will hardly be possible to avoid leaving behind some Jew traders here and there, who in the absence of other possibilities simply must stay for the sake of supplying the troops. In such cases, however, prompt Aryanization of these enterprises is to be sought and the emigration of the Jews is to be completed later, in accord with the locally competent German administrative authorities.

(2) For the preservation of German economic interests in the occupied territories, it is obvious that Jewish-owned essential or war industries and enterprises, as well as those important for the Four Year Plan, must be kept up for the time being.

In these cases also, prompt Aryanization is to be sought, and the emigration of the Jews is to be completed later.

(3) Finally, the food situation in the occupied territories must be taken into consideration. For instance, as far as possible, real estate owned by Jewish settlers is to be provisionally entrusted to the care of neighbouring German or even Polish farmers, to be worked by them together with their own, so as to assure harvesting of the crops still in the fields or renewed cultivation.

With regard to this important question, contact is to be made with the agricultural expert of the Chief of the Civil Administration.

(4) In all cases in which the interest of the Security Police on one hand and those of the German Civil Administration on the other cannot be reconciled, I am to be informed in the fastest way before the particular measures in question are carried out, and my decision is to be awaited.

IV

The chiefs of the Einsatzgruppen will report to me continuously on the following matters:

(1) Numerical survey of the Jews present in their territories (broken down as indicated above, if possible). The numbers of Jews who are being evacuated from the countryside and of those who are already in the cities are to be reported separately.

(2) Names of cities which have been designated as concentration points.

(3) Deadlines set for the Jews to migrate to the cities.

(4) Survey of all Jewish-owned essential or war industries and enterprises, as well as those important for the Four Year Plan, within their areas.

If possible, the following should be specified:

a. Kind of enterprise (also statement on possible conversion into enterprises that are truly essential or war-related, or important for the Four Year Plan);

b. Which of these enterprises need to be Aryanized most promptly (in order to forestall any kind of loss)?

What kind of Aryanization is suggested? Germans or Poles? (This decision depends on the importance of the enterprise.)

c. How large is the number of Jews working in these enterprises (including leading positions)?

Can the enterprise simply be kept up after the removal of the Jews, or will such continued operation require assignment of German or Polish workers? On what scale?

Insofar as Polish workers have to be introduced, care should be taken that they are mainly brought in from the former German provinces, so as to begin the weeding out of the Polish element there. These questions can be carried out only through involvement and participation of the German labour offices which have been set up.

V

For the attainment of the goals set, I expect total deployment of all forces of the Security Police and the Security Service.

The chiefs of neighbouring Einsatzgruppen are to establish contact with each other immediately so that the territories concerned will be covered completely.

VI

The High Command of the Army, the Plenipotentiary for the Four Year Plan (Attention: Secretary of State *Neumann*), the Reich Ministries of the Interior (Attention: Secretary of State *Stuckart*), for Food and for Economy (Attention: Secretary of State *Landfried*), as well as the Chiefs of Civil Administration of the Occupied Territory have received copies of this decree.

[Signed] *Heydrich*

Mass Arrests in Łódź, October 1939
DAWID SIERAKOWIAK

Sierakowiak was one of the 200,000 Jews living in Łódź when the Nazis occupied the city. It lay in the western half of Poland as defined by the Pact with the Soviet Union, which took the eastern part of the country.

It's been three days since the mass arrests began. Thousands of teachers, doctors, and engineers, Jews and Poles, have been taken from their homes together with their families (infants have not been spared), and hurried to the market halls, and from there to various German jails. All old activists, former legionnaires, even simply rich people share the same fate. Groups of more prominent people are often dispatched immediately into the next world. The repairman who came to fix the tap said that his wife and some engineers have been arrested. They could not touch the engineer because he's sick (the last phase of tuberculosis). So the Germans sealed the apartment with him and his servant inside. They were, for all practical purposes, condemned to death from hunger. His merciful neighbours lowered a string with bread (challah) so the servant could catch it through the window.

In the evening Mrs Pomeranc came for a visit. She had been to the Jewish Community Council and learned what's really going on. It's true that Łódź is to be cleared of Jews. All the poor who register at the Jewish Community Council receive 50 złotys per person and are literally thrown out of the city: they are taken to Koluszki by train, and are let loose into the world from there. Mrs Pomeranc was advised at the Jewish administration to wait. We, too, considered various plans for departure, but in the end nothing came of them, and we have to wait. Either they will throw us out, or they will not ... In any case, the Hitlerjugendpartei [Hitler Youth Party] leader gave a huge speech, and what he said could be summed up in one sentence: 'We will exterminate the Jews because there is no place for them in the Reich!'

With the Nazi invasion of Poland, two million Polish Jews came under German authority. In line with Heydrich's directive of that month, Jews – invariably stripped of their worldly goods – were herded into ghettos. Sierakowiak was one of them. He died in the Łódź ghetto, probably from tuberculosis, in 1943.

Perhaps as many as 5,000 defenceless Polish Jews were executed by German soldiers and SS between September and October 1939. Everywhere Jews were robbed at gunpoint. One witness, David Wdowinski, a psychiatrist in Warsaw, recalled an incident that befell one Jewish family:

They [three German officers] demanded money and jewellery and threatened the woman at the point of a gun ... Suddenly one of the officers noticed a small medallion hanging around the neck of the little boy. This child had been ill from birth. He had petit mal, a form of epilepsy ... The only thing which gave this child any comfort was this very medallion. In the presence of the officers the child was taken with a seizure ... One of the officers watching the child said: 'I see that the child is ill. I am a doctor, but a Jew-kid is not a human being,' and he tore the medallion off the neck of the little boy.

A Konzentrationslager *is Built at* Oświęcim, Poland, February 1940
SS-OBERSTURMBANNFÜHRER RUDOLF HOESS

Fifty miles west of Kraków, Oświęcim lay in the zone of Poland annexed by Nazi Germany in 1939. The Germans knew it as Auschwitz. The first transports of prisoners arrived there in May 1940, these being criminals relocated from Germany. A transport of Poles – including Jews – arrived in the following month. Under Hoess, Auschwitz grew to become the largest concentration camp in the Third Reich, consisting of Auschwitz I (Administration), Auschwitz II–Birkenau (the extermination camp from 1942 onwards) and Auschwitz III–Monowitz (also known as Buna, a labour camp for the nearby I. G. Farben works). There were also forty-five satellite camps.

When the question of building a new camp at Auschwitz became urgent, the authorities had not far to go for a commandant. Loritz was glad to let me go, so that he could find a commander of the protective custody camp more to his liking. This was Suhren, later to be Commandant of Ravensbrück, who had been Loritz's adjutant in the General SS.

I therefore became Commandant of the quarantine camp which was to be built at Auschwitz.

It was far away, in the back of beyond, in Poland. There the inconvenient Hoess could exercise his passion for work to his heart's content. That was what Glücks, the Inspector of Concentration Camps, had intended. It was in these circumstances that I took up my new task.

I had never anticipated being made a commandant so quickly, especially as some very senior protective custody camp commanders had been waiting a long time for a commandant's post to fall vacant.

My task was not an easy one. In the shortest possible time I had to construct a transit camp for 10,000 prisoners, using the existing complex of buildings which, though well-constructed, had been completely neglected, and were swarming with vermin. From the point of hygiene, practically everything was lacking. I had been told in Oranienburg, before setting off, that I could not expect much help, and that I would have to rely largely on my own resources. In Poland I would find everything that had been unobtainable in Germany for years!

It is much easier to build a completely new concentration camp than to construct one quickly out of a conglomeration of buildings and barracks which require a large amount of constructional alteration. I had hardly arrived in Auschwitz before the Inspector of the Security Police and of the Security Service in Breslau was enquiring when the first transports could be sent to me!

It was clear to me from the very beginning that Auschwitz could be made into a useful camp only through the hard and untiring efforts of everyone, from the Commandant down to the lowest prisoner.

But in order to harness all the available manpower to this task, I had to ignore all concentration camp tradition and customs. If I was to get the maximum effort out of my officers and men, I had to set them a good example. When reveille sounded from the SS rankers, I too must get out of bed. Before they had started their day's work, I had already begun mine. It was late at night before I had finished. There were very few nights in Auschwitz when I could sleep undisturbed by urgent telephone calls.

Deportation, Plock, March 1941
MOSCHE SHKLAREK

In the early hours of that morning the house shuddered from violent knocks on the door and from the savage cries of the Germans, 'Filthy Jews, outside!' Within a few moments we found ourselves huddled together in a crowd of the town's Jews on Sheroka Street.

With the help of the *Volksdeutsche* and with cruel blows and many murders, they loaded the assembled ones on to trucks, crowding them tightly, and the long convoy drove out of town. We were not permitted to take anything with us, not even something else to wear other than what we had put on in our terrified haste.

On the same day, after hours of difficult travelling, the trucks came to a stop in the midst of Dzialdowo camp, at the entrance to the town of Mlawa. Two rows of Germans, equipped with clubs and whips, stood in a line several tens of metres long, extending from the trucks to the camp gate.

We were ordered to jump out of the trucks and run the gauntlet towards the gate. Before the first ones to jump had managed to set foot on the torture-pass, the clubs and whips flew and a torrent of blows rained down on the runners' heads. With difficulty and desperate haste, each one hurried to reach the camp gate, people falling and being trampled under their brothers' feet in their frantic race.

Only an isolated few managed to get through the gate without being wounded by the blows and lashes of the Germans. In the aftermath of this act of terror, scores of slain bodies were left lying and were buried next to the single privy which was provided for the men and women who lived in the camp.

The hundreds of wounded and injured lay without any medical care in the stables that were full of mud and dung, and into which we had been squeezed and packed without room enough to free our aching limbs. In this camp we endured days of torment and distress, thirst and hunger.

Shklarek was later sent to the ghetto at Częstochowa.

A Jewish Girl Risks a Visit to the Cinema, Vienna, 1940
RUTH KLUGER

Unable to afford the *Reichsfluchsteuer*, the tax paid to the Reich which allowed Jews to emigrate, Ruth Kluger and her mother 'got stuck' in Vienna. Almost every public activity was denied to Viennese Jewish children, including going to the cinema.

In 1940, when I was eight or nine, the local movie theatre showed Walt Disney's *Snow White*. I loved movies. I had been weaned on Mickey Mouse shorts and traded pictures of Shirley Temple with classmates.

I badly wanted to see this film, but since I was Jewish, I naturally wasn't permitted to. I groused and bitched about this unfairness, until finally my mother proposed that I should leave her alone and just go and forget about what was permitted and what wasn't.

I hesitated a bit at this unexpected go-ahead, for it was a Sunday, we were known in the neighbourhood, and to go to a movie right there in broad daylight was a kind of dare. My mother couldn't accept the absurdity of blatant discrimination. She assured me that no one would care who sat in an audience of children. I shouldn't think I was that important, and I should stop being a coward, because she was never a coward, not even when she was my age. So of course I went, not only for the movie, but to prove myself. I bought the most expensive type of ticket, thinking that sitting in a loge would make me less noticeable, and thus I ended up next to the nineteen-year-old baker's daughter from next door with her little siblings, enthusiastic Nazis one and all.

I sweated it out for the next ninety minutes and have never before or afterwards understood so little of what happened on the screen. All I could think of was whether the baker's daughter was really glaring at me, or if I was only imagining it. The wicked queen of the film merged with my neighbour, her fairy-tale malice a poor imitation of the real thing, and it was I, and no innocent princess, who was lost in the woods, offered poisoned apples, and in fear of glass coffins.

Why didn't I get up and walk out? Perhaps in order not to face my mother, or because any move might attract attention. Perhaps merely because one doesn't leave a theatre before the film is over, or most likely, because this solution didn't occur to me, frightened as I was. Consider that I still wonder why my people didn't leave Vienna in time – and perhaps there is a family resemblance between that question and why I stayed glued to my seat.

When the lights came on, I wanted to wait until the house had emptied out, but my enemy stood her ground and waited, too. She told her little brothers to hush and fixed me sternly. There I was, trapped, as I had surmised. The baker's daughter put on her gloves and coat and finally addressed me.

She spoke firmly and with conviction, in the manner of a member of the *Bund Deutscher Mädchen*, the female branch of the Hitler Youth, to which she surely belonged. Hadn't I seen the sign at the box office? (I nodded, what else could I do? It was a rhetorical question.) Didn't I know what it meant? I could read, couldn't I? It said 'No Jews'. I had broken a law. She was using her best High German – none of Vienna's easygoing dialect for this patriotic occasion. If it happened again she would call the police. I was lucky that she was letting me off this once.

The story of Snow White can be reduced to one question: who is entitled to live in the king's palace and who is the outsider? The baker's daughter and I followed this formula. She, in her own house, the magic mirror of her racial purity before her eyes, and I, also at home here, a native, but without permission and at this moment expelled and exposed. Even though I despised the law that excluded me, I still felt ashamed to have been found out. For shame doesn't arise from the shameful action, but from discovery and exposure. If I had got away with my transgression, I would have been proud of my daring. But I had been unmasked. W. B. Yeats writes of a man 'among his enemies':

How in the name of Heaven can he escape
That defiling and disfigured shape
The mirror of malicious eyes
Casts upon his eyes until at last
He thinks that shape must be his shape?

The common lot of the outcast is self-contempt. I might have felt better had I known this poem, which I committed to memory some ten years later.

It was over pretty soon. The girl had asserted the superiority of her Germanic forefathers as opposed to the vermin race I belonged to, and there was nothing more to say. I was in a state of shock. This was new and terrible. Tears welled up, but I held them back. The usher, an older woman, helped me into my coat and handed me my purse, which I was about to leave on the seat. She was sorry for me and said a few soothing words. I nodded, incapable of answering because I was choking on my tears of humiliation, but grateful for this bit of kindness, these alms for the poor.

Kluger was later transported to the ghetto at Theresienstadt, then Auschwitz. She survived the Holocaust.

'People were being hanged for nothing':
Terror in the Łódź Ghetto, c. 1940
MICHAEL ETKIND

In some ghettos the Jews were forced into labour on behalf of the Nazi war economy, in others they were simply left to die by the 'natural' means of starvation and disease, but in all these places there were random acts of Nazi terror. Etkind was a Jewish schoolboy in Łódź in 1940.

... various notices appeared; for example, Jews were not allowed to walk on the main street which was renamed Adolf Hitler Strasse. They were not allowed to go into parks, swimming pools, or cinemas and theatres. All the money in the bank was frozen, all property belonging to Jews automatically confiscated. Then Jews had to wear an armband with the Star of David on it to show that they were Jews; somebody started making them and you bought them at the street corners. The death penalty was imposed for the slightest deviation from the order. People were being hanged for nothing, just to terrorize the population. I am very squeamish and found it strange that, out of morbid curiosity, people would go to where corpses were hanging in the square.

Medical Experiments at Dachau, 1941–5
FRANZ BLAHA

This is taken from Blaha's deposition to the post-war military tribunal at Nuremberg.

I, Franz Blaha, being duly sworn, depose and state as follows:

I was sent as a prisoner to the Dachau Concentration Camp in April 1941, and remained there until the liberation of the camp in April 1945. Until July 1941 I worked in a Punishment Company. After that I was sent to the hospital and subjected to the experiments in typhoid being conducted by Dr Mürmelstadt. After that I was to be made the subject of an experimental operation, and only succeeded in avoiding this by admitting that I was a physician. If this had been known before I would have suffered, because intellectuals were treated very harshly in the Punishment Company. In October 1941 I was sent to work in the herb plantation, and later in the laboratory for processing herbs. In June 1942, I was taken into the hospital as a surgeon. Shortly afterwards I was directed to conduct a stomach operation on twenty healthy prisoners. Because I would not do this I was put in the autopsy room, where I stayed until April 1945. While there I performed approximately 7,000 autopsies. In all, 12,000 autopsies were performed under my direction.

From mid-1941 to the end of 1942 some 500 operations on healthy prisoners were performed. These were for the instruction of the SS medical students and doctors and included operations on the stomach, gall bladder, spleen and throat. These were performed by students and doctors of only two years' training although they were very dangerous and difficult. Ordinarily they would not have been done except by surgeons with at least four years' surgical practice. Many prisoners died on the operating table and many others from later complications. I performed autopsies on all these bodies. The doctors who supervised these operations were Lang, Mürmelstadt, Wolter, Ramsauer and Kahr. Standartenführer Dr Lolling frequently witnessed these operations.

During my time at Dachau I was familiar with many kinds of medical experiments carried on there with human victims. These persons were never volunteers but were forced to submit to such acts. Malaria experiments on about 1,200 people were conducted by Dr Klaus Schilling between 1941 and 1945. Schilling was personally asked by Himmler to conduct these experiments. The victims were either bitten by mosquitoes or given injections of malaria sporozoites taken from mosquitoes. Different kinds of treatment were applied, including quinine, pyrifer, neosalvarsan, antipyrin, pyramidon and a drug called 2515 Behring. I performed autopsies on bodies of people who died from these malaria experiments. Thirty to forty died from the malaria itself. Three to four hundred died later from diseases which proved fatal because of the physical condition resulting from the malaria attacks. In addition there were deaths resulting from poisoning due to overdoses of neosalvarsan and pyramidon. Dr Scholling was present at the time of my autopsies on the bodies of his patients.

In 1942 and 1943 experiments on human beings were being conducted by Dr Sigismund Rascher to determine the effects of changing air pressure. As many as twenty-five persons were put at one time into a specially constructed van in which pressure could be increased or decreased as required. The purpose was to find out the effects of high altitude and of rapid parachute descents on human beings. Through a window in the van I have seen the people lying on the floor of the van. Most of the prisoners who were made use of died as a result of these experiments, from internal haemorrhages of the lungs or brain. The rest coughed blood when taken out. It was my job to take the bodies out and to send the internal organs to Munich for study as soon as they were found to be dead. About 400 to 500 prisoners were experimented on. Those not dead were sent to invalid blocks and liquidated shortly afterwards. Only a few escaped.

Rascher also conducted experiments on the effect of cold water on human beings. This was done to find a way for reviving aviators who had fallen into the ocean. The subject was placed in ice-cold water and kept there until he was unconscious. Blood was taken from his neck and tested each time his body temperature dropped one degree. This drop was determined by a rectal thermometer. Urine was also periodically tested. Some men lasted as long as twenty-four to thirty-six hours. The lowest body temperature reached was nineteen degrees C., but most men died at twenty-five degrees C., or twenty-six degrees C. When the men were removed from the ice water attempts were made to revive them by artificial warmth from the sun, from hot water, from electro-therapy or by animal warmth. For this last experiment prostitutes were used and the body of the unconscious man was placed between the bodies of two women. Himmler was present at one such experiment. I could see him from one of the windows in the street between the blocks. I have personally been present at some of the cold-water experiments when Rascher was absent, and I have seen notes and diagrams on them in Rascher's laboratory. About 300 persons were used in these experiments. The majority died. Of those who lived many became mentally deranged. Those not killed were sent to invalid blocks and were killed, just as were the victims of the air-pressure experiments. I only know two who survived – a Jugoslav and a Pole, both of whom have become mental cases.

Liver-puncture experiments were performed by Dr Brachtl on healthy people, and on people who had diseases of the stomach and gall bladder. For this purpose a needle was jabbed into the liver of a person and a small piece of liver was extracted. No anaesthetic was used. The experiment is very painful and often had serious results, as the stomach or large blood vessels were often punctured and haemorrhage resulted. Many persons died of these tests, for which Polish, Russian, Czech and German prisoners were employed. Altogether these experiments were conducted on about 175 people.

Phlegmone experiments were conducted by Dr Schütz, Dr Babor, Dr Kieselwetter and Professor Lauer. Forty healthy men were used at a time, of whom twenty were given intra-muscular, and twenty intravenous, injections of pus from diseased persons. All treatment was forbidden for three days, by which time serious inflammation and in many cases general blood poisoning had occurred. Then each group were divided again into groups of ten. Half were given chemical treatment with liquid and special pills every ten minutes for twenty-four hours. The rest were treated with sulphonamide and surgery. In some cases all of the limbs were amputated. My autopsy also showed that the chemical treatment had been harmful and even caused perforations of the stomach wall. For these experiments Polish, Czech and Dutch priests were ordinarily used. Pain was intense in such experiments. Most of the 600 to 800 persons who were used finally died. Most of the others became permanent invalids and were later killed.

In the autumn of 1944 there were sixty to eighty persons who were subjected to salt-water experiments. They were locked in a room and for five days were given nothing to swallow but salt water. During this time their urine, blood and excrement were tested. None of these prisoners died, possibly because they received smuggled food from other prisoners. Hungarians and gypsies were used for these experiments.

It was common practice to remove the skin from dead prisoners. I was commanded to do this on many occasions. Dr Rascher and Dr Wolter in particular asked for this human skin from human backs and chests. It was chemically treated and placed in the sun to dry. After that it was cut into various sizes for use as saddles, riding breeches, gloves, house slippers and ladies' handbags. Tattooed skin was especially valued by SS men. Russians, Poles and other inmates were used in this way, but it was forbidden to cut out the skin of a German. This skin had to be from healthy prisoners and free from defects. Sometimes we did not have enough bodies with good skin and Rascher would say 'All right, you will get the bodies.' The next day we would receive twenty or thirty bodies of young people. They would have been shot in the neck or struck on the head so that the skin would be uninjured. Also we frequently got requests for the skulls or skeletons of prisoners. In those cases we boiled the skull or the body. Then the soft parts were removed and the bones were bleached and dried and reassembled. In the case of skulls it was important to have a good set of teeth. When we got an order for skulls from Oranienburg the SS men would say, 'We will try to get you some with good teeth.' So it was dangerous to have a good skin or good teeth.

The Commandant of Auschwitz is Ordered to Construct a Mass Extermination Facility, Summer 1941
RUDOLF HOESS

Although Chelmno (Kulmhof) was the first sole-purpose extermination camp, or *Vernichtungslager*, Auschwitz II was the Nazi leadership's preferred killing gound because of its easy rail access and its isolation.

In the summer of 1941, I cannot remember the exact date, I was suddenly summoned to the Reichsführer SS, directly by his adjutant's office. Contrary to his usual custom, Himmler received me without his adjutant being present and said in effect:

'The Führer has ordered that the Jewish question be solved once and for all and that we, the SS, are to implement that order.

'The existing extermination centres in the east are not in a position to carry out the large actions which are anticipated. I have therefore earmarked Auschwitz for this purpose, both because of its good position as regards communications and because the area can easily be isolated and camouflaged. At first I thought of calling in a senior SS officer for this job, but I changed my mind in order to avoid difficulties concerning the terms of reference. I have now decided to entrust this task to you. It is difficult and onerous and calls for complete devotion notwithstanding the difficulties that may arise. You will learn further details from Sturmbannführer Eichmann of the Reich Security Head Office who will call on you in the immediate future.

'The departments concerned will be notified by me in due course. You will treat this order as absolutely secret, even from your superiors.

After your talk with Eichmann you will immediately forward to me the plans of the projected installations.

'The Jews are the sworn enemies of the German people and must be eradicated. Every Jew that we can lay our hands on is to be destroyed now during the war, without exception. If we cannot now obliterate the biological basis of Jewry, the Jews will one day destroy the German people.'

* * *

On receiving these grave instructions, I returned forthwith to Auschwitz, without reporting to my superior at Oranienburg.

Shortly afterwards Eichmann came to Auschwitz and disclosed to me the plans for the operations as they affected the various countries concerned. I cannot remember the exact order in which they were to take place. First was to come the eastern part of Upper Silesia and the neighbouring parts of Polish territory under German rule, then, depending on the situation, simultaneously Jews from Germany and Czechoslovakia, and finally the Jews from the West: France, Belgium and Holland. He also told me the approximate numbers of transports that might be expected, but I can no longer remember these.

We discussed the ways and means of effecting the extermination. This could only be done by gassing, since it would have been absolutely impossible to dispose by shooting of the large numbers of people that were expected, and it would have placed too heavy a burden on the SS men who had to carry it out, especially because of the women and children among the victims.

Eichmann told me about the method of killing people with exhaust gases in lorries, which had previously been used in the east. But there was no question of being able to use this for these mass transports that were due to arrive in Auschwitz. Killing with showers of carbon monoxide while bathing, as was done with mental patients in some places in the Reich, would necessitate too many buildings and it was also very doubtful whether the supply of gas for such a vast number of people would be available. We left the matter unresolved. Eichmann decided to try and find a gas which was in ready supply and which would not entail special installations for its use, and to inform me when he had done so. We inspected the area in order to choose a likely spot. We decided that a peasant farmstead situated in the north-west corner of what later became the third building sector at Birkenau would be the most suitable. It was isolated and screened by woods and hedges, and it was also not far away from the railway. The bodies could be placed in long, deep pits dug in nearby meadow. We had not at that time thought of burning the corpses. We calculated that after gas-proofing the premises then available, it would be possible to kill about 800 people simultaneously with a suitable gas. These figures were borne out later in practice …

By the will of the Reichsführer SS, Auschwitz became the greatest human extermination centre of all time.

When in the summer of 1941 he himself gave me the order to prepare installations at Auschwitz where mass exterminations could take place, and personally to carry out these exterminations, I did not have the slightest idea of their scale or consequences. It was certainly an extraordinary and monstrous order. Nevertheless the reasons behind the extermination programme seemed to me right. I did not reflect on it at the time: I had been given an order, and I had to carry it out. Whether this mass extermination of the Jew was necessary or not was something on which I could not allow myself to form an opinion, for I lacked the necessary breadth of view.

If the Führer had himself given the order for the 'final solution of the Jewish question', then, for a veteran National Socialist and even more so for an SS officer, there could be no question of considering its merits. 'The Führer commands, we follow' was never a mere phrase or slogan. It was meant in bitter earnest.

Death by gassing had been the fate of mentally 'defective' Germans since 1939. In addition to Chelmno and Auschwitz, there were *Vernichtungslager* at Belzec, Sobibór, Majdanek and Treblinka. There was also gassing of inmates on a more minor scale at Dachau, Mauthausen, Oranienburg (also known as Sachsenhausen), Ravensbrück, Neuengamme, Stutthof, and Natzweiler concentration camps. The main poison gas used in the camps, Zyklon (Cyclon) B, prussic acid, was manufactured by I. G. Farben's subsidiary, Degesch.

Auschwitz: The Gas Trial, 3 September 1941
RUDOLF HOESS

In accordance with a secret order issued by Hitler, these Russian *politruks* and political commissars were combed out of all the prisoner-of-war camps by special detachments from the Gestapo. When identified, they were transferred to the nearest concentration camp for liquidation. It was made known that these measures were taken because the Russians had been killing all German soldiers who were party members or belonged to special sections of the NSDAP, especially members of the SS, and also because the political officials of the Red Army had been ordered, if taken prisoner, to create every kind of disturbance in the prisoner-of-war camps and their places of employment and to carry out sabotage wherever possible.

The political officials of the Red Army thus identified were brought to Auschwitz for liquidation. The first, smaller transports of them were executed by firing squads.

While I was away on duty, my deputy, Fritzsch, the commander of the protective custody camp, first tried gas for these killings. It was a preparation of prussic acid, called Zyklon B, which was used in the camp as an insecticide and of which there was always a stock on hand. On my return, Fritzsch reported this to me, and the gas was used again for the next transport.

The gassing was carried out in the detention cells of Block II. Protected by a gas-mask, I watched the killing myself. In the crowded cells death came instantaneously the moment the Zyklon B was thrown in. A short, almost smothered cry, and it was all over. During this first experience of gassing people, I did not fully realize what was happening, perhaps because I was too impressed by the whole procedure. I have a clearer recollection of the gassing of 900 Russians which took place shortly afterwards in the old crematorium, since the use of Block II for this purpose caused too much trouble. While the transport was detraining, holes were pierced in the earth and concrete ceiling of the mortuary. The Russians were ordered to undress in an anteroom; they then quietly entered the mortuary, for they had been told they were to be deloused. The whole transport exactly filled the mortuary to capacity. The doors were then sealed and the gas shaken down through the holes in the roof. I do not know how long this killing took. For a little while a humming sound could be heard. When the powder was thrown in, there were cries of 'Gas!', then a great bellowing, and the trapped prisoners hurled themselves against both the doors. But the doors held. They were opened several hours later, so that the place might be aired. It was then that I saw, for the first time, gassed bodies in the mass.

It made me feel uncomfortable and I shuddered, although I had imagined that death by gassing would be worse than it was. I had always thought that the victims would experience a terrible choking sensation. But the bodies, without exception, showed no signs of convulsion. The doctors explained to me that the prussic acid had a paralyzing effect on the lungs, but its action was so quick and strong that death came before the convulsions could set in, and in this its effects differed from those produced by carbon monoxide or by a general oxygen deficiency.

The killing of these Russian prisoners-of-war did not cause me much concern at the time. The order had been given, and I had to carry it out. I must even admit that this gassing set my mind at rest, for the mass extermination of the Jews was to start soon and at that time neither Eichmann nor I was certain how these mass killings were to be carried out. It would be by gas, but we did not know which gas or how it was to be used. Now we had the gas, and we had established a procedure.

Life inside the Warsaw Ghetto, 1941–2
ANONYMOUS

After the time of the German invasion 393,950 Jews lived in Warsaw, a third of the city's population. The ghetto in the city, into which all Warsaw's Jews were herded, was formally established on 15 November 1940. The *Judenrat* was the official Jewish community council, as prescribed by Heydrich.

The Germans came to the ghetto with trucks to haul away the furniture. Most possessions – furniture, pictures, carpets, and the like – had been collected from the majority of the Jewish apartments even before the district was closed off. Practically every German visit to a Jewish home was accompanied by some brutality. They kicked and beat the inhabitants at every opportunity: if someone was a little too slow answering questions, or if he didn't carry the furniture adroitly enough, or mostly for no reason at all. One German gentleman punched my fifty-year-old neighbour in the eye because she took too long to find the whisk broom he had requested, even though the hallway was completely dark. They squeezed her husband's nose with pliers because he didn't say goodbye; the punishment was for a lapse of courtesy. Similar incidents could be listed ad infinitum.

The Germans didn't stop plundering inside the ghetto until the typhus epidemic began to gain strength. The disease had broken out in the first months after the Germans entered Warsaw, clearly due to the growing hunger and poverty. Food rations were incalculably small: other than dark bread, which was supplied irregularly, and vegetables, which were scarcely ever available, there was practically nothing to eat, especially no meat or fat of any kind. People were undernourished; their nerves were exhausted; they neglected their apartments, which became increasingly filthy. If they didn't have money to buy their children a bit of bread, how were they going to pay for a bar of soap?

I know this side of life in the Warsaw Ghetto very well because I spent a long time working with the building committee on Ogrodowa Street. Assigned to my building were about thirty families (approximately 150 people) who lived in a small wooden shack set off at right angles to the main building and who had no electricity, gas, or water. Among them were a carriage driver whose horses had been taken by the Germans, a seamstress with two children whose husband – a provincial schoolteacher – had been killed, a bakery worker with ten mouths to feed, and so on. Ten or twenty people were crammed into each room: old parents, small children, or young people who had been removed from their places of work and were trying to earn a few pennies for bread by trading on the streets. They struggled with the difficult conditions as well as they could, but it was an uphill battle. Prices kept rising, while their strength and resources kept dwindling. Shortages of shoes and clothing left a severe mark. Hunger and cold often kept people confined to bed for weeks on end. The building committee organized a kitchen to feed the children, distributed packages for the holidays, paid for medicine and medical treatments, offered whatever aid or loans it could, procured clothes, sought employment for those able to work, and maintained a heated and lit community room where people could sit during the day. More than a dozen building committees set up a public kitchen on

Ogrodowa Street, which served soup daily to several hundred of the poorest people.

Not only did the building committees fill an important role by bringing aid to the impoverished populace, they frequently also helped awaken their political consciousness. The committees were headed by people with ties to the working masses and were generally opposed by the *Judenrat*, which disapproved of independent programmes. The *Judenrat* wanted to transform the committees into agencies that would implement its own agenda by pressuring the residents in their charge. To this end the *Judenrat* imposed a variety of payments and taxes on the committees, clearly designed to reduce the committees' available funds.

Whereas some committees continued operating several months into the liquidation actions, the one on Ogrodowa ceased operations when a new shift in the ghetto's boundaries relocated the streets to the Aryan side. This was in 1941. The soup kitchen was closed at the same time, depriving many people in the neighbourhood of a hot bowl of soup and needed nutrition. Hunger grew increasingly severe. More and more patients complained to their doctors of swelling due to hunger, and more and more corpses lay on the ghetto streets. Pale, emaciated children with huge, horribly hungry eyes sobbed and moaned and asked for bread. Living skeletons covered in rags became an increasingly common sight. There was scarcely a night when you didn't hear the groans of people dying on the street. The typhus spread. Doctors made superhuman efforts to control the disease: daily rounds of assigned buildings, lectures maintaining hygiene, attempts to obtain soap rations and disinfectants, and long hard hours in the hospital. But the epidemic grew, owing to the conditions inside the ghetto. Hundreds of dirty, starving Jews who had been declared unfit for work in the labour camps were relocated in Warsaw, and even more people were resettled from the provinces. Typhus decimated the population – in private homes, public shelters, children's boarding houses, and in the *punkty*.

These last, shelters for homeless refugees, had their own desperate, tragic story. They housed masses of people who had been deprived of their homes and shipped in from outside the city without any possessions or means of support. The agency responsible for their welfare put these people up wherever it could and struggled to keep them alive. But what kind of life was it, with over a dozen – or even several dozen – people to a room, lacking even the most primitive cots for sleeping, and, worst of all, with no food, no hope for tomorrow, no energy to go on living? A few lucky ones managed to break out and move in with some distant relative, miraculously discovered, where they would add to the poverty already reigning in that household. Some stayed put for as long as it took for a merciful death to bring an end to their suffering.

The mortality rate rose. On average, some 4,000 people died each month. As the poverty and hunger worsened, tuberculosis also became epidemic and wrought horrible devastation up to the very end of the ghetto's existence. It was impossible to fight. Thousands of adults and children died because they were getting no fat, no milk, no sugar. The hospitals were overflowing and the doctors despaired at their powerlessness.

Life in the ghetto never flowed smoothly. News of every event, regardless of its significance, was passed from mouth to mouth. One day a small Jewish boy was killed on Biala Street as he attempted to pull a carrot lying in the gutter on the Aryan side through a hole in the fence. A German spotted him, inserted his gun in the hole, and killed the boy with one well-aimed shot. Was it so strange that this incident should have moved thousands of people? Another case involved a notorious gendarme known as Frankenstein, who had vowed he would personally kill a thousand Jews. From a window of the building at Elektoralna 6, I once saw this murderer at work in the courtyard, killing the concierge, who refused to say where another Jew had run off, supposedly a smuggler who had caught Frankenstein's eye.

During the winter of 1942, people were going barefoot on the streets. But that no longer made much impression; by then the ghetto residents had grown indifferent even to the dry shrivelled faces and dull stares of children who were alive but unable to walk, whose mouths could no longer form words, and whose speech was reduced to a terrifying gibberish. Their eyes showed neither tears nor hunger, but only death, painting its features inside their faces. For the most part these children sat near the courthouse; people learned to pass by these living human horrors calmly, just as they passed corpses.

The Germans started filming inside the ghetto. One day they drove to the *Judenrat* and ordered a lavish banquet to be staged in the home of the council president, with a number of elegantly dressed guests. That was filmed along with several other banquets staged in various other apartments. They also filmed in restaurants and cafés. They even took the camera to the Jewish bath house, or *mikvah*, but that day no dirty, starving Jews were allowed inside; the Germans rounded up well-dressed people from off the street. They filmed a Jewish funeral as well. Inside the ghetto, especially in 1942, all funerals followed the same pattern. A collective hearse – a large box divided into two floors, each of which held three or four litters – arrived for the corpse; it could be pulled by a single person if there was only one deceased. The German film crew staged a different kind of funeral. The hearse was decorated with flowers and pulled by two beautifully festooned horses, while a sumptuously dressed rabbi led the procession. Of course no funerals like that ever happened in the ghetto. It was obvious that the films were designed as propaganda.

Life Inside the Warsaw Ghetto II, 1941–2
NATAN ZELICHOWER

The people of the ghetto street formed one huge mass of castaways doomed to extinction, subsisting on a daily diet of anguished news and heart-wrenching notices. With its relentless reports of dead and dying friends and acquaintances, the street served as a constant memento mori, a terrible whip in the hands of a merciless executioner, flogging into sobriety any drunken hopes for a better tomorrow. But the street was also a true life-giving artery. Shadowy figures emerged from the depths of the blackened city to feed off the street like leeches, and these in turn fed others, even to the point of nourishing delusions of a bright future built on easy living and abundant earnings.

Raw nerves cried out at the slightest touch. The most trivial matter would set women crowded around a kitchen stove to quarrelling. Every pot became the subject of a spat, every spoon sparked anger, every child's cry triggered a mother's sharp reaction. The ghetto lived in a constant tense clamour that grew worse with every piece of bad news and rarely if ever was silenced. Even the seemingly quiet nights only muffled but did not still this unbroken lament.

Everyone stayed alert. No one left home without asking, 'What's it like out today?' Once outside, people focused trained eyes on their surroundings, searching for danger. Pedestrians traded words of warning that could suddenly shift the direction of traffic. Mere mention of a threat, the slightest gesture, could send a crowd of several thousand back inside, leaving the street empty and bare.

Danger could swoop down like a hawk. A black limousine would pull up at a street corner; a Gestapo officer would step out and casually survey the crowd. He would choose his victims, summon them with his finger, shove them into the car, and speed off towards the destroyed buildings on Dzielna Street, just opposite the Pawiak prison. There they would be subjected to a meticulous search and then shot in the head, while the car would return to the ghetto in search of new prey. This private hunting became a favourite sport among dignitaries of the new regime in need of immediate financial relief. If they appeared on a street the traffic would slow down, although it never stopped altogether. After the limousine left, people would diligently enquire who had been taken away – then return to business, trading, shouting, haggling, consoling ... and waiting for the next black limousine.

During the night, soldiers would make the rounds of certain buildings accompanied by members of the SP; they would pound on doors using their rifle-butts and nightsticks. Dozens of men whose names had been listed in advance would be dragged from their homes. These dazed, terrified victims would be led to some side street, lined up against a wall, and gunned down on the spot. Then the perpetrators would briskly ring the doorbells of the buildings nearest the corpses and order the concierges to stack the bodies in the entranceways and wash the blood off the pavement. A few hours later, crowds of people would step over the same spot completely unaware of what had taken place there. The only news of these incidents travelled through word of mouth, as people passed along the victims' names – at least for a day or two, until the next execution.

The Jews did not believe in their own extinction. At the very centre of the 'spiritual refuge' sat God, who, having led them through the Red Sea, would surely knock down the walls of the ghetto. While the executions filled people with terror and wrenched their hearts with fear, there was always some space left for reasoning: methods such as this might enable the Germans to eliminate a few thousand, or let's say, even tens of thousands, but surely not half a million people! Logically speaking then, since not everyone inside the ghetto was doomed, each person had a chance of escaping alive. And the best defence against execution was faith – an unwavering faith in divine protection, along with vigilance and cleverness to avoid getting caught in a round up. In time, though, none of these defences could withstand the cunning techniques devised by the Germans.

The SP (*Sluzba Porzadkowa*) was the Jewish police force in the ghetto. Zelichower survived the Holocaust, and was liberated from Buchenwald in April 1943. His wife and daughter both perished.

Smuggling in the Warsaw Ghetto, 1941
PERETZ OPOCZYNSKI

In every ghetto the smuggling of food became a way of life. Opoczynski was a Polish journalist.

Kożla Alley

The ghetto wall cuts across Franciszkańska Street right at Kożla Alley. From the distance you don't see it; only when you stand at the corner of the alley does it become visible, and then in its entirety, as it is. It is an alley, narrow and small, with odd old-fashioned[?]* and antiquated buildings, courtyards[?], twisting entryways, and tumbledown stairways. Here and there, a narrow many-windowed five-storey house shoots up between two antiquated buildings, a sign that small flats had been here, working people, artisans, and street-vendors.

These forlorn, uprearing buildings, squeezed in between the antiquated little houses, destroy the symmetry of the alley and give an impression of something chaotic, untrammelled[?], neglected and disregarded even before the war ...

In front of every house is a dense mass of fruit and vegetable carts and food stands. The food stands are small. On a chair or a small table a woman sets out a few small sacks of two or three kilograms of rye, coarse, and 'ration' flour; or groats, millet, and barley. Other types of food, like beans and white flour, are not usually seen[?] on these stands, but can be had in the stores. The prices here are of course a

---

* Illegible portions of the original are indicated by a bracketed question mark; reconstructions are in brackets.

little cheaper than in other streets; after all, it is Koźla Alley. Still, they are dear enough for a great part of Warsaw Jews, whom the ghetto has robbed of their livelihood and left with idle, useless hands and whose only possibility for sustaining a bare existence is by selling, little by little, their clothes and household effects at the poor man's flea market.

The booths, stands, and carts block the street. Every booth is besieged not so much by customers as by those who want to buy, but don't have the wherewithal. The volume of business is large, but negligible in weight. Rare the housewife who buys a whole kilo of potatoes, beets, or carrots. People buy ten decagrams or less. People buy a single apple, and anyone who buys a quarter kilogram is a super housekeeper.[?] People come to find out how high the market stands today, if prices have fallen. They swallow their mortification and leave with a searing pain of shame that they are penniless …

The traffic of the rickshaws, the distinctive means of locomotion of the Warsaw Ghetto, which … [?] was taken from as far away as the Japanese and Chinese. The rickshaw is a big help in Koźla Alley, not so much because now there are no droshkies and wagons, since the Germans confiscated the Jewish drivers' horses – that would still not be intolerable. The Warsaw Jewish porter, you may be sure, can carry a fine load of flour on his back. But what's the use if you don't dare do it in the open? For the Gestapo agent's eye is on the lookout. With the rickshaw, it's another story. The Jews have perfected the rickshaw in ways the Chinese never dreamed of. Under the seat is a space where you can stow a few bundles of flour, and sit up there on the plush seat as innocent as you please: I'm just taking a little ride.

But not everyone who carries food from Koźla Alley uses a rickshaw. Most go on foot, and indeed these are the mainstay of Koźla, the receivers and their helpers, the 'strollers'. They can't afford rickshaws; their rickshaws are their own backs on to which they often load three or four bags of flour, groats, and other sorts of food at one time. A bag may weigh fifteen kilograms, yet off they go. The market at the corner of Koźla Alley, the congestion among the vegetable buyers, and the rickshaws block the way for the 'stroller' and other buyers at Koźla. Each stride brings curses from the crowd. [The 'stroller' who hears these curses] hurries. He sweats and pants and tries [to get rid] of his bundles as soon as possible, because a Gestapo agent [is around] and has terrified him.

The movement and the danger [are] not so great all through the day, for the smuggler doesn't want to and can't keep the goods in storage; he must get the goods off his hands as quickly as possible. Just as feverishly and hurriedly as it is smuggled into his house, so quickly must he get it out. Only then can he relax, with no evidence to incriminate him.

Night-time Smuggling

Night-time smuggling supplies the smugglers' shops with plenty of everything: vegetables and fruit, groceries, meat and poultry[?], honey, and whatever one's heart desires. Even good drink, too. The city needs to eat in the morning, the 'strollers' need a whole day for their work. At five o'clock summer mornings you can see them hauling bags of food, sacks of potatoes, cans of milk. Their faces fresh, washed by the morning, these people have the spirit of working people who eat their fill, and the feeling of assurance and of strength – amid the swarm of swollen feet.

Night-time smuggling is only a part of all the [smuggling], and cannot supply the ghetto with everything it requires in the few night hours, especially in summer, when the smuggler never gets the goods he ordered at the specified time. When you ask the smuggler if he will have such and such provision later, he will always answer: 'I don't know. If they get it over to me, I'll have it. Everything depends on when they can pass it over from there.'

Night-time the smuggling goes by way of the rooftops, through tight openings, through cellars, and even over the ghetto wall itself. In short: wherever possible. Daytime, in contrast, it goes much more simply, although not without dodges and very often with inventiveness, a Jewish head. As the Mishna has it: 'He who sees a place where miracles happened to Israel ...'

Koźla Alley has several even-numbered houses in which non-Jews live, but whose entrances and gates have been walled up. Their entrances are on the other side, on Freta Street, that is, outside the ghetto. Only the windows of some apartments look out on Koźla. This is indeed a blessing not only for the few non-Jews who occupy these apartments, but also for the Jews. And, let's be honest, not only for the Jews of Koźla Alley, for the smugglers, but for all the Jews in Warsaw. Smuggling, to be sure, is basically a dirty business, a noose on the neck of the hunger-swollen consumer, but, nevertheless, under the terrible conditions of the great prison into which Warsaw Jews have been corralled, the ghetto walls, it is the only salvation for the surviving remnants. Who knows? Some day perhaps we ought to erect a monument to the smuggler for [the] risks [he took] because consequently he thereby saved a good part of Jewish Warsaw from starving to death.

Grated Windows

The windows of the non-Jewish apartments were secured from top to bottom with wire grating, supposedly to fence the building off from the Jewish street. Actually the gratings are a good way to bring off the smuggling. Inside, right at the grates, the Gentile inserts a wooden trough, the kind you see in the mills. The trough reaches[?] through the grating, and when the Gentile pours a sack of rye into it, the rye drains through the grating right into the sack in the hands of the Jewish smuggler of Kozła Alley. In a wink the sack is full, and Meyer Bomke, the tall porter, with shoulders like a Russian peasant, whisks it on his back like a feather and vanishes, as he must.

Cereal, millet, granulated sugar,[?] and other foods are smuggled the same way. Only flour is smuggled in paper bags ... through upstairs windows. From above, the Polish smuggler lowers a rope to the pavement. There the Jewish smuggler ties the paper bags to the rope. The Pole hoists the rope with the paper bags, fills them with flour, then lowers the rope with single bags of flour, which are [promptly] seized by the smugglers who spirit them away. In order not to cut his hands, the Pole wears heavy cotton gloves, through which the rope slides smoothly.

When the time comes to lower the merchandise, the ground-floor windows are besieged. Around the smugglers are their wives, their sons and daughters, porters[?] talking to the Poles. But only those can buy who are entitled, according to the smugglers.

Often you can hear one smuggler arguing with another at the 'non-Jewish' window: 'Jakie, rat! You stinker! The devil take you! You won't get near that window again! I swear, I'll fix you good!'

'Meyer, shove off! Hurry up. Look how he works.'

'Mendel, blazes take you, why are you standing there![?] Here, take this to the market.'

... People scramble for merchandise and the smuggled goods are quickly removed. A heave, a shove, a yank, and the merchandise is stowed away in the half-closed dark stores ... Broad shouldered women, red-cheeked, with callused hands[?] wink nervously, keeping a lookout to the end of the alley, where it meets Franciszkańska, to see if someone is coming, driving, riding. And, suddenly the air is pierced by a hoarse warning scream: 'Passover!'

The warning is picked up on all sides and [all] doors are slammed shut and bolted. Padlocks are hung up outside. Some of the smugglers remain inside, others go out to keep watch. They lean against the store, as if to say they have nothing better to do. The Poles above speedily hoist up the ropes, and Kozla becomes quiet. The atmosphere grows more[?] in tense anticipation. The smuggling routine has ground to a halt.

For it is 'Passover'. Some non-Jew with a briefcase has turned up. No one knows who he is, but probably he is a police agent So they wait. When the Pole upstairs, too impatient to wait, has the nerve to lower the rope again, shouting to the Jews below: 'There is no more Passover', they send up a warning with the contemptuous manner of the more experienced: 'Hold on, Passover is still around.'

The Poles deliver milk to Kozla Alley at about seven in the morning, elsewhere still earlier. Large tin cans of standard litre capacity are set outside the windows of the ground-floor apartments. A thick hose equipped with a measuring device is passed through the wire mesh of the grates. One turn of the tap and out pours a white stream of rich milk, diffusing the aroma of cow sheds, and quickly fills the cans. Even more quickly it is dispatched from the window into the stores, where milkmen and women are already waiting with containers to deliver the milk home to their customers.

Berl the Souse

The Jewish smugglers, receivers of the milk, are provided with tasters to see if the milk is pure, unadulterated, but that is only for themselves. They don't care if the customers are fooled, in fact they manage to somehow, because, after all, it's not a matter of justice, but a matter of profit[?]; a plump drumstick or gizzard, and a drink, which a man like Mr Berl must have. Indeed, this Mr Berl has prepared the cans in his place in such a way that they contain a goodly quantity of water mixed with a sort of white froth, and that's the way he does business. When a woman comes to the window and insists on buying the milk as it flows directly from the Pole's hose, to be sure of its purity, he argues that it will cost her six złotys.

The accounting is quite simple.

Actually we've run ahead of ourselves. The work plan or, more accurately, the daily smuggling plan begins not with milk, but with vegetables. Not everybody can buy bread, but a beetroot, on the other hand, a potato, or carrot, are precious foods in wartime, much in demand.

Solly the Skirt, a squat man with round red cheeks like Simhat Torah apples, and doughy hands stuck in his pockets, starts selling at dawn: smuggled potatoes, greens, and also eggs, creamery butter, honey, and sometimes also non-kosher fats. His wife, Rosie, with a big backside, fleshy lips, and puffy beringed fingers, stands at the scales; time and again she lifts a bag of flour and asks this one and that one what he's buying, how much he pays, and giddap – we're off again. If she doesn't like the price, she shouts in her mannish voice: 'Beat it, phonies, we'll send [a delivery boy] to your house[?]. Too bad you can't do with less than pure white flour.'

Solly stands nearby on his stumpy legs, frowns, his squinty eyes with whitish brows dusted with flour summon up the sleepiness of a baker. He keeps his hands in his pockets; the watch chain over his well-filled waistcoat gleams sumptuously, as if to say: Damn your hides, you paupers! The hell I'll give you such flour for that price. Solly the Skirt knows what flour is. After all, he was a baker before the war.

One of his six or eight partners, Izzy the Face, who is two heads taller but has the same oaken shoulders, also stands around with his hands in the pockets of his lumber jacket and does nothing. He just watches to see if the 'capital' is growing. His people sit at the counter, adding, counting, and taking in money. The young man at the till keeps track, and, at each transaction, he opens the drawer crammed with paper money and closes it. The Polish money which the Germans issued, with reproductions of the Chopin monument and Piast's portrait, lies piled up in heaps like greasy waste paper. Hundreds, five hundreds, and fifties, fifties, fifties – mountains. The young fellow, with the shiny boots and the expensive cigarette in his mouth after a good breakfast, shows contempt both for the money and those who provide it. So much money is piled before him, so much inflated paper, that he imagines he's not short of money. Indeed he too has forgotten what people without money look like, and he waits impatiently for the paupers to pay up, so he can grab it fast.

Izzy the Face has nothing to do. He hangs around the shop, his floury visored cap down over his eyes, looking like a ferocious dog.

Also the third, fourth, and fifth partners are in the store. Once they were well-to-do truckers, soft-drink producers, tanners. Now they are smugglers. One of them sits with one leg propped up on the counter, munching a drumstick, a pickle for dessert, loftily eyeing the customers ...

Only the women, the partners' wives, are nimble. They are experts on eggs, butter, and all the other foods, and they are dying for that big take. One complains to the other that for thirty złotys she cannot get anything for her children to eat, but of course she's lying. She wants to make herself out to be a poor slob. Both women know very well that this is said only for the customers, so they won't envy her. Look, upon my word, even the top smugglers of the Koźla can't afford to spend more than thirty złotys for breakfast. But of course it's not true, because nowadays a kilo loaf of bread costs twenty złotys, and what about butter and milk and cheese and indeed a fresh egg, which a smuggler's child simply must have for breakfast – things that hundreds of thousands of Jewish children in town see only in their delirious dreams. The twenty-złoty loaf is a sure guarantee that the smuggler's children will have all those good things. It also ensures Solly's peace of mind and that of his partners, as well as the nervous helter-skelter of their wives.

Meanwhile, we're still at the start of the day, at the sale of potatoes. Right away the sale of other foods will begin and then comes the real hullabaloo. You can never know, two hours later a miracle can happen – someone will start a rumour that the Germans are invading Russia. At dawn troops were seen marching over the bridge to Praga. That's enough. The Gentile smugglers understand such sensational news as well as their Jewish counterparts, and prices suddenly soar. That's all they need. When prices soar, things get brisk in Koźla. There is a scramble for the merchandise. Every bag of food lowered from the Polish windows is instantly seized in the pincer-like grip of the strong iron paws of the tough Jewish porters, who grab the goods for the rich traders in the markets. No one can compete with them.

Hundreds of Jews then throng the street, as on festivals in front of the synagogue, portly, well-fed. They make deals and talk politics. The pavement is thickly littered with cigarette butts and stubs, at a time when a cigarette costs sixty groszy, about ten to twelve times the pre-war price.

Pedlars circulate in the crowd with little boxes of cakes, shouting, 'Come on, let's go, who'll take a chance?' Numbers are drawn from a small sack; some lose and some even win a pastry. A couple of smuggler lads besiege the cake peddlers and devour the cakes with such insolent gusto, it is sickening to look at their greasy faces. Street singers and players drop in here in the hope of earning something in this land of plenty, but who appreciates them? The fiddle screeches, the singer sings: 'I don't wanna give away my ration card, I wanna live a little more.' But it has no effect. This street comes alive, starts to move and surge only when the whisper spreads: 'Another quarter, half a złoty ... two ... rye flour 24½ ...' That's the prettiest music in the alley.

Who cares about the corpse, or rather the dying man who has chosen to lie down right in front of Solly's place and plans to die right under the smugglers' feet? On Ostrowska, Wołyńska, even on Franciszkańska, and the Nalewki, the dead lie in the streets as though they were at home. Jews arise in the morning, go out and know they will find dead bodies there – one, two, five, ten corpses of famine, the bloated dead who hungered through the war and, hungering, attained death, desired yet hated. But here in Koźla Alley? A squashed fly or a louse – who pays it heed?

The smugglers are in shiny boots and fine jackets. The cool September sun gilds their pampered faces. They nibble on the caramels and pastries which the sweets-pedlars bring them, and they never even hear the whir of the death-bullet as it whizzes by.

'Hey, boy, look out! Auntie's coming!'

He means Basha, a red-head, one of the 'strollers'. It is nine, ten o'clock in the morning. The food smuggling is in full swing. The strollers stuff their knapsacks with the plenty of Koźla Alley and carry it to the bakers. The strollers earn twenty, at most thirty, groszy on each kilo of food, and they have to lug many loads. Some make dozens of trips daily to the alley for fresh food supplies. They have wives and children, they work hard, walk a lot, carry many loads, want to eat, indeed, must eat. For bread and potatoes alone they need fifty złotys a day, if not a whole hundred. Without them [the smuggler would be] helpless. The smuggler knows it, but he likes to make a living too, no less than anyone else who has hired hands.

Basha, a tall girl with big feet, strides like a boy, and zips across the street with the sacks of flour like a demon. One-two and she's there and back with an empty knapsack and a handful of paper money. Before you look around, she's out and back inside again and so on continuously. Not slower than Basha is old Zelig, a man in his seventies, from childhood accustomed to lugging loads … He also comes to the alley sometimes twenty times a day.

Not all the strollers have the same luck. There are some women strollers who can barely manage to drag their swollen legs. They have to plead for eight or ten kilos of flour at one time, and the smugglers regard them as nuisances they can't get rid of. They do them a favour and throw them a few kilos of flour, as though it were a despised handout to these pesky recipients, but this is just for appearances' sake. At bottom they know how to appreciate the value of every stroller[?] because he helps them quickly to unload the forbidden fruit, to avoid tangling with a stray gendarme, a Polish policeman or a Junak.

Yesterday there was a pretty piece of business. Right after a good deal on all sides, the Germans appeared unexpectedly at night – different Germans who had not been 'fixed' – and they did a real piece of mischief: They confiscated food worth tens of thousands of złotys and, besides, it cost a fortune to get off with only the losses. During the tumult three boundary guards fell from the roof and were killed on the spot. Well, after all, they do live from boundary money.

The system of boundary money is a complicated one, reminiscent of the wide range of means through which circulating and profit-seeking capital has at all times tried to benefit and, under all circumstances, to ensure its income. There are Polish and Jewish boundary men. The Poles smuggle the merchandise, brought by Christian suppliers to the Jews. The Jewish boundary men deliver to the Jewish smugglers on the Jewish side. The boundary men keep accounts so know how many tons of provisions are smuggled in, and for every kilo they get a percentage. The boundary men have their own people who watch the buying and selling and make sure they won't be cheated.

The boundary men have a hard lot. Standing on the roof means they are always in mortal danger. But what won't a Jew do to earn his bread?

Koźla Alley gives thousands of Jews their livelihood. The barrowmen, who cart away vegetables and fruit, and the porters who live off it. Outside every smuggler shop are always a couple of porters who grab the lowered bags of flour, sacks of grain and other provisions and deliver them to their designated places. Besides their regular earnings, the porters have staked out a new claim – a package fee on every sack of food that leaves Koźla Alley.

At the corner of Franciszkańska stands Zelig the Paw, a stolid personage in a Polish peasant hat with a lacquered visor that he wears at a rakish angle, ready to spring on anyone carrying a package:

'Stop!' he hisses. 'Don't be bashful, uncle, hand over fifty for a package fee.'

'Me – fifty?' replies the passer-by, trying to look innocent.

'Yeah, fifty and make it quick.'

The other gives in. Otherwise Zelig the Paw lets him have the feel of a real paw so that he sees stars. Against such an argument all pleas are useless, so he cries and pays.

Noon Rest in Kożla Alley

At noon everything quietens down in Kożla. All the supplies of smuggled provisions have already been sold. The porters sit on the shop steps, the smugglers take a nap on the counters in the empty stores and Kożla Alley rests, preparing itself for the afternoon smuggling, which starts at about four or five.

You never know if the afternoon prices will be the same as the morning prices. This you can tell only when they lower the supplies through the windows. In the courage of the first smuggler who carries off his bags of flour, of the porter and the boundary men, the entire alley [senses] the change on the bourse and, like a sudden wind across a wheat field on a hot summer day, a murmur gusts through the street: 'Higher'.

Not only the barrowmen, porters, strollers, milkmen, and boundary men live off the alley. Thousands of grocery stores live partly off it, naturally raising their prices. Last but not least, Kożla Alley supports tens of thousands of Jews who even with money in their pocket would die of hunger if the alley did not serve as their granary.

Time will tell.

Whoever will endure, whoever will survive the diseases that range in the ghetto because of the dreadful congestion, the filth and uncleanness, because of having to sell your last shirt for half a loaf of bread, whoever will be that hero, will tell the terrible story of a generation and an age when human life was reduced to the subsistence of abandoned dogs in a desolate city.

Operation Barbarossa, the Nazi invasion of the Soviet Union (and Soviet-occupied Poland), began on 22 June 1941. In the wake of the German armed forces went four Einsatzgruppen. Their orders, transmitted orally, was to kill Jews, from the Baltic to the Black Sea. Other German forces, Wehrmacht and SS troops, frequently went on Jew-killing rampages, either of their own volition or after being stirred up by senior commanders. Field Marshal von Reichenau, commander of the German Sixth Army, informed his men that the essential aim of the campaign against 'the Jewish-Bolshevist system' (the Nazis consistently conflated Socialism with the 'conspiracies' of international Jewry) was the 'complete crushing of its means of power':

> This poses tasks for the troops that go beyond the one-sided routine of conventional soldiering. In the Eastern region, the soldier is not merely a fighter according to the rules of the art of war, but also the bearer of an inexorable national idea and the avenger of all bestialities inflicted upon the German people and its racial kin.
>
> Therefore the soldier must have full understanding for the necessity of a severe but just atonement on Jewish sub-humanity.

Where the killing of Jews was controlled, Einsatzgruppen ensured that they killed local Jewish leaders first, to destroy a community's morale and ability to retaliate. In the first forty days of Barbarossa, more Jews were killed than between the eighteen-month period 20 January 1933 to 21 June 1941.

Diary of an SS Executioner, Drohobycz, Galicia, 12–28 July 1941
SS-HAUPTSCHARFÜHRER FELIX LANDAU

Landau, an SS Sergeant Major (Master Sergeant), volunteered for an Einsatzkommando – known universally as an 'EK' – on 30 June 1941.

12 July 1941

At 6.00 in the morning I was suddenly awoken from a deep sleep. Report for an execution. Fine, so I'll just play executioner and then grave-digger, why not? Isn't it strange, you love battle and then have to shoot defenceless people. Twenty-three had to be shot, amongst them two women. They are unbelievable. They even refused to accept a glass of water from us.

I was detailed as marksman and had to shoot any runaways. We drove one kilometre along the road out of town and then turned right into a wood. There were only six of us at that point and we had to find a suitable spot to shoot and bury them. After a few minutes we found a place.

The death candidates assembled with shovels to dig their own graves. Two of them were weeping. The others certainly have incredible courage. What on earth is running through their minds during these moments? I think that each of them harbours a small hope that somehow he won't be shot. The death candidates are organized into three shifts as there are not many shovels.

Strange, I am completely unmoved. No pity, nothing. That's the way it is and then it's all over. My heart beats just a little faster when involuntarily I recall the feelings and thoughts I had when I was in a similar situation.

On 24 July 1934 in the Bundeskanzleramt, when I was confronted with the machine-gun barrels of the Heimwehr, then there were moments when I came close to weakening. I would not have allowed it to show. No, that would have been out of the question with my character. 'So young and now it's all over.'

Those were my thoughts, then I pushed these feelings aside and in their place came a sense of defiance and the realization that my death would not have been in vain. And here I am today, a survivor, standing in front of others in order to shoot them. Slowly the hole gets bigger and bigger. Two of them are crying continuously. I keep them digging longer and longer: they don't think so much when they're digging.

While they are working they are in fact calmer. Valuables, watches and money are put into a pile. When all of them have been brought to stand next to one another on a stretch of open ground, the two women are lined up at one end of the grave ready to be shot first.

Two men had already been shot in the bushes by our Kriminal Kommissar; I did not see this as I had to keep my eyes on the others. As the women walked to the grave they were completely composed. They turned round. Six of us had to shoot them.

The job was assigned thus: three at the heart, three at the head. I took the heart. The shots were fired and the brains whizzed through the air. Two in the head is too much. They almost tear it off. Almost all of them fell to the ground without a sound. Only with two of them it didn't work. They screamed and whimpered for a long time. Revolvers were no use. The two of us who were shooting together had no failures.

The penultimate group had to throw those who had already been shot into the mass grave then line up and fall in themselves. The last two had to place themselves at the front edge of the grave so that they would fall in at just the right spot.

Then a few bodies were rearranged with a pickaxe and after that we began the grave-digging work. I came back dog tired but the work went on. Everything in the building had to be straightened up. And so it went on without respite.

28 July 1941

In the evening we drive into town. Here we experience things it is impossible to describe. We drive to the prison. The streets tell of murder. We would like to take a closer look at everything, but it is impossible to enter the gas-chambers and cellars of the prison without gas-masks. In a side turning we notice some Jewish corpses covered with sand. We look at each other in surprise. One living Jew rises up from among the corpses. We dispatch him with a few shots.

Eight hundred Jews have been herded together; they are to be shot tomorrow. We drive further along the street. Hundreds of Jews with bloodstained faces, with bullet holes in the head, broken limbs and gouged-out eyes, run ahead of us. One of the Jews carries another one, who is bleeding to death.

We drive to the Citadel. Here we see things no one has ever seen on earth before. It is absolutely impossible to describe them. Two soldiers stand at the entrance to the citadel. Wielding sticks as thick as fists, they lash furiously at the crowd. Jews are being pushed out from inside. Covered with blood, they collapse on top of one another – they scream like pigs – we stand and look on.

Who gave the order to kill the Jews? No one! Somebody ordered them to be set free.

They were all murdered because we hate them.

Himmler Watches a Demonstration Shooting of Jews, Minsk, August 1941
SS GENERAL KARL WOLFF

Heinrich Himmler, Reichsführer of the SS, was the prime architect of the genocide of the Jews, the man who shaped Hitler's dream into a concrete plan. Karl Wolff was the Reichsführer Liaison Officer at Hitler's HQ.

An open grave had been dug and they had to jump into this and lie face downwards. And sometimes when one or two rows had already been shot, they had to lie on top of the people who had already been shot and then they were shot from the edge of the grave. And Himmler had never seen dead people before and in his curiosity he stood right up at the edge of this open grave – a sort of triangular hole – and was looking in.

While he was looking in, Himmler had the deserved bad luck that from one or other of the people who had been shot in the head he got a splash of brains on his coat, and I think it also splashed into his face, and he went very green and pale; he wasn't actually sick, but he was heaving and turned round and swayed, and then I had to jump forward and hold him steady and then I led him away from the grave.

After the shooting was over, Himmler gathered the shooting squad in a semi-circle around him and, standing up in his car, so that he would be a little higher and be able to see the whole unit, he made a speech. He had seen for himself how hard the task which they had to fulfil for Germany in the occupied areas was, but however terrible it all might be, even for him as a mere spectator, and how much worse it must be for them, the people who had to carry it out, he could not see any way round it.

They must be hard and stand firm. He could not relieve them of this duty; he could not spare them. In the interests of the Reich, in this hopefully Thousand Year Reich, in its first decisive great war after the take-over of power, they must do their duty however hard it may seem. He appealed to their sense of patriotism and their readiness to make sacrifices. Well, yes – and then he drove off. And he left this – this police unit to sort out the future for themselves, to see if and how far they could come to terms with this – within themselves, because for some it was a shock which lasted their whole lives.

*Operational Situation Report from Einsatzgruppe C, Kiev, USSR,
7 October 1941*
SS-GRUPPENFÜHRER DR OTTO RASCH

I
KIEV

An advance commando of the Sonderkommando 4a, led by SS Obersturmführer Häfner and Janssen, fifty men strong, arrived on 19 September 1941, with the fighting troops in Kiev. The main commando of the Sonderkommando 4a reached Kiev on 25 September 1941, after SS Standartenführer Blobel had already been in Kiev on 21 and 22 September. The advance commando of the Einsatzgruppe staff, Police Captain Krumme, SS Obersturmführer Dr Krieger and Breun and SS Oberscharführer Braun, arrived in Kiev on 21 September 1941. The Einsatzgruppe staff followed on 25 September 1941 ...

The Army first of all systematically secured public buildings, factories, and stocks of the scarcest goods, so that no large-scale plunder occurred either by members of the Army or by the population. Reports on mines and other explosive material in public buildings and apartment houses were made by the population in great numbers from the very first day of the occupation of Kiev. On 20 September 1941, a delayed-action mine exploded in the citadel where Artillery Headquarters were located ... On 24 September 1941, an explosion occurred in the offices of the Rear Area German Military Headquarters and developed during the day into a large fire, because of the lack of water. A large part of the city centre and several large buildings in the suburbs were destroyed by further explosions and resulting fires. In order to control the fire, the Army was forced to blow up more buildings to prevent the fire from spreading to other districts. As a result of these necessary explosions, the office of the Einsatzgruppe headquarters and of the Sonderkommando 4a had to be evacuated ...

II
EXECUTIONS AND OTHER MEASURES

Public feeling against the Jews was very strong, partly because of the better economic situation of the Jews under the Bolshevist regime and their activities as NKVD informers and agents, partly because of the explosions and the resulting fires (which deprived about 25,000 people of shelter). As an added factor, it was proved that the Jews participated in the arson. The population expected appropriate retaliatory measures by the German authorities. Consequently, all Jews of Kiev were ordered, in agreement with the city commander, to appear on Monday, 29 September, by 8 a.m., at a designated place. These announcements were posted throughout the city by members of the Ukrainian militia. At the same time it was announced orally that all Jews were to be resettled. In collaboration with the Einsatzgruppe staff and 2 commandos of the Police Regiment South, the Sonderkommando 4a executed 33,771 Jews on 29 and 30 September. Money, valuables, underwear, and clothing were confiscated and placed in part at the disposal of the NSV for the use of *Volksdeutsche* and in part given to the city's administrative authorities for the use of the needy population.

It was accomplished without interference. No incidents occurred. The 'resettlement measure' against the Jews was approved throughout by the population. The fact that in reality the Jews were liquidated was hardly known until now; in the light of the latest experiences, however, there would scarcely have been objections. The measures were also approved by the Army. The Jews who were not caught before, as well as those who returned to the city little by little after their flight, were in each case treated appropriately.

Round-up Report of Einsatzgruppe A to 15 October 1941

Einsatzgruppe A, after preparing vehicles for action, proceeded to their area of concentration, as ordered, on 23 June 1941, the second day of the campaign in the East. Army Group North, consisting of the 16th and 19th Armies and Tank Group 4, had begun their advance the day before. Our task was, with all dispatch, to establish personal contact with the commanders of the Armies and with the Commander of the Army of the rear area. It must be stressed that cooperation with the Armed Forces was from the start under General Höpner, it was very close, almost cordial. Misunderstandings with some authorities which cropped up in the first days were settled principally through personal discussions ...

For the Security Police it appeared, at the start of the Eastern campaign, that its special work had to be done not only in rear areas, as was provided for in the original agreements with the High

Command of the Army, but also in the combat areas, and this, on the one hand, because the consolidation of the rear area of the armies was delayed because of the quick advance and, on the other hand, because the subversive Communist activity and the fight against partisans took place intensively within the areas of actual warfare ...

To carry out the tasks of the Security Police, it was desirable to enter into the larger towns together with the Armed Forces. We had our first experiences in this direction when a small advance squad under my command entered Kovno together with the advance units of the Armed Forces on 25 June 1941. When the other larger towns, specifically Libau, Mitau, Riga, Dorpat, Reval, and the larger suburbs of Leningrad were captured, a Security Police commando was always with the first troop units. Above all, Communist functionaries and Communist documentary material had to be seized, and the Armed Forces themselves had to be safeguarded against surprise attacks inside the towns; the troops themselves were usually not able to take care of that because of their small numbers. For this purpose the Security Police, immediately after entry, set up volunteer formations of trustworthy indigenous residents of all three Baltic provinces who successfully performed their duties under our command ...

Similarly, in the first hours after our entry, even under considerable hardships, native anti-Semite elements were induced to start pogroms against Jews. In conformity with orders, the Security Police was determined to solve the Jewish question with all means and full decisiveness. It was, however, desirable that the Security Police should not be visible, at least in the beginning, since the extraordinarily harsh measures would attract attention even in German circles. It had to be demonstrated to the world that the native population itself took the first measures by way of natural reaction against decades-long suppression by the Jews and against the terror exercised by the Communists in the preceding period.

After reaching the Dvina River and therewith Riga, the Einsatzgruppe, to begin with, detached itself from the further advance of the Army Group North, and concentrated its forces on the pacification of the Lithuanian and Latvian area ...

A. THE BALTIC AREA

I   *Organization Measures*

(1) Formation of auxiliary police and police troops:

89

In view of the extensiveness of the area of operations and the great number of Security Police tasks, it was intended from the very start to obtain the cooperation of the trustworthy population for the fight against the vermin in their land – that is, particularly the Jews and Communists. While directing the first spontaneous self-purging actions, which will be reported about elsewhere, care had to be taken that trustworthy elements should be harnessed to the purging job and assigned to regular auxiliary organs of the Security Police …

In Lithuania, at the start of the Eastern campaign, activist nationalist elements formed so-called partisan units in order to take part in the struggle against Bolshevism …

II *Mopping-up and Security of the Area of Operations*
(1) Instigation of self-purging operations:

Considering that the people of the Baltic countries had suffered very heavily under the dominion of Bolshevism and Jewry during the period they were incorporated in the USSR, it was to be expected that after liberation from foreign rule they would render harmless most of the enemies left behind after the retreat of the Red Army. The task of the Security Police was to set these self-purging aspirations in motion and to direct them into the proper channels in order to accomplish the purpose of the mopping-up operations as quickly as possible. It was no less important, for the time to come, to adduce the well-established and demonstrable fact that the liberated populace itself took the severest measures against the Bolshevist and Jewish enemy on its own, and hence no instructions by German authorities should be discernible.

In Lithuania this was achieved for the first time by the readiness of the partisans in Kovno. Surprisingly, it was not easy at first to set in motion a pogrom against the Jews on a large scale. Klimatis, the leader of the partisan unit mentioned above, who was used primarily for this purpose, succeeded in initiating a pogrom on the basis of instructions given to him by a small advance unit operating in Kovno. He worked in such a way that no German order or German instigation was discernible. During the first pogrom on the night of 25 to 26 June, the Lithuanian partisans eliminated over 1,000 Jews, set fire to several synagogues or otherwise destroyed them, and burned down a Jewish quarter of about sixty buildings. On subsequent nights, about 2,300 Jews were made harmless in a similar way. In other parts of Lithuania similar actions followed the example of Kovno, though on a smaller scale, and extended to the Communists who had been left behind.

These self-purging operations went smoothly because the Army authorities, who had been apprised, were understanding of this procedure. From the beginning it was obvious that only the first days after the occupation would offer the opportunity for carrying out pogroms. After the disarmament of the partisans, the self-purging operations automatically ceased.

It proved much more difficult to set in motion similar mopping-up operations and pogroms in Latvia. Essentially, this was because the entire stratum of national leadership, especially in Riga, had been murdered or deported by the Soviets. Nevertheless, through appropriate influence, the Latvian auxiliary police did set in motion a pogrom against the Jews in Riga, in the course of which all synagogues were destroyed and about 400 Jews were killed. As the population of Riga quietened quickly, further pogroms were not feasible.

So far as possible, both in Kovno and in Riga, motion-picture films and still photographs showed that the first spontaneous executions of Jews and Communists were carried out by Lithuanians and Latvians …

(2) Combating Communism:

The fight against Communism and Jewry stood in the forefront of Security Police work in all parts of the area of operations …

(3) The fight against Jewry:

It was to be expected from the first that the Jewish problem in the East could not be solved by pogroms alone. On the other hand, in accordance with the basic orders, the mopping-up work of the Security Police had as its goal the annihilation, as comprehensive as possible, of the Jews. Sonderkommandos reinforced by selected units – partisan detachments in Lithuania, units of the Lettish auxiliary police in Latvia – therefore carried out extensive executions both in the towns and in the countryside. The operations of the execution commandos were performed without trouble. In assigning Lithuanian and Lettish forces to the execution commandos, men were chosen whose relatives had been murdered or deported by the Russians.

Especially severe and comprehensive measures became necessary in Lithuania. In some places – especially in Kovno – the Jews had armed themselves and participated actively in guerrilla warfare and committed arson. Besides, the Jews in Lithuania had worked hand in hand most actively with the Soviets.

The sum total of Jews liquidated in Lithuania amounts to 71,105.

In the pogroms in Kovno, 3,800 Jews were eliminated; in the smaller towns about 1,200 Jews.

Also in Latvia the Jews participated in acts of sabotage and arson after the entry of the German Armed Forces. In Dvinsk so many fires were started by Jews that a large part of the town was lost. The electric power station was burned out. The streets which were mainly inhabited by Jews remained unscathed.

In Latvia up to now a total of 30,000 Jews was executed. Five hundred were rendered harmless by pogroms in Riga.

Of the 4,500 Jews living in Estonia at the beginning of the Eastern campaign, most fled with the retreating Red Army. About 2,000 stayed behind. About 1,000 Jews lived in Reval alone.

The arrest of all male Jews over sixteen years of age is nearly finished. With the exception of the doctors and the Elders of the Jews who were appointed by the Sonderkommandos, they were executed by the Estonian Home Guard under the supervision of Sonderkommando 1a. In Reval and Pernau able-bodied female Jews from sixteen to sixty years of age were arrested and put to peat-cutting or other required labour.

At present a camp is being constructed in Harku, in which all Estonian Jews are to be assembled, so that Estonia will shortly be free of Jews.

After the first larger executions in Lithuania and Latvia, it soon became apparent that an absolute annihilation of the Jews was not feasible, at least not at the present moment. Since handicrafts in Lithuania and Latvia are for the most part in Jewish hands and many occupations (especially glaziers, plumbers, stove-fitters, shoe-makers) consist almost exclusively of Jews, a large number of Jewish craftsmen is indispensable at present for repairing installations of vital importance, for the reconstruction of destroyed towns, and for work of military importance. Although employers aim to replace Jewish labour with Lithuanian or Lettish labour, it is not yet possible to replace all employed Jews, especially not in the larger towns. In cooperation with the labour offices, however, all Jews who are no longer fit for work are being arrested and will be executed in small batches.

In this connection it should be mentioned that some authorities in the Civil Administration offered resistance, at times quite considerable, to carrying out executions of large scope.

The killings on 29 and 30 September were the infamous Babi Yar massacre.

Escape from Babi Yar, 29 September 1941
DINA PRONICHEVA

Babi Yar is a ravine ten miles north-west of Kiev's centre. Pronicheva was one of the few Jews to escape the mass shootings there. She later told her story to the Russian writer Anatoli Kuznetsov (A. Anatoli).

All around and beneath her she could hear strange submerged sounds, groaning, choking and sobbing: many of the people were not dead yet. The whole mass of bodies kept moving slightly as they settled down and were pressed tighter by the movements of the ones who were still living.

Some soldiers came out on to the ledge and flashed their torches down on the bodies, firing bullets from their revolvers into any which appeared to be still living. But someone not far from Dina went on groaning as loud as before.

Then she heard people walking near her, actually on the bodies. They were Germans who had climbed down and were bending over and taking things from the dead and occasionally firing at those which showed signs of life.

Among them was the policeman who had examined her papers and taken her bag: she recognized him by his voice.

One SS-man caught his foot against Dina and her appearance aroused his suspicions. He shone his torch on her, picked her up and struck her with his fist. But she hung limp and gave no signs of life. He kicked her in the breast with his heavy boot and trod on her right hand so that the bones cracked but he didn't use his gun and went off, picking his way across the corpses.

A few minutes later she heard a voice calling from above:

'Demidenko! Come on, start shovelling!'

There was a clatter of spades and then heavy thuds as the earth and sand landed on the bodies, coming closer and closer until it started falling on Dina herself.

Her whole body was buried under the sand but she did not move until it began to cover her mouth. She was lying face upwards, breathed in some sand and started to choke, and then, scarcely realizing what she was doing, she started to struggle in a state of uncontrollable panic, quite prepared now to be shot rather than be buried alive.

With her left hand, the good one, she started scraping the sand off herself, scarcely daring to breathe lest she should start coughing; she used what strength she had left to hold the cough back. She began to feel a little easier. Finally she got herself out from under the earth.

The Ukrainian policemen up above were apparently tired after a hard day's work, too lazy to shovel the earth in properly, and once they had scattered a little in they dropped their shovels and went away. Dina's eyes were full of sand. It was pitch dark and there was the heavy smell of flesh from the mass of fresh corpses.

Dina could just make out the nearest side of the sandpit and started slowly and carefully making her way across to it; then she stood up and started making little foot-holds in it with her left hand. In that way, pressed close to the side of the pit, she made steps and so raised herself an inch at a time, likely at any moment to fall back into the pit.

There was a little bush at the top which she managed to get hold of. With a last desperate effort she pulled herself up and, as she scrambled over the ledge, she heard a whisper which nearly made her jump back.

'Don't be scared, lady! I'm alive too.'

It was a small boy in vest and pants who had crawled out as she had done. He was trembling and shivering all over.

'Quiet!' she hissed at him. 'Crawl along behind me.'

And they crawled away silently, without a sound.

Motyn, the boy, was killed by the Germans as he fled.

'It is impossible to live with this knowledge': A Kiev Citizen on the Shootings at Babi Yar, Kiev, 2 October 1941
LUKIANOVSKA FRIEDHOF

A resident of Kiev, Friedhof confided to her diary:

Everybody is saying now that the Jews are being murdered. No, they have been murdered already. All of them, without exception – old people, women and children. Those who went home on Monday (29 September) have also been shot.

People say it in a way that does not leave any doubt. No trains left Lukianovska cemetery at all. People saw cars with warm shawls and other things driving away from the cemetery. German 'accuracy'. They'd already sorted the loot!

A Russian girl accompanied her girlfriend to the cemetery, but crawled through the fence from the other side. She saw how naked people were taken towards Babi Yar and heard shots from a machine gun. There are more and more rumours and accounts. They are too monstrous to believe. But we are forced to believe them, for the shooting of the Jews is a fact.

A fact which is starting to drive us insane. It is impossible to live with this knowledge. The women around us are crying. And we? We also cried on 29 September, when we thought they were taken to a concentration camp. But now? Can we really cry? I am writing, but my hair is standing on end.

'There are still Jews!' Ukrainian Militia and Police Assist the SS in Mass Murder, Stanislawów, Galicia, 1941
ANONYMOUS

The Einsatzgruppen were willingly helped in their bloody work by Latvian, Ukranian, Rumanian and Lithuanian policemen and auxiliaries.

I felt quite certain that my labour card would serve to shield and save me. So I went out and even took a pregnant woman with me in order to pass her through as my wife. (Her husband had fled with the Red Army.) According to the official announcement all forced workers and their wives were to be released.

No sooner had I entered the street than I was attacked by a gang of Ukrainian young ruffians shouting wildly, 'Look! There are still Jews!' They whistled. The Ukrainian militia appeared and began dragging me along with all the other Jews.

A blind old woman aged 104 who lived in my courtyard was also dragged along, and no attention was paid to all her entreaties to be allowed to remain where she was.

I was ordered to carry the old woman on my back, while at my side strode two companions. One pushed me along with his rifle-butt and shouted that I was going too slowly and idly; while the other kept on hitting me for being in such a hurry.

Beaten and bleeding, I dragged my way to the town hall square. Not a single Jew of all those I saw there were uninjured. They were wounded and bruised, and blood was running on all sides. From the square they were loaded on huge lorries which afterwards returned empty. Then the Germans and Ukrainians began to hurry up very much indeed and ordered them all to line up in three rows, each three men deep.

These rows began to drag along, covering a length of three kilometres and containing many thousand Jews. We were driven to the road behind the town, towards the new Jewish cemetery at Batory. When we approached we understood the full horror of the situation. The sound of shots reached us from the cemetery.

We were driven into the cemetery with cruel, brutal beatings. I saw that the Germans were driving the people standing on the one side towards the graves, while those standing on the other were being permitted merely to stand and watch. Then came an order, 'Hand over all valuables!' I used the tumult and hubbub, and crossed over to the side of the watchers.

The German stormtroopers together with the Ukrainian police took up their stations beside the machine guns. Fifteen of the stormtroopers shot, and fifteen others loaded the guns. The Jews leapt naked into the graves. The bullets hit them while jumping.

Three graves had been dug there. The work of excavation had lasted for about a fortnight. It had been done by young Ukrainians who were members of the Petlura organization. The Germans then explained to the Jewish Council that the Ukrainians were preparing stations for anti-aircraft against Bolshevik air attack. Nobody even imagined that 6,000 Jews would meet with their deaths at this place.

The graves were deep, the naked people fell one on the other, whether dead or alive. The heap of bodies grew higher and higher. I stood and gazed. Early in the morning the murderers had stationed a group of Jews to watch the scene. This was far worse than death, and many people of our group, who could bear it no longer, burst out with shouts, 'Take us and murder us as well!' And the murderers satisfied them, and began dragging people from our ranks off to the graves as well.

My turn came. The only thing I had in mind was to reach the grave as soon as possible so that an end might be made of it all. 'Take off your clothes!' I was ordered, and quickly stood naked. Three of us approached the grave. There were shots. Two of us fell. Suddenly something strange happened. There came an order, 'Cease fire!' The stormtroopers standing ready stopped their shooting. I stood astonished and confused. One of the murderers approached me and said, 'Jew, you are lucky. You are not going to die. Dress again, quickly.'

The graves were filled to overflowing. All round lay the dead, strangled, trodden underfoot, wounded. Those of us who remained alive felt ourselves to be infinitely unfortunate. There were about 1,700 of us left in the cemetery grounds. We were afraid to move from the spot. One of those in command of the action announced that 'the action was completed', and that the survivors might return to their homes.

Field Report, 1 December 1941
KARL JAGER, COMMANDING OFFICER
EINSATZKOMMANDO 3

Einsatzkommando 3 was an extermination unit of Einsatzgruppe A, attached to Army Group North during Operation Barbarossa, the invasion of Russia.

1 December 1941

Secret Reich Business!   5 copies

4th copy

Complete list of executions carried out in the EK 3 area up to 1 December 1941

Security police duties in Lithuania taken over by Einsatzkommando 3 on 2 July 1941.

On my instructions and orders the following executions were conducted by Lithuanian partisans:

4.7.41	Kauen-Fort VII	416 Jews, 47 Jewesses	463
6.7.41	Kauen-Fort VII	Jews	2,514

Following the formation of a raiding squad under the command of SS-Obersturmführer Hamman and 8–10 reliable men from the Einsatzkommando, the following actions were conducted in cooperation with Lithuanian partisans:

7.7.41	Mariampole	Jews	32
8.7.41	Mariampole	14 Jews, 5 Comm. Officials	19
8.7.41	Girkalinei	Comm. Officials	6
9.7.41	Wendziogala	32 Jews, 2 Jewesses, 1 Lithuanian (f.), 2 Lithuanian Comm., 1 Russian Comm.	38
9.7.41	Kauen-Fort VII	21 Jews, 3 Jewesses	24
14.7.41	Mariampole	21 Jews, 1 Russ., 9 Lith. Comm.	31
17.7.41	Babtei	8 Comm. Officals (inc. 6 Jews)	8
18.7.41	Mariampole	39 Jews, 14 Jewesses	53
19.7.41	Kauen-Fort VII	17 Jews, 2 Jewesses, 4 Lith. Comm., 2 Comm. Lithuanians (f.), 1 German Comm.	26
21.7.41	Panevezys	59 Jews, 11 Jewesses, 1 Lithuanian (f.), 1 Pole, 22 Lith. Comm., 9 Russ. Comm.	103

22.7.41	Panevezys	1 Jew	1
23.7.41	Kedainiai	83 Jews, 12 Jewesses, 14 Russ. Comm., 15 Lith. Comm., 1 Russ. O-Politruk	125
25.7.41	Mariampole	90 Jews, 13 Jewesses	103
28.7.41	Panevezys	234 Jews, 15 Jewesses, 19 Russ. Comm., 20 Lith. Comm.	288

Total carried forward   3,384

Sheet 2

Total carried over   3,384

29.7.41	Rasainiai	254 Jews, 3 Lith. Comm.	257
30.7.41	Agriogala	27 Jews, 11 Lith. Comm.	38
31.7.41	Utena	235 Jews, 16 Jewesses, 4 Lith. Comm., 1 robber/murderer	256
31.7.41	Wendziogala	13 Jews, 2 murderers	15
1.8.41	Ukmerge	254 Jews, 42 Jewesses, 1 Pol. Comm., 2 Lith. NKVD agents, 1 mayor of Jonava who gave order to set fire to Jonava	300
2.8.41	Kauen-Fort IV	170 Jews, 1 US Jewess, 33 Jewesses, 4 Lith. Comm.	209
4.8.41	Panavezys	362 Jews, 41 Jewesses, 5 Russ. Comm., 14 Lith. Comm.	422
5.8.41	Rasainiai	213 Jews, 66 Jewesses	279
7.8.41	Uteba	483 Jews, 87 Jewesses, 1 Lithuanian (robber of corpses of German soldiers)	571
8.8.41	Ukmerge	620 Jews, 82 Jewesses	702
9.8.41	Kauen-Fort IV	484 Jews, 50 Jewesses	534
11.8.41	Panavezys	450 Jews, 48 Jewesses, 1 Lith., 1 Russ.	500
13.8.41	Alytus	617 Jews, 100 Jewesses, 1 criminal	719

Date	Place	Description	Number
14.8.41	Jonava	497 Jews, 55 Jewesses	552
15–16.8.41	Rokiskis	3,200 Jews, Jewesses, and J. Children, 5 Lith. Comm., 1 Pole, 1 partisan	3207
9–16.8.41	Rasainiai	294 Jewesses, 4 Jewish children	298
27.6–14.8.41	Rokiskis	493 Jews, 432 Russians, 56 Lithuanians (all active communists)	981
18.8.41	Kauen-Fort IV	689 Jews, 402 Jewesses, 1 Pole (f.), 711 Jewish intellectuals from Ghetto in reprisal for sabotage action	1,812
19.8.41	Ukmerge	298 Jews, 255 Jewesses, 1 Politruk, 88 Jewish children, 1 Russ. Comm.	645
22.8.41	Dunaburg	3 Russ. Comm., 5 Latvian, incl. 1 murderer, 1 Russ. Guardsman, 3 Poles, 3 gypsies (m.), 1 gypsy (f.), 1 gypsy child, 1 Jew, 1 Jewess, 1 Armenian (m.), 2 Politruks (prison inspection in Dunanburg	21
Total carried forward			16,152

Sheet 3

Date	Place	Description	Number
Total carried forward			16,152
22.8.41	Aglona	Mentally sick: 269 men, 227 women, 48 children	544
23.8.41	Panevezys	1,312 Jews, 4,602 Jewesses, 1,609 Jewish children	7,523
18–22.8.41	Kreis Rasainiai	466 Jews, 440 Jewesses, 1,020 Jewish children	1,926
25.8.41	Obeliai	112 Jews, 627 Jewesses, 421 Jewish children	1,160
25–26.8.41	Seduva	230 Jews, 275 Jewesses, 159 Jewish children	664

Date	Place	Details	Total
26.8.41	Zarasai	767 Jews, 1,113 Jewesses, 1 Lith. Comm., 687 Jewish children, 1 Russ. Comm. (f.) 2,569	
28.8.41	Pasvalys	402 Jews, 738 Jewesses, 209 Jewish children	1,349
26.8.41	Kaisiadorys	All Jews, Jewesses, and Jewish children	1,911
27.8.41	Prienai	All Jews, Jewesses, and Jewish children	1,078
27.8.41	Dagda and Kraslawa	212 Jews, 4 Russ. POW's	216
27.8.41	Joniskia	47 Jews, 165 Jewesses, 143 Jewish children	355
28.8.41	Wilkia	76 Jews, 192 Jewesses, 134 Jewish children	402
28.8.41	Kedainiai	710 Jews, 767 Jewesses, 599 Jewish children	2,076
29.8.41	Rumsiskis and Ziezmariai	20 Jews, 567 Jewesses, 197 Jewish children	784
29.8.41	Utena and Moletai	582 Jews, 1,731 Jewesses, 1,469 Jewish children	3,782
13–31.8.41	Alytus and environs	233 Jews	233
1.9.41	Mariampole	1,763 Jews, 1,812 Jewesses, 1,404 Jewish children, 109 mentally sick, 1 German subject (f.), married to a Jew, 1 Russian (f.)	5,090
Total carried over			47,814

Sheet 4

Total carried over			47,814
28.8–2.9.41	Darsuniskis	10 Jews, 69 Jewesses, 20 Jewish children	99

	Carliava	73 Jews, 113 Jewesses, 61 Jewish children	247
	Jonava	112 Jews, 1,200 Jewesses, 244 Jewish children	1,556
	Petrasiunai	30 Jews, 72 Jewesses, 23 Jewish children	125
	Jesuas	26 Jews, 72 Jewesses, 46 Jewish children	144
	Ariogala	207 Jews, 260 Jewesses, 195 Jewish children	662
	Jasvainai	86 Jews, 110 Jewesses, 86 Jewish children	282
	Babtei	20 Jews, 41 Jewesses, 22 Jewish children	83
	Wenziogala	42 Jews, 113 Jewesses, 97 Jewish children	252
	Krakes	448 Jews, 476 Jewesses, 97 Jewish children	1,125
4.9.41	Pravenischkis	247 Jews, 6 Jewesses	253
	Cekiske	22 Jews, 64 Jewesses, 60 Jewish children	146
	Seredsius	6 Jews, 61 Jewesses, 126 Jewish children	193
	Velinona	2 Jews, 71 Jewesses, 86 Jewish children	159
	Zapiskis	47 Jews, 118 Jewesses, 13 Jewish children	178
5.9.41	Ukmerge	1,123 Jews, 1,849 Jewesses, 1,737 Jewish children	4,709
25.8–6.9.41	Mopping-up in: Rasainiai Georgenburg	16 Jews, 412 Jewesses, 415 Jewish children	843

9.9.41	Alytus	287 Jews, 640 Jewesses, 352 Jewish children	1,279
9.9.41	Butrimonys	67 Jews, 370 Jewesses, 303 Jewish children	740
10.9.41	Merkine	223 Jews, 640 Jewesses, 276 Jewish children	854
10.9.41	Varena	541 Jews, 141 Jewesses, 149 Jewish children	831
11.9.41	Leipalingis	60 Jews, 70 Jewesses, 25 Jewish children	155
11.9.41	Seirijai	229 Jews, 384 Jewesses, 340 Jewish children	953
12.9.41	Simnas	68 Jews, 197 Jewesses, 149 Jewish children	414
11–12.9.41	Uzusalis	Reprisal against inhabitants who fed Russ. Partisans; some in possession of weapons	43
26.9.41	Kauen-F.IV	412 Jews, 615 Jewesses, 581 Jewish children (sick and suspected epidemic cases)	1,608
Total carried over			66,159

Sheet 5

Total carried over			66,159
2.10.41	Zagare	633 Jews, 1,107 Jewesses, 496 Jewish children (as these Jews were being led away a mutiny rose, which was however immediately put down; 150 Jews were shot immediately; 7 partisans wounded)	2,236
4.10.41	Kauen-F.IX	315 Jews, 712 Jewesses, 818 Jewish children (reprisal after German police officer shot in ghetto)	1,845

29.10.41	Kauen-F.IX	2,007 Jews, 2,920 Jewesses, 4,273 Jewish children (mopping up ghetto of superfluous Jews)	9,200
3.11.41	Lazdijai	485 Jews, 511 Jewesses, 539 Jewish children	1,535
15.11.41	Wilkowiski	36 Jews, 48 Jewesses, 31 Jewish children	115
25.11.41	Kauen-F.IX	1,159 Jews, 1,600 Jewesses, 175 Jewish children (resettlers from Berlin, Munich and Frankfurt am Main)	2,934
29.11.41	Kauen-F.IX	693 Jews, 1,155 Jewesses, 152 Jewish children (resettlers from Vienna and Breslau)	2,000
29.11.41	Kauen-F.IX	17 Jews, 1 Jewess, for contravention of ghetto law, 1 Reichs German who converted to the Jewish faith and attended rabbinical school, then 15 terrorists from the Kalinin group	34
EK 3 detachment in Dunanberg in the period 13.7–21.8.41:		9,012 Jews, Jewesses and Jewish children, 573 active Comm.	9,585
EK 3 detachment in Wilna:			
12.8–1.9.41	City of Wilna	425 Jews, 19 Jewesses, 8 Comm. (m.), 9 Comm. (f.)	461
2.9.41	City of Wilna	864 Jews, 2,019 Jewesses, 817 Jewish children (sonderaktion because German soldiers shot at by Jews)	3,700
Total carried forward			99,084

Sheet 6

Total carried forward			99,804
12.9.41	City of Wilna	993 Jews, 1,670 Jewesses, 771 Jewish children	3,334
17.9.41	City of Wilna	337 Jews, 687 Jewesses, 247 Jewish children and 4 Lith. Comm.	1,271
20.9.41	Nemencing	128 Jews, 176 Jewesses, 99 Jewish children	403
22.9.41	Novo-Wilejka	468 Jews, 495 Jewesses, 196 Jewish children	1,159
24.9.41	Riesa	512 Jews, 744 Jewesses, 511 Jewish children	1,767
25.9.41	Jahiunai	215 Jews, 229 Jewesses, 131 Jewish children	575
27.9.41	Eysisky	989 Jews, 1,636 Jewesses, 821 Jewish children	3,446
30.9.41	Trakai	366 Jews, 483 Jewesses, 597 Jewish children	1,446
4.10.41	City of Wilna	432 Jews, 1,115 Jewesses, 436 Jewish children	1,983
6.10.41	Semiliski	213 Jews, 359 Jewesses, 390 Jewish children	962
9.10.41	Svenciany	1,169 Jews, 1,840 Jewesses, 717 Jewish children	3,726
16.10.41	City of Wilna	382 Jews, 507 Jewesses, 257 Jewish children	1,146
21.10.41	City of Wilna	718 Jews, 1,063 Jewesses, 586 Jewish children	2,367
25.10.41	City of Wilna	1,776 Jewesses, 812 Jewish children	2,578
27.10.41	City of Wilna	946 Jews, 184 Jewesses, 1,203 Jewish children	1,203
30.10.41	City of Wilna	382 Jews, 789 Jewesses, 362 Jewish children	1,553
6.11.41	City of Wilna	340 Jews, 749 Jewesses, 252 Jewish children	1,341

19.11.41	City of Wilna	76 Jews, 77 Jewesses, 18 Jewish children	171
19.11.41	City of Wilna	6 POW's, 8 Poles	14
20.11.41	City of Wilna	3 POW's	3
25.11.41	City of Wilna	9 Jews, 46 Jewesses, 8 Jewish children, 1 Pole for possession of arms and other military equipment	64

EK 3 detachment in Minsk from 28.9–17.10.41:

	Pleschnitza	620 Jews, 1,285 Jewesses, 1,126 Jewish children and 19 Comm.	3,050
	Bischolin		
	Scak		
	Bober		
	Uzda		

| Prior to EK 3 taking over security police duties, Jews liquidated by pogroms and executions (including partisans) | 4,000 |
| Total | 137,346 |

Today I can confirm that our objective, to solve the Jewish problem for Lithuania, has been achieved by EK 3. In Lithuania there are no more Jews, apart from Jewish workers and their families.

The distance between [*sic*] the assembly point to the graves was on average 4 to 5 Km.

I consider the Jewish action more or less terminated as far as Einsatzkommando 3 is concerned. Those working Jews and Jewesses still available are needed urgently and I can envisage that after the winter this workforce will be required even more urgently. I am of the view that the sterilization programme of the male worker Jews should be started immediately so that reproduction is prevented. If despite sterilization a Jewess becomes pregnant she will be liquidated.

(signed) Jäger
SS-Standartenführer

It was estimated at the International Military Tribunal in 1945 that the Einsatzgruppen, aided by sympathizers in the overrun regions, shot some two million Jews.

'I tried to get closer to the corpses to take a last look at my nearest and dearest': An Eye-witness at Chelmno, January 1942
SZLAMEK BAJLER

Bajler was a young Jew from the village of Izbica Kujawska, north of Chelmno in the annexed region of Poland known as Wathgau. He was arrested in a round-up in Izbica in early-January 1942, and forced to work in Chelmno Waldlager, where he witnessed the murder of some 1,600 Jews from his village – including his own family – as well as local gypsies. After a week he managed to escape to the Warsaw Ghetto where he was persuaded to write a report on what he had witnessed at Chelmno. Bajler did so under the pen name 'Yakov Grojanowski'.

Tuesday, 6 January 1942
We arrived at 12.30 p.m. We were pushed out of the lorry. From here onwards we were in the hands of black-uniformed SS men, all of them high-ranking *Reich* Germans. We were ordered to hand over all our money and valuables. After this fifteen men were selected, I among them, and taken down to the cellar rooms of the *Schloss* [castle]. We fifteen were confined in one room, the remaining fourteen in another. Down in the cellar it was pitch dark. Some Ethnic Germans on the domestic staff provided us with straw. Later a lantern was brought. At around eight in the evening we received unsweetened black coffee and nothing else. We were all in a depressed mood. One could only think of the worst, some were close to tears. We kissed and took leave of each other. It was unimaginably cold and we lay down close together. We spent the whole night without shutting our eyes. We only talked about the deportation of Jews, particularly from Kolo and Dąbie. The way it looked, we had no prospect of ever getting out again.

Wednesday, 7 January 1942
At seven in the morning, the gendarme on duty knocked and ordered us to get up. It took half an hour till they brought us black coffee and bread from our provisions. We drew some meagre consolation from this and told each other there was a God in heaven; we would, after all, be going to work.

At about 8.30 we were led into the courtyard. Six of us had to go into the second cellar room to bring out two corpses. The dead were from Klodawa, and had hanged themselves. They were conscript grave-diggers. Their corpses were thrown on a lorry. We met the other fourteen enforced grave-diggers from Izbica. As soon as we came out of the cellar we were surrounded by twelve gendarmes and Gestapo men with machine guns. We got on the lorry. Our escorts were six gendarmes with machine guns. Behind us came another vehicle with ten gendarmes and two civilians. We drove in the direction of Kolo for about seven kilometres till turning left into the forest; after half a kilometre we halted at a clear path. We were ordered to get down and line up in double file.

An SS man ordered us to fall in with our shovels, dressed, despite the frost, only in shoes, underwear, trousers and shirts. Our coats, hats, gloves, etc., had to remain in a pile on the ground. The two civilians took all the shovels and pick-axes down from the lorry. Eight of us who weren't handed any tools had to take down the corpses. Already on our way into the forest we saw about fourteen men, enforced grave-diggers from Klodawa, who had arrived before us.

The eight men without tools carried the two corpses to the ditch and threw them in. We didn't have to wait long before the next lorry arrived with fresh victims. It was specially constructed. It looked like a normal large lorry, in grey paint, with two hermetically closed rear doors. The inner walls were of steel metal. There weren't any seats. The floor was covered by a wooden grating, as in public baths, with straw mats on top. Between the driver's cab and the rear part were two peepholes. With a torch one could observe through these peepholes if the victims were already dead.

Under the wooden grating were two tubes about fifteen centimetres thick which came out of the cab. The tubes had small openings from which gas poured out. The gas generator was in the cab, where the same driver sat all the time. He wore a uniform of the SS death's head units and was about forty years old. There were two such vans.

When the lorries approached we had to stand at a distance of five metres from the ditch. The leader of the guard detail was a high-ranking SS man, an absolute sadist and murderer. He ordered that eight men were to open the doors of the lorry. The smell of gas that met us was overpowering. The victims were gypsies from Łódź. Strewn about the van were all their belongings: accordions, violins, bedding, watches and other valuables. After the doors had been open for five minutes orders were screamed at us, 'Here! You Jews! Get in there and turn everything out!'

The work didn't progress quickly enough. The SS leader fetched his whip and screamed, 'The devil, I'll give you a hand straight away!' He hit out in all directions on people's heads, ears and so on, till they collapsed. Three of the eight who couldn't get up again were shot on the spot. When the others saw this they clambered back on their feet and continued the work with the last reserves of energy … The corpses were thrown one on top of another, like rubbish on a heap. We got hold of them by the feet and the hair. At the edge of the ditch stood two men who threw in the bodies. In the ditch stood an additional two men who packed them in head to feet, facing downwards. If any space was left, a child was pushed in. Every batch comprised 180–200 corpses. For every three vanloads twenty men were used to cover up the corpses. At first this had to be done twice, later up to three times, because nine vans arrived (that is nine times sixty corpses). At exactly twelve noon we had to put our shovels down and to climb out of the ditch. We were surrounded by guards all the time. We even had to excrete on the spot. We went to the spot where our belongings were. We had to sit on them close together. We were given cold bitter coffee and a frozen piece of bread. That was our lunch. That's how we sat [for] half an hour. Afterwards we had to line up, were counted and led back to work.

What did the dead look like? They weren't burned or black; their faces were unchanged. Nearly all the dead were soiled with excrement. At about five o'clock we stopped work. The eight men who had worked with the corpses had to lie on top of them face downwards. An SS man with a machine gun shot at their heads.

We dressed quickly and took the shovels with us. We were counted and escorted to the lorry by gendarmes and SS men. We had to put the shovels away. Then we were counted again and pushed into the lorry. The journey to the *Schloss* took about fifteen minutes. We travelled together with the men from Klodawa and talked very quietly together, so the gendarmes sitting at the back shouldn't hear us.

It turned out that there were many more rooms in the *Schloss*. We numbered twenty in our room, with fifteen more in the adjacent one. There weren't any other enforced grave-diggers. As soon as we came into the cold and black cellar we threw ourselves down on the straw and cried about everything that had befallen us.

With Bajler in the cellar was fifty-five-year-old Gershon Praschker, who invited his fellow prisoners to say the prayer of confession before death.

It was a very depressing sight. The sergeant-major knocked at the door, shouting 'Quiet, you Jews, or I shoot!' We continued the prayer softly with choking voices.

At 7.30 in the evening they brought us a pot of thin kohlrabi soup. We couldn't swallow anything for crying and pain. It was very cold and we had no covers at all. One of us exclaimed, 'Who knows who among us will be missing tomorrow?' We pressed close together and lapsed into exhausted fitful sleep haunted by terrible dreams. We slept for about four hours. Then we ran about the room, freezing cold and debating the fate that was in store for us.

Thursday, 8 January 1942
The day starts in more or less similar fashion to yesterday, although high-ranking SS men came to visit. Their identity is not mentioned, but they were driving in a limousine. The identity of one of the 'eight' who worked with the corpses is known: nineteen-year-old Mechel Wiltschinski from Izbica. Together with his fellows he was shot in the ditch at the end of the working day ... Two hours later the first lorry arrived full of gypsies. I state with 100 per cent certainty that the executions had taken place in the forest. In the normal course of events the gas vans used to stop about one hundred metres from the mass graves. In two instances the gas vans, which were filled with Jews, stopped twenty metres from the ditch. This happened once on this Thursday, the other time on Wednesday the 14th ... Our comrades from among the 'eight' told us there was an apparatus with buttons in the driver's cab. From this apparatus two tubes led into the van. The driver (there were two execution gas vans, and two drivers – always the same) pressed a button and got out of the van. At the same moment frightful screaming, shouting and banging against the sides of the van could be heard. That lasted for about fifteen minutes. Then the driver re-boarded the van and shone an electric torch into the back to see if the people were already dead. Then he drove the van to a distance of five metres from the ditch.

There were nine transports to be buried, of which seven were full of gypsies and two of Jews. Back in the cellar, the Jewish grave-diggers were ordered by the guards to sing.

I began to sing 'Hear, O Israel: the eternal one is our God, the eternal one is unique'. Those assembled repeated each verse in depressed tones. Then I continued: 'Praised be His name and the splendour of His realm for ever and ever', which the others repeated after me three times. The gendarme insisted that we go on. I said, 'Friends and honourable people, we shall now sing the *Hatikvah.*' And we sang the anthem with our heads covered. It sounded like a prayer. After this the gendarme left and bolted the door with three locks. Later that evening the prisoners had to sing again. They had to repeat: 'We thank Adolf Hitler for everything'.

By five in the morning everybody was awake because of the cold. We had a conversation. Getzel Chrzastowski, a member of the Bund, and Eisenstab, both from Klodawa (Einstab owned a furrier's there), had lost their belief in God because He didn't concern himself with injustice and suffering. In contrast others, myself included, remained firm in our belief and said, like Mosche Asch (a worthy man from Izbica), that the time of the Messiah was at hand.

Friday, 9 January 1942
The bottom of the ditch was about one and a half metres wide, the top five metres, and its depth was five metres. The mass graves extended a long way. If a tree stood in the way it was felled. Among the 'eight' today were Abraham Zalinski, thirty-two years old, Zalman Jakubowski, fifty-five and the earlier mentioned Gershon Praschker, all from Izbica. They were killed as usual. On arrival back at the courtyard of Schloss Kulmhof we were disagreeably surprised to see a new transport. They were probably a new batch of grave-diggers: sixteen men from Izbica and sixteen from Bugaj. Among those from Izbica were 1. Mosche Lesek, forty years old, 2. Avigdor Palanski, twenty years old, 3. Steier, thirty-five years old, 4. Knoll, forty-five years old, 5. Izchak Preiss, forty-five years old, 6. Jehuda Lutzinski, fifty-one years old, 7. Kalman Radzewski, thirty-two years old, 8. Menachem Archijowski, forty years old. Among those from Bugaj was my friend and comrade Haim Reuben Izbizki, thirty-five years old.

Twenty of the old grave-diggers, together with five new ones, were driven into another room in the cellar. This room was somewhat smaller than the previous one. There we found bedding, underwear, trousers, suits, as well as foodstuffs (bread, dripping, and sugar). These items belonged to the new grave-diggers.

We heard voices from the adjacent room. I banged at the wall and shouted at a spot where a missing brick let the air through. I asked if H. R. Izbizki was in the room. He came to the wall. I asked if at least his mother and sister had escaped. The guard interrupted our conversation.

Afterwards the new arrivals gave us some political news. They said the Russians had already retaken Smolensk and Kiev, and were making their way towards us. We wished they would with God's assistance come and destroy this terrible place.

Seven to eight transports were buried this day, at first gypsies as yesterday but the last two containing Jewish victims.

They were younger and older people with suitcases and rucksacks. On their clothes a Jewish star was affixed front and back. We assumed they were diseased camp inmates whom the Nazis wanted to get rid of in this manner. They were buried with their belongings. These events shook us to the core because up until then we had hoped that Jews in the camps would survive these terrible times.

Saturday, 10 January 1942
At about eleven o'clock the first van loaded with victims arrived. Jewish victims were treated in this way: the Jewish men, women and children were in their underwear. After they had been tossed out of the van, two Germans in plain clothes stepped up to them to make a thorough check if anything had been hidden. If they saw a necklace round a throat they tore it off. They wrenched rings from fingers, and pulled gold teeth out of mouths. They even examined anuses (and, in the case of women, genitals). The entire examination was done most brutally.

Eisenstab told us he had no further reason for living since his wife and fifteen-year-old only daughter had just been buried. But his fellows restrained him from asking the Germans to shoot him. Today seven transports arrived.

Sunday, 11 January 1942
We were told we wouldn't have to work because it was Sunday. After the morning prayer and the prayer for the dead we remained in our

paradisiacal cellar. We didn't recite the prayer of penitence. We again talked about ourselves, politics and God. Everybody wanted to hold out until liberation.

Monday, 12 January 1942
At 7 a.m. they brought us coffee and bread. Some of the men from Izbica (who had lately lived in Kutno) drank up all the coffee. The others got very annoyed and said we were already facing death and had to behave with dignity.

At 8.30 we were already at work. At 9.30 the first gas van appeared. Among the 'eight' were Aharon Rosenthal, Schlomo Babiacki and Schmuel Bibedgal, all of them aged between fifty and sixty ... On this day we were absolutely slave-driven. They wouldn't even wait till the gas smell had evaporated.

Nine vans then arrived, each containing sixty Jews from Klodawa:

My friend Getzel Chrzastowski screamed terribly for a moment when he recognized his fourteen-year-old-son, who had just been thrown into the ditch. We had to stop him, too, from begging the Germans to shoot him. We argued it was necessary to survive this suffering, so we might revenge ourselves later and pay the Germans back.

After an escaped Jew warned others in the locality of their likely fate at Chelmno, those arriving in the transports were initially met with reassuring kindness:

When they arrived at the *Schloss* they were at first treated most politely. An elderly German, around sixty, with a long pipe in his mouth, helped the mothers to lift the children from the lorry. He carried babies so that the mothers could alight more easily and helped dotards to reach the *Schloss*.

The unfortunate ones were deeply moved by his gentle and mild manner. They were led into a warm room which was heated by two stoves. The floor was covered with wooden gratings as in a bath house. The elderly German and the SS officer spoke to them in this room. They assured them they would be taken to the Łódź Ghetto. There they were expected to work and be productive. The women would look after the household, the children would go to school, and so on.

In order to get there, however, they had to undergo delousing. For that purpose they needed to undress down to their underwear. Their clothes would be passed through hot steam. Valuables and documents should be tied up in a bundle, and handed over for safekeeping.

Whoever had kept banknotes, or had sewn them into their clothes, should take them out without fail, otherwise they would get damaged in the steam oven. Moreover they would all have to take a bath. The elderly German politely requested those present to take a bath and opened a door from which 15–20 steps led down. It was terribly cold there. Asked about the cold, the German said gently they should walk a bit further: it would get warmer. They walked along a lengthy corridor to some steps leading to a ramp. The gas van had driven up to the ramp.

The polite behaviour ended abruptly and they were all driven into the van with malicious screams. The Jews realized immediately they were facing death. They screamed, crying out the prayer 'Hear, O Israel'.

At the exit of the warm room was a small chamber in which Goldmann hid. After he had spent twenty-four hours there in the icy cold and was already quite stiff, he decided to look for his clothes and to save himself. He was caught and pushed in among the grave-diggers.

The next morning Goldmann was ordered to lie in a ditch and was shot.

Tuesday, 13 January 1942
On this day the transports were brimful – roughly ninety corpses in each van. On this day the Jewish community at Bugemin was liquidated ... [and] ... we buried approximately 800 Jews from Bugaj. We buried nine transports; after work, five of the men who had unloaded the corpses were shot. When in our cellar, Michael Worbleznik burst into tears; he had lost his wife, two children and his parents ...

Thursday, 15 January 1942
On this occasion we rode in a bus. Monik Halter called across to me [that] the windows of the vehicle could be easily opened with a hook. The thought of escape had lodged in my brain all the time.

At 8 a.m. we were already at the place of work. At ten o'clock the first victims arrived, again from Izbica. Till noon we dispatched four overloaded transports. One van waited in line after the next.

At midday I received the sad news that my brother and parents had just been buried. I tried to get closer to the corpses to take a last look at my nearest and dearest. Once I had a clod of frozen earth tossed at me, thrown by the benign German with the pipe. The second time 'Big Whip' shot at me. I don't know if the shot missed me deliberately, or by accident. One thing is certain: I remained alive. I suppressed my anguish and concentrated on working fast so as to forget my dreadful situation for five minutes.

I remained lonely as a piece of stone. Out of my entire family, which comprised sixty people, I am the only one who survived. Towards evening, as we helped to cover the corpses, I put my shovel down.

Michael Podklebnik followed my example and we said the prayer of the mourners together. Before leaving the ditch five of the 'eight' were shot. At seven in the evening we were taken back home. All those who hailed Izbica were in absolute despair. We had realized that we should never see our relatives again. I was quite beside myself and indifferent to everything.

In the next room, we had learned, were eighteen grave-diggers from Łódź. We heard through the wall that Rumkowski (the elder of the Jewish there) had ordered the deportation of 750 families.

Friday, 16 January 1942
… the victims came from Łódź. Some of them looked starved and showed signs of having been beaten and injured; one could gauge the degree of famine in Łódź. We felt great pity when we saw how they had hungered for a long time merely to perish in such a cruel manner. The corpses hardly weighed anything. Where previously three transports were put in layers one on top of the other, now there was room for four.

In the afternoon 'Big Whip' again drank a bottle of schnapps; afterwards he began to deal murderous blows with his whip.

On Friday they started to pour chloride on the graves because of the stench caused by the many corpses.

On this day eight transports were buried; at the end of the day seven of the 'eight' were shot.

Saturday, 17 January 1942
We buried seven overloaded transports. We had finished the work at five o'clock when a car suddenly appeared with the order to shoot sixteen men. This was obviously punishment for the escape of Abraham Rois. (He had run away at ten o'clock on Friday night.) Sixteen men were selected. They had to lie down in groups of eight, face downwards, on top of the corpses, and were shot through the head with machine guns.

Sunday, 18 January 1942
We learned at breakfast that we would have to go to work. At eight o'clock we were already at the place of work. Twenty new pick-axes and shovels were taken down from the lorry. We now realized that 'production', far from coming to an end, was on the increase. Because it was Sunday not all the gendarmes were on duty. We consumed our lunch in the grave. They probably wanted to make sure that we didn't attack any of them. We didn't even attempt to hurl ourselves upon our executioners. The guns levelled at us filled us with too much fear.

On this day no one was shot at the end of work.

After the evening prayer we decided to run away, no matter what the cost. I asked Kalman Radzewski to give me a few marks because I didn't have a single pfennig. He gave me fifty marks which he had sewn into his clothing. The escape of Rois was an example that had made a deep impression on me because he got out through a cellar window.

Monday, 19 January 1942
We again boarded the bus in the morning. I let all the others get on in front of me and was the last one aboard. The gendarme sat in front. On this day no SS men rode behind us. To my right was a window which could be opened easily. During the ride I opened the window. When the fresh cold air streamed in I caught fright and quickly shut the window again. My comrades, among them Monik Halter in particular, encouraged me, however. After I made a decision, I softly asked my comrades to stand up so the draught of cold air shouldn't reach the gendarmes. I quickly pulled the window pane out of its

frame, pushed my legs out and turned around. I held on to the door with my hands and pressed my feet against the hinges. I told my colleagues they should put the window pane back immediately after I had jumped. I then jumped at once.

When I hit the ground I rolled for a bit and scraped the skin off my hands. The only thing that mattered to me was not to break a leg. I turned round to see if they had noticed anything on the bus but it continued its journey.

I lost no time but ran as fast as I could across fields and woods. After an hour I stood before the farm of a Polish peasant. I went inside and greeted him in the Polish manner: 'Blessed be Jesus Christ'.

While I warmed myself I asked cautiously about the distance to Chelmno. It was only three kilometres. I also received a piece of bread which I put in my pocket. As I was about to go the peasant asked me if I was a Jew – which I absolutely denied. I asked him why he suspected me, and he told me they were gassing Jews and gypsies at Chelmno. I took my leave with the Polish greeting and went away.

Life Inside the Warsaw Ghetto III, January 1942
JEWISH SOCIETY FOR SOCIAL WELFARE (*ZYDOWSKIE TOWARZYSTWO OPIEKI SPOLECZNEJ*)

The *Zydowskie Towarzystwo Opieki Spolecznej* was the Warsaw branch of the *Zydowska Samopomoc Spoleczna*, the largest of the Jewish communal self-help organizations in the *Generalgouvernement*, the area of Poland reserved for Jews.

January 1942 was the hardest month for the refugees generally and especially for the residents of the locale at Dzika and Niska Streets. There is no misfortune and illness which they did not experience in the time they have spent in Warsaw.

Hunger, sickness, and want are their constant companions and death is the only visitor in their homes.

In the last months of the past year the typhus epidemic raged there, not bypassing child or adult; hundreds of families were shattered – fathers and mothers passed away, children's lives were cut down, and the last Mohicans among the aged are expiring most hideously. This January there were only isolated cases of typhus in the locales mentioned, yet the refugees fell like flies from cold and exhaustion; the mortality reached 539, or 18 per cent of their number.

Now the newly organized body for refugee care is working in the locales, trying to alleviate the poverty and improve the sorrowful plight of the unfortunate refugees.

The most serious affliction now in the locales is dysentery and its accompanying rash.

The number of refugees declines from day to day. Now, as of the end of January, there are 2,977 refugees in the locales. The locales at Dzika 7, 9, and 11 have been liquidated. A large children's residential centre is being organized at No. 9.

If help for the refugee locale is not increased, if the sanitary-hygienic conditions are not improved, if the indifference on the part of the Warsaw Jewish community to the expiring refugees is not combated and the mortality is not halted, this locale, which is dubbed a 'refugee town', will become a 'refugee village'.

The situation at the end of the month is as follows:

9 Stawkt Street

The total number of refugees at the end of the month – 1,100; rooms – 170. The rooms are generally not heated. There is no heated room at all in the locale. No running water, and toilets are not working. Typhus – isolated cases. As of now, there are among the refugees 200 who are not exempt from the meal charges. The number of deaths in this locale was 280, the mortality here the highest: *25 per cent of all residents* …

The highest mortality turns out to be among children. The next highest is the age group 20–40. Refugees of advanced age are rare cases.

The deceased refugees come from: Rawa, Łowicz, Zakroczym, Lipno, Skierniewice, Nowy Dwór, Biezuń, Warka, Góra-Kalwaria, Sokołów, Cracow, Aleksandrów, Głowno, Sierpce, Żyrardów, Kałuszyn, Mszczonów, Błonie, Drobin, Kowal, Wyszków, Kutno, Częstochowa, Leszno, Raciąż, Słupce, Błędów, Grójec, Płońsk, Otwock, Tarczyn, Stryków, Zgierz.

3 Dzika Street

Number of residents – 1,613; rooms – 153. Only the orphans' rooms and children's club room are heated. No running water, and toilets are not working. About 10 per cent are exempt from meal charges. The locale has a diverse population (employable, beggars, and ordinary criminals), as the locale directors remark, because of poor nutrition, lack of occupation, and low cultural standard …

Unfortunately for the locale, persons stricken with dysentery remain here and even persons with broken limbs are not sent to the hospital. The locale still lacks plank beds. The refugees are in rags and tatters. Some are completely naked.

The number of deceased during the month was 183. The mortality rate is 11.5 per cent …

9 Dzika Street

The locale at 9 Dzika is being transformed into a large children's residence. The building is dirty, corridors and stairs with mud and excrement. The upper storeys are being prepared for the children. Meantime the children are in the most horrible sanitary conditions. Nutrition is inadequate, but tolerable in comparison to living in the conditions in the locales.

The number of children is 191. During the month 87 children were admitted. The children come from the following cities: Poznań, Zgierz, Łódź, Brzeziny, Żuromin, Stryków, Aleksandrów, Sierpce, and Kałuszyn. Besides the cities mentioned, there are also a small number of children from Warsaw.

No running water, and toilets are not working. Dysentery stalks the children's centre. A large number of children suffer from rashes. The children are naked and barefoot. Several children sleep on one plank bed.

During the month 63 children died.

The mortality among children has reached 33 per cent of the total.

The children still do not get supplementary food rations from the management.

19 Dzika Street

The locale holds 136 refugees. Rooms – 8. The rooms are unheated. Running water works partially. One toilet is in operation. There have been no typhus cases, but, in contrast, there have been three cases of dysentery. There are also cases where the refugee does not get a midday meal, because some are not exempt from meal charges.

Only the children's club room is heated.

There were 13 deaths, among them five children, 10 per cent of all ...
Some comments on conclusions to be drawn:

a. Births: 0. In December, one birth – a stillborn child.
b. Deaths: Children up to 14 years – 42 per cent.
c. Deaths are doubtless the result of harsh living and sanitary-hygienic conditions in the above-mentioned locales.

PART III: ASH

The Final Solution,
20 January 1942–1946

The Final Solution had already begun with the Einsatzgruppen: the Wannsee Conference, held in a suburban villa on the outskirts of Berlin, was convened to coordinate a more effective mass extermination of Europe's Jews. Fifteen representatives of party and state apparatus attended this meeting about the *Endlosung*, which was chaired by Reinhard Heydrich. Adolf Eichmann took the minutes. The ensuing protocols do not explicitly mention extermination, hiding behind what Eichmann called 'office speak' (euphemisms to make mass murder innocuous, even mundane), but no one at the conference was under any illusions. What Heydrich meant by 'practical experience is already being collected' was that experiments had been carried out with gas chambers at Auschwitz and the other death camps. Heydrich's striving for efficiency combined with mass gassing would bring the Holocaust to four million European Jews between 1942 and 1945.

Minutes of the Wannsee Conference, Berlin, 20 January 1942
SS OBERSTURMBANNFÜHRER ADOLF EICHMANN

Secret Reich Business!
30 copies
16th copy

Minutes of discussion.
I.
The following persons took part in the discussion about the final solution of the Jewish question which took place in Berlin, am Grossen Wannsee No. 56/58 on 20 January 1942.

Gauleiter Dr Meyer and Reichsamtleiter Dr Leibbrandt	Reich Ministry for the Occupied Eastern territories
Secretary of State Dr Stuckart	Reich Ministry for the Interior
Secretary of State Neumann	Plenipotentiary for the Four Year Plan
Secretary of State Dr Freisler	Reich Ministry of Justice
Secretary of State Dr Bühler	Office of the Government General
Under Secretary of State Dr Luther	Foreign Office

SS-Oberführer Klopfer   Party Chancellery
Ministerialdirektor Kritzinger   Reich Chancellery
SS-Gruppenführer Hofmann   Race and Settlement Main Office
SS-Gruppenführer Müller   Reich Main Security Office
SS-Obersturmbannführer
Eichmann
SS-Oberführer Dr Schöngarth   Security Police and SD
Commander of the Security Police
and the SD in the
Government General
SS-Sturmbannführer Dr Lange   Security Police SD
Commander of the Security Police
and the SD for the General-District
Latvia, as deputy of the Commander
of the Security Police and the SD
for the Reich Commissariat 'Eastland'.

II.

At the beginning of the discussion Chief of the Security Police and of the SD, SS-Obergruppenführer Heydrich, reported that the Reich Marshal had appointed him delegate for the preparations for the final solution of the Jewish question in Europe and pointed out that this discussion had been called for the purpose of clarifying fundamental questions. The wish of the Reich Marshal to have a draft sent to him concerning organizational, factual and material interests in relation to the final solution of the Jewish question in Europe makes necessary an initial common action of all central offices immediately concerned with these questions in order to bring their general activities into line. The Reichsführer-SS and the Chief of the German Police (Chief of the Security Police and the SD) was entrusted with the official central handling of the final solution of the Jewish question without regard to geographic borders. The Chief of the Security Police and the SD then gave a short report of the struggle which has been carried on thus far against this enemy, the essential points being the following:

a)   the expulsion of the Jews from every sphere of life of the German people,
b)   the expulsion of the Jews from the living space of the German people.

In carrying out these efforts, an increased and planned acceleration of the emigration of the Jews from Reich territory was started, as the only possible present solution.

By order of the Reich Marshal, a Reich Central Office for Jewish Emigration was set up in January 1939 and the Chief of the Security Police and SD was entrusted with the management. Its most important tasks were

a) to make all necessary arrangements for the preparation for an increased emigration of the Jews,
b) to direct the flow of emigration,
c) to speed the procedure of emigration in each individual case.

The aim of all this was to cleanse German living space of Jews in a legal manner.

All the offices realized the drawbacks of such enforced accelerated emigration. For the time being they had, however, tolerated it on account of the lack of other possible solutions of the problem.

The work concerned with emigration was, later on, not only a German problem, but also a problem with which the authorities of the countries to which the flow of emigrants was being directed would have to deal. Financial difficulties, such as the demand by various foreign governments for increasing sums of money to be presented at the time of the landing, the lack of shipping space, increasing restriction of entry permits, or the cancelling of such, increased extraordinarily the difficulties of emigration. In spite of these difficulties, 537,000 Jews were sent out of the country between the takeover of power and the deadline of 31 October 1941. Of these

approximately 360,000 were in Germany proper on 30 January 1933
approximately 147,000 were in Austria (Ostmark) on 15 March 1939
approximately 30,000 were in the Protectorate of Bohemia and Moravia on 15 March 1939.

The Jews themselves, or their Jewish political organizations, financed the emigration. In order to avoid impoverished Jews remaining behind, the principle was followed that wealthy Jews have to finance the emigration of poor Jews; this was arranged by imposing a suitable tax, i.e., an emigration tax, which was used for financial arrangements in connection with the emigration of poor Jews and was imposed according to income.

Apart from the necessary Reichsmark exchange, foreign currency had to be presented at the time of landing. In order to save foreign exchange held by Germany, the foreign Jewish financial organizations were – with the help of Jewish organizations in Germany – made responsible for arranging an adequate amount of foreign currency. Up to 30 October 1941, these foreign Jews donated a total of around 9,500,000 dollars.

In the meantime the Reichsführer-SS and Chief of the German Police had prohibited emigration of Jews due to the dangers of an emigration in wartime and due to the possibilities of the East.

III.

Another possible solution of the problem has now taken the place of emigration, i.e. the evacuation of the Jews to the East, provided that the Führer gives the appropriate approval in advance.

These actions are, however, only to be considered provisional, but practical experience is already being collected which is of the greatest importance in relation to the future final solution of the Jewish question.

Approximately 11 million Jews will be involved in the final solution of the European Jewish question, distributed as follows among the individual countries:

Country	Number
A. Germany proper	131,800
Austria	43,7000
Eastern territories	420,000
General Government	2,284,000
Bialystok	400,000
Protectorate Bohemia and Moravia	74,200
Estonia – free of Jews	
Latvia	3,500
Lithuania	34,000
Belgium	43,000
Denmark	5,600
France/occupied territory	165,000
unoccupied territory	700,000

Greece	69,600
Netherlands	160,800
Norway	1,300
B. Bulgaria	48,000
England	330,000
Finland	2,300
Ireland	4,000
Italy including Sardinia	58,000
Albania	200
Croatia	40,000
Portugal	3,000
Rumania including Bessarabia	342,000
Sweden	8,000
Switzerland	18,000
Serbia	10,000
Slovakia	88,000
Spain	6,000
Turkey (European portion)	55,500
Hungary	742,800
USSR	5,000,000
Ukraine	2,994,684
White Russia excluding Bialystok	446,484
Total	over 11,000,000

The number of Jews given here for foreign countries includes, however, only those Jews who still adhere to the Jewish faith, since some countries still do not have a definition of the term 'Jew' according to racial principles. The handling of the problem in the individual countries will meet with difficulties due to the attitude and outlook of the people there, especially in Hungary and Rumania. Thus, for example, even today the Jew can buy documents in Rumania that will officially prove his foreign citizenship.

The influence of the Jews in all walks of life in the USSR is well known. Approximately five million Jews live in the European part of the USSR, in the Asian part scarcely ¼ million.

The breakdown of Jews residing in the European part of the USSR according to trades was approximately as follows:

Agriculture 9.1 per cent
Urban workers 14.8 per cent
In trade 20.0 per cent
Employed by the state 23.4 per cent
In private occupations such as medical profession, press, theatre, etc.
32.7 per cent

Under proper guidance, in the course of the final solution the Jews are
to be allocated for appropriate labour in the East. Able-bodied Jews,
separated according to sex, will be taken in large work columns to
these areas for work on roads, in the course of which action doubtless
a large portion will be eliminated by natural causes.

The possible final remnant will, since it will undoubtedly consist of
the most resistant portion, have to be treated accordingly, because it is
the product of natural selection and would, if released, act as the seed
of a new Jewish revival (see the experience of history).

In the course of the practical execution of the final solution,
Europe will be combed through from west to east. Germany proper,
including the Protectorate of Bohemia and Moravia, will have to be
handled first due to the housing problem and additional social and
political necessities.

The evacuated Jews will first be sent, group by group, to so-called
transit ghettos, from which they will be transported to the East.

SS-Obergruppenführer Heydrich went on to say that an important
pre-requisite for the evacuation as such is the exact definition of the
persons involved.

It is not intended to evacuate Jews over sixty-five years old, but to
send them to an old-age ghetto – Theresienstadt is being considered
for this purpose.

In addition to these age groups – of the approximately 280,000 Jews
in Germany proper and Austria on 31 October 1941, approximately
30 per cent are over sixty-five years old – severely wounded veterans
and Jews with war decorations (Iron Cross I) will be accepted in the
old-age ghettos. With this expedient solution, in one fell swoop many
interventions will be prevented.

The beginning of the individual larger evacuation actions will
largely depend on military developments. Regarding the handling
of the final solution in those European countries occupied and

influenced by us, it was proposed that the appropriate expert of the Foreign Office discuss the matter with the responsible official of the Security Police and SD.

In Slovakia and Croatia the matter is no longer so difficult, since the most substantial problems in this respect have already been brought near a solution. In Rumania the government has in the meantime also appointed a commissioner for Jewish affairs. In order to settle the question in Hungary, it will soon be necessary to force an adviser for Jewish questions on to the Hungarian government.

With regard to taking up preparations for dealing with the problem in Italy, SS-Obergruppenführer Heydrich considers it opportune to contact the chief of police with a view to these problems.

In occupied and unoccupied France, the registration of Jews for evacuation will in all probability proceed without great difficulty.

Under Secretary of State Luther calls attention in this matter to the fact that in some countries, such as the Scandinavian states, difficulties will arise if this problem is dealt with thoroughly and that it will therefore be advisable to defer actions in these countries. Besides, in view of the small numbers of Jews affected, this deferral will not cause any substantial limitation.

The Foreign Office sees no great difficulties for south-east and western Europe.

SS-Gruppenführer Hofmann plans to send an expert to Hungary from the Race and Settlement Main Office for general orientation at the time when the Chief of the Security Police and SD takes up the matter there. It was decided to assign this expert from the Race and Settlement Main Office, who will not work actively, as an assistant to the police attaché.

IV.

In the course of the final solution plans, the Nuremberg Laws should provide a certain foundation, in which a pre-requisite for the absolute solution of the problem is also the solution to the problem of mixed marriages and persons of mixed blood.

The Chief of the Security Police and the SD discusses the following points, at first theoretically, in regard to a letter from the chief of the Reich chancellery:

1)   Treatment of Persons of Mixed Blood of the First Degree
Persons of mixed blood of the first degree will, as regards the final solution of the Jewish question, be treated as Jews.

From this treatment the following exceptions will be made:

a)   Persons of mixed blood of the first degree married to persons of German blood if their marriage has resulted in children (persons of mixed blood of the second degree). These persons of mixed blood of the second degree are to be treated essentially as Germans.

b)   Persons of mixed blood of the first degree, for whom the highest offices of the Party and State have already issued exemption permits in any sphere of life. Each individual case must be examined, and it is not ruled out that the decision may be made to the detriment of the person of mixed blood.

The pre-requisite for any exemption must always be the personal merit of the person of mixed blood. (Not the merit of the parent or spouse of German blood.)

Persons of mixed blood of the first degree who are exempted from evacuation will be sterilized in order to prevent any offspring and to eliminate the problem of persons of mixed blood once and for all. Such sterilization will be voluntary. But it is required to remain in the Reich. The sterilized 'person of mixed blood' is thereafter free of all restrictions to which he was previously subjected.

2)   Treatment of Persons of Mixed Blood of the Second Degree
Persons of mixed blood of the second degree will be treated fundamentally as persons of German blood, with the exception of the following cases, in which the persons of mixed blood of the second degree will be considered as Jews:

a)   The person of mixed blood of the second degree was born of a marriage in which both parents are persons of mixed blood.

b)   The person of mixed blood of the second degree has a racially especially undesirable appearance that marks him outwardly as a Jew.

c)   The person of mixed blood of the second degree has a particularly bad police and political record that shows that he feels and behaves like a Jew.

Also in these cases exemptions should not be made if the person of mixed blood of the second degree has married a person of German blood.

3)   Marriages between Full Jews and Persons of German Blood.
Here it must be decided from case to case whether the Jewish partner will be evacuated or whether, with regard to the effects of such a step on the German relatives, [this mixed marriage] should be sent to an old-age ghetto.

4)   Marriages between Persons of Mixed Blood of the First Degree and Persons of German Blood
a) Without Children.
If no children have resulted from the marriage, the person of mixed blood of the first degree will be evacuated or sent to an old-age ghetto (same treatment as in the case of marriages between full Jews and persons of German blood, point 3.)

b)   With Children.
If children have resulted from the marriage (persons of mixed blood of the second degree), they will, if they are to be treated as Jews, be evacuated or sent to a ghetto along with the parent of mixed blood of the first degree. If these children are to be treated as Germans (regular cases), they are exempted from evacuation as is therefore the parent of mixed blood of the first degree.

5)   Marriages between Persons of Mixed Blood of the First Degree and Persons of Mixed Blood of the First Degree or Jews.
In these marriages (including the children) all members of the family will be treated as Jews and therefore be evacuated or sent to an old-age ghetto.

6)   Marriages between Persons of Mixed Blood of the First Degree and Persons of Mixed Blood of the Second Degree.

In these marriages both partners will be evacuated or sent to an old-age ghetto without consideration of whether the marriage has produced children, since possible children will as a rule have stronger Jewish blood than the Jewish person of mixed blood of the second degree.

SS-Gruppenführer Hofmann advocates the opinion that sterilization will have to be widely used, since the person of mixed blood who is given the choice whether he will be evacuated or sterilized would rather undergo sterilization.

State Secretary Dr Stuckart maintains that carrying out in practice of the just mentioned possibilities for solving the problem of mixed marriages and persons of mixed blood will create endless administrative work. In the second place, as the biological facts cannot be disregarded in any case, State Secretary Dr Stuckart proposed proceeding to forced sterilization.

Furthermore, to simplify the problem of mixed marriages, possibilities must be considered with the goal of the legislator saying something like: 'These marriages have been dissolved.'

With regard to the issue of the effect of the evacuation of Jews on the economy, State Secretary Neumann stated that Jews who are working in industries vital to the war effort, provided that no replacements are available, cannot be evacuated.

SS-Obergruppenführer Heydrich indicated that these Jews would not be evacuated according to the rules he had approved for carrying out the evacuations then underway.

State Secretary Dr Bühler stated that the General Government would welcome it if the final solution of this problem could be begun in the General Government, since on the one hand transportation does not play such a large role here nor would problems of labour supply hamper this action. Jews must be removed from the territory of the General Government as quickly as possible, since it is especially here that the Jew as an epidemic carrier represents an extreme danger, and on the other hand he is causing permanent chaos in the economic structure of the country through continued black market dealings. Moreover, of the approximately 2½ million Jews concerned, the majority are unfit for work.

State Secretary Dr Bühler stated further that the solution to the Jewish question in the General Government is the responsibility of the Chief of the Security Police and the SD and that his efforts would be supported by the officials of the General Government. He had only one request, to solve the Jewish question in this area as quickly as possible.

In conclusion, the different types of possible solutions were discussed, during which discussion both Gauleiter Dr Meyer and State Secretary Dr Bühler took the position that certain preparatory activities for the final solution should be carried out immediately in the territories in question, in which process alarming the populace must be avoided.

The meeting was closed with the request of the Chief of the Security Police and the SD to the participants that they afford him appropriate support during the carrying out of the tasks involved in the solution.

The first mass gassings of Jews at Auschwitz began in February 1942. Although the extermination of European Jewry would now largely be achieved with Zyklon B, the Nazis did not neglect the bullet.

'The cries and screams of the children could be heard': Mass Execution at Krepiec Forest, Poland, 22 April 1942
ANDRZEJ WOJCIK

The Krepiec forest is one of the largest mass execution sites of Jews in Poland. Although the incident witnessed by Wojcik – a Pole living nearby – took place in April 1942, executions had been occurring in the forest since May 1940 and they would only end in October 1942, when the gas chambers at Majdanek were fully functioning.

On 22 April 1942 I was at home and suddenly I noticed that six or seven trucks, full of children between two and fourteen years of age, arrived at the forest. The children were driven down to the pits and the Germans shot them. From the place of the murder the cries and screams of the children could be heard. In all this lasted from 2 a.m. until 6 a.m. The Germans were in helmets and blue uniforms. It is difficult for me to say from which formation they were. Visibility was difficult because at the beginning it was still dark. I observed the massacre from a distance of about fifty metres. I don't know how many children were killed. They were transported by trucks, completely overcrowded.

About 8 a.m. nine trucks full of Jews arrived at the forest. The area was surrounded by Lithuanian soldiers. I know this because people described them to me as Lithuanians. The Jews were driven down from the trucks and they were led to the same place where the children were murdered. Some of the Jews held their children in their arms. I observed the massacre from a distance of about 150 metres but from a different direction than before. Germans drove the Jews down to the pits. There were horrible screams. A group of six SS officers and Lithuanians shot into the Jews who were already in the pits. I'm sure that they were SS men because on their caps they had death's head insignia and on their sleeves the signs of SS. The execution lasted from 8 a.m. until 8 p.m. I observed these murders the entire time. I heard from people that a Jewess escaped from the mountain of bodies but that later, attempting to escape, she was shot in a field.

The next day I went to the place of the executions and I noticed that the pits were covered partially by earth and partially by bushes. Legs, hands and heads stood out from the pits. The earth around the pits was covered in blood. I was there about twenty minutes.

Inside the Crematorium at Auschwitz:
The View of a Sonderkommando, May 1942
FILIP MÜLLER

Prisoner 29236, Müller was a Slovakian Jew who arrived on one of the earliest transports to Auschwitz. He began working in a 'Sonderkommando', a unit of inmates whose prime job was disposing of corpses in the camp's crematoria, almost immediately. He was one of the very few Sonderkommandos to survive the Holocaust: the SS administration regularly culled these workers who were, after all, prime witnesses to their crimes against the Jews.

We had been running for about 100 metres, when a strange flat-roofed building loomed up before us. Behind it a round redbrick chimney rose up into the sky. Through a wooden gate the two guards led us into a yard which was separated from the outside world by a wall. To our right was the building we had seen, with an entrance in the middle.

Above the door hung a wrought-iron lamp. Under it stood an SS man who, according to his insignia, was an *Unterscharführer*. He was still young, with sandy hair and a commanding presence, and I learned later that his name was Stark. In his hand he held a horsewhip. He greeted us with the words: 'Get inside, you scum!' Then, belabouring us with his whip, he drove us through the entrance into a passage with several doors which were painted pale blue. We were confused and did not know which way we were meant to go. 'Straight ahead, you shits!' Stark shouted, opening one of the doors. The damp stench of dead bodies and a cloud of stifling, biting smoke surged out towards us. Through the fumes I saw the vague outlines of huge ovens. We were in the cremation room of the Auschwitz crematorium. A few prisoners, the Star of David on their prison uniforms, were running about. As the glow of the flames broke through the smoke and fumes, I noticed two large openings: they were cast-iron incinerators. Prisoners were busy pushing a truck heaped with corpses up to them. Stark pulled open another door. Flogging Maurice and me, he hustled us into a larger room next door to the cremation plant.

We were met by the appalling sight of the dead bodies of men and women lying higgledy-piggledy among suitcases and rucksacks. I was petrified with horror for I did not know then where I was and what was going on. A violent blow accompanied by Stark yelling: 'Get a move on! Strip the stiffs!' galvanized me into action. Before me lay the corpse of a woman. With trembling hands and shaking all over I began to remove her stockings. It was the first time in my life that I had touched a dead body. She was not yet quite cold. As I pulled the stocking down her leg, it tore. Stark who had been watching, struck me again, bellowing: 'What the hell d'you think you are doing? Mind out, and get a move on! These things are to be used again!' To show us the correct way he began to remove the stockings from another female corpse. But he did not manage to take them off without at least a small tear.

I was like one hypnotized and obeyed each order implicitly. Fear of more blows, the ghastly sights of piled-up corpses, the biting smoke, the humming of fans and the flickering of flames, the whole infernal chaos, had paralyzed my sense of orientation as well as my ability to think. It took some time before I began to realize that there were people lying there at my feet who had been killed only a short while before. But what I could not imagine was how so many people could have been killed at one time.

When Stark returned he ordered Maurice and myself to the cremation room. Handing each of us a long crow-bar and a heavy hammer he ordered us to remove the clinker from the grates of those ovens which were not then in use. Neither Maurice nor I had ever done any work like this before, so we did not know what we were supposed to do. Instead of hammering the crow-bars into the clinker on the grates we thrust them into the ash pit and damaged the fire-brick lining. When Stark discovered the damage we had done, he hustled us back into the room where the corpses were and fetched a prisoner called Fischl – later to become our foreman – who went on with cleaning the grates.

Maurice and I continued stripping corpses. Cautiously I began to look around. I noticed that there were some small greenish-blue crystals lying on the concrete floor at the back of the room. They were scattered beneath an opening in the ceiling. A large fan was installed up there, its blades humming as they revolved. It struck me that where the crystals were scattered on the floor there were no corpses, whereas in places further away, particularly near the door, they were piled high.

My stay in the camp had undermined my health. I was weakened by starvation, my feet were swollen and the sole raw from wearing rough wooden clogs. It was therefore not surprising that, with the constant rush and hurry, I longed for a moment of rest. I kept a watchful eye on Stark and waited for a chance to take a breather while he was not looking. My moment came when he went across to the cremation room. Out of the corner of my eye I noticed a half-open suitcase containing food. Pretending to be busy undressing a corpse with one hand, I ransacked the suitcase with the other. Keeping one eye on the door in case Stark returned suddenly I hastily grabbed a few triangles of cheese and a poppyseed cake. With my filthy, blood-stained fingers I broke off pieces of cake and devoured them ravenously. I had only just time to pocket a piece of bread when Stark returned. He clearly thought we were slacking and shouted at us to work faster. An hour later we had undressed about 100 corpses. There they lay, naked and ready to be cremated.

In another suitcase I found a round box of cheese and several boxes of matches with Slovakian labels. And as I looked a little more closely at the faces of the dead, I recoiled with horror when I discovered among them a girl who had been at school with me. Her name was Yolana Weis. In order to make quite sure I looked at her hand because Yolana's hand had been deformed since childhood. I had not been mistaken: this was Yolana. There was another dead body which I recognized. It was that of a woman who had been our neighbour in Sered, my home town. Most of the dead were dressed in civilian clothes, but there were a few wearing military uniforms. Two wide, red stripes on the back of their jackets and the letters SU in black showed them to be Soviet prisoners-of-war.

Meanwhile Fischl had finished cleaning the grates. Now all six ovens were working, and Stark ordered us to drag the naked corpses across the concrete floor to the ovens. There Fischl went from corpse to corpse, forcing their mouths open with an iron bar. When he found a gold tooth he pulled it out with a pair of pliers and flung it into a tin. Stripped and robbed of everything, the dead were destined to become victims of the flames and to be turned into smoke and ashes. Final preparations were now in hand. Stark ordered the fans to be switched on. A button was pressed and they began to rotate. But as soon as Stark had checked that the fire was drawing well they were switched off again. At his order 'Shove 'em in!' each one of us set to work doing the job he had been given earlier.

I now began to realize the dangerous position in which I found myself. At that moment I had only one chance to stay alive, even if only for a few hours or days. I had to convince Stark that I could do anything he expected from a crematorium worker. And thus I carried out all his orders like a robot.

Coming from the room where I had been undressing corpses into the cremation room, there were two ovens on the left and four on the right. A depression roughly twenty to twenty-five centimetres deep and one metre wide ran across the room and in this rails had been laid. This track was about fifteen metres long. Leading off from the main track were six branch rails, each four metres long, going straight to the ovens. On the main track was a turn-table which enabled a truck to be moved on to the branch tracks. The cast-iron truck had a box-shaped superstructure made of sheet metal, with an overall height and width of just under one metre. It was about eighty centimetres long. An iron hand-rail went right across its entire width at the back. A loading platform made of strong sheet metal and not quite two metres long jutted out in the front; its side walls were twelve to fifteen centimetres high. Open at the front, the platform was not quite as wide as the mouth of the oven so that it fitted easily into the muffle. On the platform there was also a box-shaped pusher made of sheet metal, higher than the side walls of the platform and rounded off at the top. It was about 40 centimetres deep, thirty to forty centimetres high, and could be moved back and forth quite easily. Before the truck was loaded, the pusher was moved to the back of the platform. To move the truck from one track to another, one 'had to hold on to the turn-table to prevent the truck from jumping off the rails as it left the turn-table.

To begin with, the corpses were dragged close to the ovens. Then, with the help of the turn-table, the truck was brought up to a branch rail, and the front edge of the platform supported by a wooden prop to prevent the truck from tipping during loading. A prisoner then poured a bucket of water on the platform to stop it from becoming too hot inside the red-hot oven. Meanwhile two prisoners were busy lifting a corpse on to a board lying on the floor beside the platform. Then they lifted the board, tipping it sideways so that the corpse dropped on the platform. A prisoner standing on the other side checked that the body was in correct position.

When the truck was finally loaded two corpses were lying on either side facing the oven while a third was wedged between them feet first. Now the time had come to open the oven door. Immediately one was overcome by the fierce heat which rushed out. When the wooden prop had been removed, two men took hold of the front end of the platform on either side, pulling it right up to the oven. Simultaneously two men pushed the truck from behind, thus forcing the platform into the oven. The two who had been doing the carrying in front, having meanwhile nipped back a few steps, now braced themselves against the hand-rail while giving the pusher a vigorous shove with one leg. In this way they helped complete the job of getting the corpses right inside the oven. As soon as the front part of the pusher was inside the oven, the truck with its platform was pulled back. In order to prevent the load of corpses from sliding out of the oven during this operation, a prisoner standing to one side thrust an iron fork into the oven pressing it against the corpses. While the platform – which had been more than three-quarters inside the oven – was being manoeuvred on its truck back on to the turn-table, the oven door was closed again.

During one such operation I was kneeling by the turn-table holding on to it with all my strength so that the truck might roll on smoothly. But, my hands being unsteady, I failed to set the turn-table exactly in line with the track, which resulted in the empty truck jumping rails as it rattled back from the oven. I felt a sharp pain in the little finger of my right hand and saw that I was bleeding. This wound nearly frightened me out of my wits. I vaguely remembered being told about ptomaine poisoning as a child. Quickly I tore a piece out of my sweaty shirt and tried to bandage my wound. At that moment nothing else seemed to matter; my mind was completely preoccupied with the wound. And then Stark appeared. He was annoyed about the derailed truck and began to hit me. I screamed with pain. Then, making one last and desperate effort, I jumped up and helped to put the truck back on to the track. Of one thing I was quite sure: any failure on my part to comply would have meant instant death.

When all six ovens were loaded, we returned to our job of stripping corpses. I worked with the greatest of care, anxiously trying to prevent my wounded finger from coming into contact with a dead body. Stark was standing in the doorway from where he could observe both rooms. My wound continued to bleed and had already soaked through my emergency bandage. Thus it happened that a little blood spilled on an undergarment just as Stark was standing near me. He noticed it at once and, raising his horsewhip, he shouted at me: 'You there, go and poke the stiffs, and be quick about it!' Although I quite failed to grasp what precisely it was he wanted me to do, I ran instinctively into the cremation room where I looked round completely at a loss. And then I saw Fischl: he walked up to one of the ovens and, lifting a flap in the lower half of the oven door, he proceeded to poke about inside the oven with a long fork. 'Come on, grab hold of this,' he whispered, 'poke the fork in and rattle it about, it'll make them burn better. Quick, or he'll kill you.' I grabbed this devil's tool and used it as Fischl had shown me, poking about among the burning disintegrating corpses as though I was poking a coal fire with a poker.

The powers that be had allocated twenty minutes for the cremation of three corpses. It was Stark's duty to see to it that this time was strictly adhered to. All at once, while I busied myself with my ghoulish task, three prisoners started to scurry around crazily in front of the ovens. They had refused to go on working and were trying to dodge Stark's blows. In the end they flung themselves on the concrete floor and, crawling on their bellies before him, implored him for pity's sake to finish them off with a bullet. Stark drove them into the room where the corpses lay and ordered them to get on with their work. But once again they threw themselves on the floor: they were beyond caring. Stark went purple with rage. His hand clutching the horsewhip was raised to come down on them in yet another vicious blow when suddenly he stopped short and simply said venomously: 'Just you wait, you lazy bastards, you've got it coming to you!' Then without another word he returned to the cremation room where he could be heard issuing orders.

When all six ovens were working, Stark hustled us next door to strip more corpses while he stayed behind in the cremation room. Meanwhile, pretending all the time to be working hard, I was trying desperately to gather new strength. Among the dead bodies I discovered our three fellow prisoners. Although they were still breathing, they were lying quite still, all their physical energy and the spiritual will to live drained out of them. They had given up.

I, on the other hand, had not yet reached that point of despair. Of course, I had no illusions: I knew with certainty that a dreadful end awaited me. But I was not yet ready to capitulate. The more menacing death grew, the stronger grew my will to survive. My every thought, every fibre of my being, was concentrated on only one thing: to stay alive, one minute, one hour, one day, one week. But not to die. I was still young, after all. The memory of my parents, my family and my early youth in my home town had faded. I was obsessed and dominated by the determination that I must not die. The heap of dead bodies which I had seen and which I was made to help remove only served to strengthen my determination to do everything possible not to perish in the same way; not to have to lie under a heap of dead bodies; not to be pushed into the oven, prodded with an iron fork and, ultimately, changed into smoke and ashes. Anything but that! I only wanted one thing: to go on living. Sometime, somehow, there might be a chance to get out of here. But if I wanted to survive there was only one thing: I must submit and carry out every single order. It was only by adopting this attitude that a man was able to carry on his ghastly trade in the crematorium of Auschwitz.

To Wear the Yellow Star or Not? The Dilemma of a Parisian Student, 7–8 June 1942
HELENE BERR

With the German invasion of Norway, Denmark, France and the Low Countries in April–May 1940 hundreds of thousands more Jews had become caught in the Nazi net. The first deportation of French Jews to the camps in the East occurred on 27 March 1942. Jews left behind were subject to the Nuremberg Laws of 1935 and their refinements. Berr was a student at the Sorbonne.

It was scorching hot when I left. I took the 92 bus. At Mme Jourdan's I met [...] and we talked about the meaning of the insignia. At that point I was determined not to wear it. I considered it degrading to do so, proof of one's submission to the Germans' laws.

This evening I've changed my mind: I now think it is cowardly not to wear it, vis-à-vis people who will.

Only, if I do wear it, I want to stay very elegant and dignified at all times so that people can see what that means. I want to do whatever is most courageous. This evening I believe that means wearing the star.

But where will it lead?

Monday, 8 June
This is the first day I feel I'm really on holiday. The weather is glorious, yesterday's storm has brought fresher air. The birds are twittering, it's a morning as in Paul Valéry. It's also the first day I'm going to wear the yellow star. Those are the two sides of how life is now: youth, beauty and freshness, all contained in this limpid morning; barbarity and evil, represented by this yellow star.

I was very courageous all day long. I held my head high, and I stared at other people so hard that it made them avert their eyes. But it's difficult.

In any case most people don't even look. The awkwardest thing is to meet other people wearing it. This morning I went out with Maman. In the street two boys pointed at us and said: 'Eh? You seen that? Jew.' Otherwise things went normally. In place de la Madeleine we ran into M. Simon, who stopped and got off his bicycle. I went back to place de l'Etoile on the métro on my own. At Etoile I went to the *Artisanat* to get my blouse, then I went to catch the 92. At the stop there was a young man and woman in the queue, and I saw the girl point me out to her companion. Then they exchanged some remarks.

Instinctively I raised my head – in full sunlight – and heard them say: 'It's disgusting.' There was a woman on the bus, probably a maid, who had smiled at me in the queue, and she turned round several times to smile at me again; a well-groomed gentleman stared at me. I couldn't make out the meaning of his stare, but I returned it with pride.

I set off again for the Sorbonne. Another working-class woman smiled at me on the métro. It brought tears to my eyes, I don't know why. There weren't many people about in the Latin Quarter. I had nothing to keep me busy at the library. Until 4.00 I whiled away the time with dreams, in the cool air of the reading room, in the brownish light seeping in through closed shutters. At 4.00 Jean Morawiecki came in. It was a relief to be able to talk to him. He sat down in front of my desk and stayed until closing time, chatting or saying nothing. He went out for half an hour to get tickets for Wednesday's concert. Meanwhile Nicole S. turned up.

When everyone had left the reading room, I got out my jacket and showed him the star. But I could not look him in the eye, so I took the star off and put in its place the tricolour brooch which I used to hold it in my buttonhole. When I looked up, I saw that this had touched his heart. I'm sure he hadn't realized. I was afraid that our friendship might suddenly be shattered or diminished. But afterwards we walked together to Sèvres-Babylone and he was very sweet. I wonder what he was thinking.

Hélène's father, managing director of Etablissements Kuhlmann, was interned in Drancy on 23 June 1942; he was released against a ransom but required to perform his job without coming into contact with the public. On 8 March 1944, Hélène and her parents were arrested in their Paris apartment and transferred to Drancy. All three died during their incarceration by the Nazis; Hélène herself was beaten to death in Bergen-Belsen while suffering from typhus just five days before the camp was liberated by the British. To the Nazis she was a routine Jew; they never discovered that she had been an active member of *L'Entraide Temporaire*, a clandestine network dedicated to saving Jewish children from deportation.

Diary of a Dutch Girl in Hiding, Netherlands, 9 July 1942–29 October 1943
ANNE FRANK

In 1942 the German-born Anne Frank and her family went into hiding in Amsterdam. Also in the 'Secret Annexe' were the three members of the Van Pels family (called by Anne the van Daan family), and later Fritz Pfeffer (Albert Dussel). Anne Frank was thirteen when she first went into hiding. 'Kitty' is the name she gave her diary, in pretence that it was an imaginary friend

Thursday, 9 July 1942
Dearest Kitty,

So there we were, Father, Mother and I, walking in the pouring rain, each of us with a satchel and a shopping bag filled to the brim with the most varied assortment of items. The people on their way to work at that early hour gave us sympathetic looks; you could tell by their faces that they were sorry they couldn't offer us some kind of transport; the conspicuous yellow star spoke for itself.

Only when we were walking down the street did Father and Mother reveal, little by little, what the plan was. For months we'd been moving as much of our furniture and apparel out of the flat as we could. It was agreed that we'd go into hiding on 16 July. Because of Margot's call-up notice, the plan had to be moved forward ten days, which meant we'd have to make do with less orderly rooms.

The hiding place was located in Father's office building. That's a little hard for outsiders to understand, so I'll explain. Father didn't have a lot of people working in his office, just Mr Kugler, Mr Kleiman, Miep and a twenty-three-year-old typist named Bep Voskuij, all of whom were informed of our coming. Mr Voskuijl, Bep's father, works in the warehouse, along with two assistants, none of whom were told anything.

Here's a description of the building. The large warehouse on the ground floor is used as a workroom and storeroom and is divided into several different sections, such as the stockroom and the milling room, where cinnamon, cloves and a pepper substitute are ground.

Next to the warehouse doors is another outside door, a separate entrance to the office. Just inside the office door is a second door, and beyond that a stairway. At the top of the stairs is another door, with a frosted window on which the word 'Office' is written in black letters. This is the big front office – very large, very light and very full. Bep, Miep and Mr Kleiman work there during the day. After passing through an alcove containing a safe, a wardrobe and a big stationery cupboard, you come to the small, dark, stuffy back office. This used to be shared by Mr Kugler and Mr van Daan, but now Mr Kugler is its only occupant. Mr Kugler's office can also be reached from the passage, but only through a glass door that can be opened from the inside but not easily from the outside. If you leave Mr Kugler's office and proceed through the long, narrow passage past the coal store and go up four steps, you find yourself in the private office, the showpiece of the entire building. Elegant mahogany furniture, a linoleum floor covered with rugs, a radio, a fancy lamp, everything first class. Next door is a spacious kitchen with a water-heater and two gas rings, and beside that a lavatory. That's the first floor.

A wooden staircase leads from the downstairs passage to the second floor. At the top of the stairs is a landing, with doors on either side. The door on the left takes you up to the spice storage area, attic and loft in the front part of the house. A typically Dutch, very steep, ankle-twisting flight of stairs also runs from the front part of the house to another door opening on to the street.

The door to the right of the landing leads to the 'Secret Annexe' at the back of the house. No one would ever suspect there were so many rooms behind that plain grey door. There's just one small step in front of the door, and then you're inside. Straight ahead of you is a steep flight of stairs. To the left is a narrow hallway opening on to a room that serves as the Frank family's living-room and bedroom. Next door is a smaller room, the bedroom and study of the two young ladies of the family. To the right of the stairs is a 'bathroom', a windowless room with just a sink. The door in the corner leads to the lavatory and another one to Margot's and my room. If you go up the stairs and open the door at the top, you're surprised to see such a large, light and spacious room in an old canalside house like this. It contains a gas cooker (thanks to the fact that it is used to be Mr Kugler's laboratory) and a sink. This will be the kitchen and bedroom of Mr and Mrs van Daan, as well as the general living-room, dining-room and study for us all. A tiny side room is to be Peter van Daan's bedroom. Then, just as in the front part of the building, there's an attic and a loft. So there you are. Now I've introduced you to the whole of our lovely Annexe!

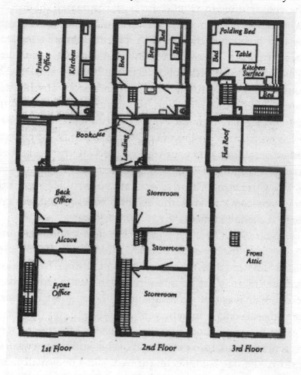

Yours, Anne

Thursday, 25 March 1943
Dearest Kitty,

Mother, Father, Margot and I were sitting quite pleasantly together last night when Peter suddenly came in and whispered in Father's ear. I caught the words 'a barrel falling over in the warehouse' and 'someone fiddling with the door'.

Margot heard it too, but was trying to calm me down, since I'd turned white as chalk and was extremely nervous. The three of us waited while Father and Peter went downstairs. A minute or two later Mrs van Daan came up from where she'd been listening to the radio and told us that Pim had asked her to turn it off and tiptoe upstairs. But you know what happens when you're trying to be quiet – the old stairs creaked twice as loud. Five minutes later Peter and Pim, the colour drained from their faces, appeared again to relate their experiences.

They had positioned themselves under the staircase and waited. Nothing happened. Then all of a sudden they heard a couple of bangs, as if two doors had been slammed shut inside the house. Pim bounded up the stairs, while Peter went to warn Dussel, who finally presented himself upstairs, though not without kicking up a fuss and making a lot of noise. Then we all tiptoed in our stockinged feet to the van Daans on the next floor. Mr van D. had a bad cold and had already gone to bed, so we gathered around his bedside and discussed our suspicions in a whisper. Every time Mr van D. coughed loudly, Mrs van D. and I nearly had a nervous fit. He kept coughing until someone came up with the bright idea of giving him codeine. His cough subsided immediately.

Once again we waited and waited, but heard nothing. Finally we came to the conclusion that the burglars had taken to their heels when they heard footsteps in an otherwise quiet building. The problem now was that the chairs in the private office were neatly grouped around the radio, which was tuned to England. If the burglars had forced the door and the air-raid wardens were to notice it and call the police, there could be very serious repercussions. So Mr van Daan got up, pulled on his coat and trousers, put on his hat and cautiously followed Father down the stairs, with Peter (armed with a heavy hammer, to be on the safe side) right behind him. The ladies (including Margot and me) waited in suspense until the men returned five minutes later and reported that there was no sign of activity in the building. We agreed not to run any water or flush the toilet; but since everyone's stomach was churning from all the tension, you can imagine the stench after we'd each had a turn in the lavatory.

Incidents like these are always accompanied by other disasters, and this was no exception. Number one: the Westertoren bells stopped chiming, and I'd always found them so comforting. Number two: Mr Voskuijl left early last night, and we weren't sure if he'd given Bep the key and she'd forgotten to lock the door.

But that was of little importance now. The night had just begun, and we still weren't sure what to expect. We were somewhat reassured by the fact that between eight-fifteen – when the burglar had first entered the building and put our lives in jeopardy – and ten-thirty, we hadn't heard a sound. The more we thought about it, the less likely it seemed that a burglar would have forced a door so early in the evening, when there were still people out on the streets. Besides that, it occurred to us that the warehouse manager at the Keg Company next door might still have been at work. What with the excitement and the thin walls, it's easy to mistake the sounds. Besides, your imagination often plays tricks on you in moments of danger.

So we went to bed, though not to sleep. Father and Mother and Mr Dussel were awake most of the night, and I'm not exaggerating when I say that I hardly got a wink of sleep. This morning the men went downstairs to see if the outside door was still locked, but all was well!

Of course, we gave the entire office staff a blow-by-blow account of the incident, which had been far from pleasant. It's much easier to laugh at these kinds of things after they've happened, and Bep was the only one who took us seriously.

Yours, Anne

P.S. This morning the toilet was clogged, and Father had to stick in a long wooden pole and fish out several pounds of excrement and strawberry recipes (which is what we use for toilet paper these days). Afterwards we burned the pole.

Friday, 29 October 1943
My dearest Kitty,

Mr Kleiman is out again: his stomach won't give him a moments's peace. He doesn't even know whether it's stopped bleeding. He came to tell us he wasn't feeling well and was going home, and for the first time he seemed really down.

Mr and Mrs van D. have had more raging battles. The reason is simple: they're broke. They wanted to sell an overcoat and a suit of Mr van D.'s, but were unable to find any buyers. His prices were much too high.

Some time ago Mr Kleiman was talking about a furrier he knows. This gave Mr van D. the idea of selling his wife's fur coat. It's made of rabbit skin, and she'd had it for seventeen years. Mrs van D got 325 guilders for it, an enormous amount. She wanted to keep the money herself to buy new clothes after the war, and it took some doing before Mr van D. could make her understand that it was desperately needed to cover household expenses.

You can't imagine the screaming, shouting, stamping of feet and swearing that went on. It was terrifying. My family stood holding its breath at the bottom of the stairs, in case it might be necessary to drag them apart. All the bickering, tears and nervous tension have become such a stress and strain that I fall into my bed at night crying and thanking my lucky stars that I have half an hour to myself.

I'm doing fine, except I've got no appetite. I keep hearing: 'Goodness, you look awful!' I must admit they're doing their best to keep me fit: they're plying me with dextrose, cod-liver oil, brewer's yeast and calcium. My nerves often get the better of me, especially on Sundays; that's when I really feel miserable. The atmosphere is stifling, sluggish, leaden. Outside, you don't hear a single bird, and a deathly, oppressive silence hangs over the house and clings to me as if it were going to drag me into the deepest regions of the underworld. At times like these, Father, Mother and Margot don't matter to me in the least. I wander from room to room, climb up and down the stairs and feel like a songbird whose wings have been ripped off and who keeps hurling itself against the bars of its dark cage. 'Let me out, where there's fresh air and laughter!' a voice within me cries. I don't even bother to reply any more, but lie down on the divan. Sleep makes the silence and the terrible fear go by more quickly, helps pass the time, since it's impossible to kill it.

Yours, Anne

The last entry in Anne Frank's diary is dated 1 August. Three days later the eight people hiding in the Secret Annexe were arrested by the SS and Dutch Security Police following a tip-off. Of the Frank family, only Anne's father survived the Holocaust. Anne Frank herself died in a typhus epidemic in Bergen-Belsen in February or March 1945.

'Now you're going to the bath house':
The Extermination Procedure at Belzec, August 1942
RUDOLF REDER

After the assassination of Reinhard Heydrich by Czech resistance fighters in May 1942, the SS instigated '*Aktion* Reinhard', by which Jews were sent to their immediate death at Sobibór, Treblinka and Belzec. Unlike Auschwitz, where there was a selection on arrival between those who would work and those who would die, at these extermination camps almost everyone was sent straight to the gassing room. Only a very small number of Jews were kept alive at Belzec to perform essential tasks as part of the 'Death Commando'. Rudolf Reder was one of only two Jews to survive Belzec.

About mid-day the train entered Belzec, a small station surrounded by small houses inhabited by the SS men. Here, the train was shunted off the main track on to a siding which ran for about another kilometre straight to the gates of the death camp. Ukrainian railwaymen also lived near the station and there was a post office nearby as well.

At Belzec station an old German with a thick, black moustache climbed into the locomotive cab. I don't know his name, but I would recognize him again, he looked like a hangman; he took over command of the train and drove it into the camp. The journey to the camp took two minutes. For months I always saw the same bandit.

The siding ran through the fields, on both sides there was completely open country; not one building. The German who drove the train into the camp climbed out of the locomotive; he was 'helping us' by beating and shouting, throwing people out of the train. He personally entered each wagon and made sure that no one remained behind. He knew about everything. When the train was empty and had been checked, he signalled with a small flag and took the train out of camp.

The whole area of Belzec was occupied by the SS – no one was allowed to approach; any individuals who stumbled accidentally into the area were immediately shot. The train entered a yard which measured about one kilometre by one kilometre and was surrounded by barbed wire and fencing about two metres high, which was not electrified. Entry to the yard was through a wooden gate covered with barbed wire. Next to the gate there was a guard house with a telephone, and standing in front of the guard house were several SS men with dogs. When the train had entered the yard the SS men closed the gate and went into the guard house.

At that moment, dozens of SS men opened the doors of the wagons shouting '*Los!*' They pushed people out with their whips and rifles. The doors of the wagons were about one metre above the ground. The people, hurried along with blows from whips, were forced to jump down, old and young alike, it made no difference. They broke arms and legs, but they had to obey the orders of the SS men. Children were injured, everyone was falling down, dirty, hungry, frightened.

Beside the SS men stood the so-called 'Zugsführers' – these were the guards in charge of the permanent Jewish death commando in the camp. They were dressed in civilian clothes, without any insignia …

The old, the sick and the babies, all those who could not walk, were placed on stretchers and taken to the edge of the huge mass graves. There, the SS man Irrman shot them and then pushed them into the graves with his rifle. Irrman was the camp expert at 'finishing off' old people and small children; a tall, dark, handsome Gestapo man, with a very normal-looking face, he lived like the other SS men in Belzec – not far from the railway station in a cottage, completely alone – and, like the others, without his family and without women.

He used to arrive at the camp early in the morning and meet the death transporters. After the victims had been unloaded from the trains, they were gathered in the yard and surrounded by armed Ukrainian SS men, and then Irrman delivered a speech. The silence was deathly. He stood close to the crowd. Everyone wanted to hear, suddenly a feeling of hope came over them. 'If they are going to talk to us, perhaps they are going to let us live after all. Perhaps we will have work, perhaps …'

Irrman spoke loudly and clearly: '*Ihr geht's jetzt baden, nachher werdet ihr zur Arbeit geschickt.*' 'Now you're going to the bath house, afterwards you will be sent to work.' That's all.

Everyone was happy, glad that they were going to work. They even clapped.

I remember those words being repeated day after day, usually three times a day – repeated for the four months of my stay here. That was the one moment of hope and illusion. For a moment the people felt happy. There was complete calm. In that silence the crowd moved on, men straight into a building on which there was a sign in big letters: *Bade und Inhalationsraume*, Bath and inhalation room.

The women went about twenty metres farther on – to a large barrack hut which measured about thirty metres by fifteen metres. There they had their heads shaved, both women and girls. They entered, not knowing what for. There was still silence and calm. Later, I knew that only a few minutes after entering, they were asked to sit on wooden stools across the barrack hut, and Jewish barbers, like automatons, as silent as the grave, came forward to shave their heads. Then they understood the whole truth, none of them could have any doubts any more.

All of them – everyone – except a few chosen craftsmen – were going to die.

The girls with long hair went to be shaved, those who had short hair went with the men – straight into the gas-chambers.

Suddenly there were cries and tears, a lot of women had hysterics. Many of them went cold-bloodedly to their deaths, especially the young girls.

There were thousands of intelligentsia, many young men and – as in all other transports – many women.

I was standing in the yard, together with a group left behind for digging graves, and was looking at my sisters, my brothers and friends being pushed to their deaths.

At the moment when the women were pushed naked, shorn and beaten, like cattle to the slaughter, the men were already dying in the gas-chambers. The shaving of the women lasted about two hours, the same time as the murder process in the chambers.

Several SS men pushed the women with whips and bayonets to the building housing the chambers; three steps led up to a hall, and Ukrainian SS men counted 750 people to each chamber. Those who did not want to enter were stabbed with bayonets and forced inside – there was blood everywhere.

I heard the doors being locked, the moaning, shouting and cries of despair in Polish and Jewish; the crying of the children and women which made the blood run cold in my veins. Then came one last terrible shout. All this lasted fifteen to twenty minutes, after which there was silence. The Ukrainian guards opened the doors on the outside of the building and I, together with all the others left over from the previous transports, began our work.

We pulled out the corpses of those who were alive only a short time ago, we pulled them using leather belts to the huge mass graves while the camp orchestra played; played from morning 'til night.

The pace of extermination increased in 1942. As many as half a million Jews were killed in that year.

The Deputy Commandant Kicks a Baby to Death, Treblinka Railway Station, 1 September 1942
FRANCISZEK ZABECKI

The writer was a railwayman at Treblinka railway station. Fugitives from the death camp and from the trains waiting to enter, frequently hid in the thicket alongside the track.

One of the SS men who had arrived at the station that day – he was Kurt Franz, Deputy Commandant of the camp – came out with his dog along the road. The dog, scenting something, pulled the SS man after it into the thicket. A Jewess was lying there with a baby; probably she was already dead. The baby, a few months old, was crying, and nestling against its mother's bosom.

The dog, let off the lead, tracked them down, but at a certain distance it crouched on the ground. It looked as if it was getting ready to jump, to bite them and tear them to pieces. However, after a time it began to cringe and whimper dolefully, and approached the people lying on the ground; crouching, it licked the baby on its hands, face and head.

The SS man came up to the scene with his gun in his hand. He sensed the dog's weakness. The dog began to wag its tail, turning its head towards the boots of the SS man. The German swore violently and flogged the dog with his stick. The dog looked up and fled. Several times the German kicked the dead woman, and then began to kick the baby and trample on its head. Later, he walked through the bushes, whistling for his dog.

The dog did not seem to hear, although it was not far away; it ran through the bushes whimpering softly; it appeared to be looking for the people. After a time the SS man came out on to the road, and the dog ran up to its 'master'. The German then began to beat it mercilessly with a whip. The dog howled, barked, even jumped up to the German's chest as if it were rabid, but the blows with the whip got the better of it. On the 'master's' command it lay down.

The German went a few paces away, and ordered the dog to stand. The dog obeyed with order perfectly. It carefully licked the boots, undoubtedly spattered with the baby's blood, under its muzzle.

'Blood flows in the streets': A Diary of the Deportations from Łódź, 4–6 September 1942
JOSEF ZELKOWICZ

Friday, 4 September 1942
The deportation of children and old people is a fact.

This morning the ghetto received a horrifying shock: what seemed improbable and incredible news yesterday has now become a dreadful fact. Children up to the age of ten are to be torn away from their parents, brothers and sisters, and deported. Old people over sixty-five are being robbed of their last life-saving plank, which they have been clutching with their last bits of strength – their four walls and their beds. They are being sent away like useless ballast.

If only they were really being 'sent away', if only there were the slightest ray of hope that these 'deportees' were being taken somewhere! That they were being settled and kept alive, ever under the worst conditions, then the tragedy would not be so enormous. After all, every Jew has always been ready to migrate; Jewish life has always been based on a capacity for adjusting to the worst conditions; every Jew has always been prepared to fold up his tent at command, to leave his home and country, and all the more so here in the ghetto, where there's no wealth, no property, no peace of mind, and where he is not attached to anything. Jewish life has always relied only on faith in the ancient Jewish God, who, the Jew feels, has never abandoned him. 'Somehow or other, everything will turn out all right. Somehow or other, we'll manage to survive, with our last bit of wretched life.'

If there were the slightest assurance, the slightest ray of hope they were being sent somewhere, then the ghetto would not be in such a turmoil over this new and unwonted evil decree. There have already been so many new and unwonted evil decrees and we have had to put up with them and, whether or not we wanted to, we had to go on living, so that we might somehow or other swallow this one too. But the fact is that no one has the least doubt, we are all certain that the people now being deported from the ghetto are not being 'sent' anywhere. They are being taken to nowhere, at least the old people. They are going to the scrap heap, as we say in the ghetto. How, then, can we be expected to make peace with this new evil decree? How can we be expected to go on living whether or not we want to?

There is simply no word, no power, no art able to transmit the moods, the laments, and the turmoil prevailing in the ghetto since early this morning.

To say that today the ghetto is swimming in tears would not be mere rhetoric. It would be simply a gross understatement, an inadequate utterance about the things you can see and hear in the ghetto of Litzmannstadt, no matter where you go or look or listen.

There is no house, no home, no family which is not affected by this dreadful edict. One person has a child, another an old father, a third an old mother. No one has patience, no one can remain at home with arms folded awaiting destiny. At home you feel forlorn, wretched, alone with your devouring cares. Just run into the street. Out there you don't feel so blind, you don't feel so abandoned. Animals, too, when they feel some sorrow, supposedly cling together, animals have mute tongues which cannot talk away their sorrows and their grief. How much more so human beings.

All hearts are icy, all hands are wrung, all eyes filled with despair. All faces are twisted, all heads bowed to the ground, all blood weeps.

Tears flow by themselves. They can't be held back. People know these tears are useless. Those who can help it refuse to see them, and those who see them – and they too shed useless tears – can't help themselves either. Worst of all, these tears bring no relief whatsoever. On the contrary. It's as though they were falling on, rather than from, our hearts. They only make our hearts heavier. Our hearts writhe and struggle in these tears like fish in poisoned waters. Our hearts drown in their own tears. But no one can help us in any way, no one can save us.

No one at all? No one in the whole ghetto who wants to, who can save us? Could there be someone after all? There must be someone who wants to, who's able to! Perhaps we still don't know who that someone is? Perhaps he's hiding somewhere, because he can't help everyone, he can't save everyone!

Maybe that's why people are scurrying all over the ghetto like poisoned mice. They're looking for that 'someone'. Maybe that's why the ghetto Jews are clutching at straws, maybe this straw is the 'someone' they're looking for. Maybe that's him over here, maybe that's him over there. Everyone is looking to revive old acquaintanceship with those who can help, everyone is looking for pull. Perhaps God will help.

And the children who don't yet understand, the little children who have no way of knowing about the Damoclean sword hanging over their innocent heads, perhaps subconsciously sense the enormous threat hovering over them, and their tiny hands cling tighter to the scrawny and shrunken breasts of their fathers and mothers.

Son of man, go out in the street. Look at all this, soak in the subconscious terror of the infants about to be slaughtered. And be strong and don't weep! Be strong and don't let your heart break, so that later on you can give a thoughtful and orderly description of just the barest essentials of what took place in the ghetto during the first few days of September in the year 1942.

Mothers run through the streets, one shoe on, one shoe off, their hair half combed, their shawls trailing on the ground. They are still holding on to their children. They can clasp them now tighter and closer to their emaciated breasts. They can still cover their bright little faces and eyes with kisses. But what will happen tomorrow, later on, in an hour?

People say: The children are to be taken from their parents as early as today. People say: The children are to be sent away as early as Monday. They are to be sent away – where?

To be sent away on Monday, to be taken away today. Meanwhile, for the moment, every mother clings to her child. Now she can still give her child everything, the very best thing in her possession – the last morsel of bread, all her love, the dearest and the best! Today the child doesn't have to wait for hours on end and cry until his father or mother figures out how much to give him from the half-pound of bread. Today they ask the child: 'Darling, would you like a piece of bread now?' And today the piece of bread that the child gets isn't dry and tasteless like always. It there's just a bit of margarine left, they spread it on. If there's any sugar left, they sprinkle it on. The ghetto lives recklessly today. No one weighs or measures. No one hordes sugar or margarine to stretch it for a whole ten days until the next ration. Today in the ghetto no one lives for the future. Today one lives for the moment and now, for the moment, every mother still has her child with her; and wouldn't she, if she could, give it her own heart, her own soul? ...

There are children who do indeed understand. In the ghetto, ten-year-old children are mature adults. They already know and understand what is in store for them. They may not as yet know why they are being torn away from their parents – they may not as yet have been told. For the moment it's enough for them to know that they are being torn away from their devoted guardians, their fathers and their loving and anxious mothers. It's hard to keep such children in one's arms or to take them by the hand. Such children weep on their own, with their own tears. Their tears are so sharp and piercing that they fall upon all hearts like poisoned arrows. But hearts in the ghetto have turned to stone. They would rather burst but they can't, and this is probably the greatest, the harshest curse. ...

The sorrow becomes greater, and the torture more senseless, when one tries to think rationally. Well, an old man is an old man. If he's lived his sixty-five years, he can convince himself, or others convince him, that he should utter something like: 'Well, thank God, I've had my share of living, in joy and sorrow, weal and woe. That's life. Probably that's fate. And anyway, you don't live for ever. So what's the difference if it's a few days, a few weeks, or even a few months sooner? Sooner or later, you've got to die, sooner or later everything's over. That's life.'

Maybe they can talk the old man into telling himself these things, maybe they can talk his family into telling themselves. But what about children who have only just been hatched, children who have only seen God's world in the ghetto, for whom a cow or a chicken is just a legendary creature, who have never in their lives so much as inhaled the fragrance of a flower, laid eyes upon an orange, tasted an apple or a pear, and who are now doomed to die? ...

The sky above the ghetto, like yesterday and the day before, is unclouded. Like yesterday and the day before, the early-autumn sun shines. It shines and smiles at our Jewish grief and agony, as though someone were merely stepping on vermin, as though someone had written a death sentence for bedbugs, a Day of Judgement for rats which must be exterminated and wiped off the face of the earth.

There are nevertheless still enough people in the ghetto who doubt, still enough people in the ghetto who continue to live with faith. There are even those who reason logically.

'This ghetto, where eighty per cent of the population performs useful work, is not one of your provincial towns which could have been made *Judenrein*, free of Jews, in half an hour. Here people are necessary, are needed for work. It's not possible that they would take people from here and send them away.'

And those who cannot argue rationally, who are just full of faith, they simply believe in miracles:

'Things like this have happened before. All through history, Jews have been threatened with bitter decrees, and deliverance has come at the last minute. There just was an air raid of Łódź for the first time since the war began. So maybe they'll withdraw the evil decree. Who can tell?' ...

Saturday, 5 September 1942.

It has begun.

It's only a few minutes after 7 a.m. now. All the people, practically the entire ghetto, are on the street. Whose nerves don't drive them out? Who can sit home? Who has peace of mind? Who can just sit with his arms folded? No one! ...

Consequently, from early morning the streets of the ghetto are busier than ever. And what a strange busyness. A silent, lifeless busyness, if one can put it that way. People don't talk to one another, as though everyone had left his tongue at home or had forgotten how to speak. Acquaintances don't greet each other, as though they feel ashamed. Everyone is rigid in motion, rigid standing in the long lines at the distribution places and rigid in the enormous lines at the vegetable places. A dead silence dominates the ghetto. No one so much as sighs or moans. Today huge, heavy stones weigh on the hearts of the ghetto residents.

People run through the ghetto streets like transmigrant spirits, perhaps like sinful souls wandering through the world of chaos. With that same stubborn silence on their clenched lips, with that same dread in their eyes – that's the way those spirits must look. People stand in line, perhaps like prisoners condemned to death, standing and waiting until their turn comes to go to the gallows. Rigidity, terror, collapse, fear, dread – there is no word to describe all the feelings that swell and grow in these petrified hearts that can't even weep, can't even scream. There is no ear that can catch the silent scream that deafens with its rigidity and that rigidifies with its deafening silence.

They run over the three ghetto bridges, like a host of hundred-headed serpents surging back and forth. The host of serpents extends forward and back. These are people hurrying and hastening. The air is pregnant with oppressiveness. Macabre tidings are in its density. The sky keeps swelling, billowing, and will soon burst, and out of the void will tumble the full horror and the full reality.

It has begun!

No one knows what, no one knows where, no one knows how. Supposing that everyone keeps silent, supposing that no one looks at anyone else, supposing that everyone avoids everyone else the way the thief avoids his pursuer, then who was the first to utter these dreadful words: 'It has begun!' ...

No one. No one spoke them. No one uttered these macabre tidings. Only the heavens burst and its spilled guts dropped those words: 'It has begun!' ...

Where has it begun? People say: 'They're already taking out all the residents of the old-age home on Dworska Street.'

People say: 'On Rybna Street there's already a truck, and they're loading it with old people and children.'

Alas, all the stories are true: they're taking them from here, from there, from everywhere, and they're already loading on Rybna Street.

It has begun.

The Jewish police made the first start. They began as if they wanted to practise their work along the line of least resistance – the old-age home. There it was as easy as pie – they were just ready to be taken. And the people there are being taken wholesale, there's no selecting and rejecting. They're all old, and so all of them are to go to the scrap heap. It's really the line of least resistance. Who is going to speak up for them, who's going to waste words for these old people who have been living on the good graces of the community for weeks and months now? ... They are being loaded on the trucks like lambs for slaughter and driven to the staging area. There they may get the condemned man's last meal consisting, supposedly, of a soup with lots of potatoes, cooked with horse bones, and later they'll be taken away from this staging area—

To the scrap heap ...

Over on Rybna Street the police have to take them out of apartments. There they are encountering resistance. There they have to cut living, palpitating limbs from bodies. There they wrench infants from their mothers' breasts. There they pull healthy molars out of mouths. On Rybna Street they tear grown children from under their parents' wings. They separate husband from wife, wife from husband, people who've been together for forty or fifty years, who've lived in sorrow and in joy, who've had children together, who've reared them together and lost them together. They've been with one another for forty or fifty years and become practically one body …

The sick, too, are being taken there, sick people who at great risk escaped from the hospital, whom mortal terror gave the strength and courage to leap over barriers, sick people who were given someone's last crust of bread, last bit of sugar, last potato just to keep them alive one more day, one more week, one more month, because the war might end and then they could perhaps get back on their feet. Also the sick are being taken.

Living limbs are cut off. Healthy molars are extracted. Palpitating bodies are halved. The anguish is great. Let someone try to describe it, he won't be able to! Let someone try to depict it, he'll only collapse! Is it any wonder that people scream? …

People scream. And their screams are terrible and fearful and senseless, as terrible and fearful and senseless as the actions causing them. The ghetto is no longer rigid; it is now writhing in convulsions. The whole ghetto is one enormous spasm. The whole ghetto jumps out of its own skin and plunges back within its own barbed wires. Ah, if only a fire would come and consume everything! If only a bolt from heaven would strike and destroy us altogether! There is hardly anyone in the ghetto who hasn't gasped such a wish from his feeble lips, whether he is affected directly, indirectly, or altogether uninvolved in the events which were staged before his very eyes and ears. Everyone is ready to die; already now, at the very start, at this very moment, it is impossible to endure the terror and the horror. Already at this moment it is impossible to endure the screams of hundreds of thousands of bound cattle slaughtered but not yet killed; impossible to endure the twitching of the pierced but unsevered throats, which let them neither die nor live.

What has happened to the Jewish police, who undertook to do that piece of work? Have their brains atrophied? Have their hearts been torn out and replaced with stones? It's hard, very hard, to answer these questions. One thing is certain – they are not to be envied. And there are also all sorts of executioners. There is an executioner who for a worthless traitor's pay would raise his hand against his brother; another, besides getting his traitor's pay, also has to be gotten drunk, otherwise his ignoble hand will fumble. And there are executioners who do their bloody work for the sake of an idea. They were told: 'So-and-so is not only useless to society, he's actually detrimental, he's got to be cleaned out.' So they act for the good of society, they do the cleaning out.

The Jewish police have been bought. They have been intoxicated. They were given hashish – their children have been exempted from the order. They've been given three pounds of bread a day for their bloody bit of work – bread to gorge themselves on and an extra portion of sausage and sugar. They work for the sake of an idea, the Jewish police do. Thus our own hands, Jewish hands, extract the molars, cut off the limbs, slice up the bodies …

No, they are not to be envied at all, the Jewish police!

The bloody page of this history should be inscribed with black letters for the so-called 'White Guard', the porters of Balut Market and of the Food Supply Office. This rabble, fearful of losing their soup during pedestrian embargo, volunteered to help in the action on condition that they get the same as had been promised the police – bread, sausage, and sugar, and the exemption of their families. Their offer was accepted. They participated voluntarily in the action.

The bloody page of this history should be inscribed with black letters for all those officials who petitioned to have some role in this action, only in order to get bread and sausage rations instead of the soup they wouldn't have gotten sitting at home …

The Seizures

O God, Jewish God, how defenceless Jewish blood has become!

Oh, God, God of all mankind, how defenceless human blood has become!

Blood flows in the streets. Blood flows over the yards. Blood flows in the buildings. Blood flows in the apartments. Not red, healthy blood. That doesn't exist in the ghetto. Three years of war, two and a half years of ghetto, have devoured the red corpuscles. All the ghetto has is pus and streaming gall, that drips, flows and gushes from the eyes, and inundates streets, yards, houses, apartments.

How can such blood satisfy the appetites of the beasts? It can only whet their appetites, nothing more!

It is no longer just a rumour, not just gossip; it is an established fact. The head of the ghetto administration, Biebow, the man most interested in the ghetto's existence, in its survival, has put himself in charge of the action. He himself directs the 'resettlement'.

People are being seized. The Jewish police are seizing them with mercy, according to orders: children under ten, old people over sixty-five, and the sick whom doctors have diagnosed as incurable …

The Jewish police have addresses. The Jewish police have Jewish concierges, and the concierges have house registers. The addresses inform that in such and such an apartment is a child who was born on such and such a date. The addresses inform that in such and such an apartment is an old man who was born so and so many years ago. A doctor comes into every apartment. He examines the occupants. He observes who is in good health and who just pretends to good health. He's had so much practice in the ghetto that a mere glance distinguishes the well from the mortally ill.

Nor does it avail the child to cling to its mother's neck with both little hands. Nor does it avail the mother to throw herself on the threshold and bellow like a slaughtered cow: 'Only over my dead body will you take my child!' It does not avail the old man to clutch the cold walls with his bony fingers and plead: 'Let me die here in peace.' It does not avail the old woman to fall on her knees, kiss their boots, and plead: 'I've already got grown-up grandchildren.' It does not avail the sick man to bury his feverish head in the damp, sweaty pillow, and moan, and shed perhaps his last tears.

Nothing avails. The police have to supply their quota. They have to seize people. They cannot show pity. But when the Jewish police take people, they do so punctiliously. When they take people, they help them weep, they help them moan. When they take people, they try to comfort them with hoarse voices, to express their anguish …

It's totally different when others come!

They enter a yard and first off is a reckless shot of a revolver. Everyone loses courage. All blood stops coursing. All throats are stopped with hot lead. The lead freezes the gasps and sobs in the throat. You tremble. No! To tremble you have to have flowing blood, but your blood refuses to circulate. It has curdled, it is rigid like water in a frost. The Jews wait, benumbed, paralyzed, helpless. They wait for what happens next.

Next comes a harsh, terse, draconic order, yelled out, and then repeated by the Jewish police. 'In two minutes everyone downstairs! No one is permitted to stay inside. All doors must be left open!'

Who can describe, depict, the crazed and wild stampede on stairways and landings, the rigid and inanimate figures who hasten to obey the order on time? No one.

Old, rheumatic, twisted sclerotic legs stumble over crooked stairs and angular stones. Young, buoyant, deer legs fly with bird-like speed. The heavy and clumsy legs of the sick heaved from their beds are bent and bowed. Swollen legs of starvelings tap blindly along. All scurry, hurry, rush out into the courtyard.

Woe to the latecomer. He will never finish that last walk. He will have to swim in his own blood. Woe to him who stumbles and falls. He will never stand up again. He will slip and fall again in his own blood. Woe to the child who is so terrified that all he can do is scream 'Mama!' He will never get past the first syllable. A reckless gunshot will sever the word in his throat. The second syllable will tumble down into his heart like a bird shot down in mid-flight. The experience of the last few hours proved this in its stark reality.

When the Jewish police take people, they take whomever they can, whoever is there. If someone has hidden and can't be taken, then he remains hidden. But when *they* come to take people, they take those who are there and those who are not there. If someone is not located, they take another in his place. If the missing man is found, he will not be seized; he will have to be carried out.

The Jewish police, further, can be bought. Not with ghetto marks of course, but with most valuable items. As long as it's hush-hush and no one can see or hear, then anyone who's got something can ransom his way out. But when *they* come to take you, you can buy your way out only with your rarest and most precious possession – your life. You can take the choice of not wishing to go, and you'll never have to go anywhere again ...

Sunday, 6 September 1942
The clock says twelve noon. It is a full-blown summer's day. It's impossible to stay indoors. No one can stay at home. Perhaps because you must stay inside, perhaps because you're surrounded by your

family and you have nothing to say to them. You yourself are indeed young. You yourself have your work certificate proving you're a useful citizen of the ghetto. Your wife is young too, and her papers are fully in order. Younger than both of you is your fourteen-year-old son, who already works. He is tall and slender and handsome, a fine figure of a lad. You have no reasons to be afraid, not for yourself, not for your wife, and not for your son. But you sit at home, listening to the sighs and shouts and screams of your neighbours, from whom pieces of flesh were torn away yesterday. You sit at home and hear yet another scream every minute from another neighbour, or mute sobs from people sick with sorrow. You sit at home and constantly hear yet another scream from a neighbour who, in his great despair over the children who were seized from him, tries to end his broken existence with a knife or by leaping from a high window. You sit at home, devoured by your own sorrow, your wife's sorrow, your son's sorrow, and the sufferings of all your neighbours and all Jews. Sitting at home like this, on and on, every time you glance at the mirror and it reflects a yellowed, sunken, confused contenance: 'You, too, are a candidate for the scrap heap!' Sitting at home, casting furtive glances at your wife who has aged dozens of years in these last two days, then looking at your beautiful son, seeing his dark hollow face and the mortal fear lurking in his deep black eyes, then all the terror around you makes you fear for yourself, makes you fear for your wife, makes you fear for your trembling child. All of you are candidates!

'Spectacles and eyeglasses of every kind are to be handed in to the medical office for utilization': Memorandum on the Disposing of the Possessions of Jews in Lublin and Auschwitz, 26 September 1942
SS-OBERGRUPPENFÜHRER AUGUST FRANK

Frank was a senior member of the SS concentration camp administration.

Top Secret
6 copies – 4th copy
Chief A/Pr./B.
Journ. No. 050/42 secr.

VS 96/42
26 September 1942
To the Chief of the SS Garrison Administration Lublin
To the Chief of Administration Concentration Camp Auschwitz
Subject: Utilization of property on the occasion of settlement and evacuation of Jews.

Without taking into account the overall regulations which are expected to be issued during October, pertaining to the utilization of mobile and immobile property of the evacuated Jews, the following procedure has to be followed with regard to the property carried by them – property, which will in all orders in the future be called goods originating from thefts, receiving of stolen goods, and hoarded goods:

1 a. Cash money in German Reich Bank notes have to be paid into the account: Economic and Administrative Main Office 158/1488 with the Reich Bank in Berlin-Schoeneberg.

   b. Foreign exchange (coined or uncoined), rare metals, jewellery, precious and semi-precious stones, pearls, gold from teeth and scrap gold have to be delivered to the SS Economic and Administrative Main Office. The latter is responsible for the immediate delivery to the German Reich Bank.

   c. Watches and clocks of all kinds, alarm clocks, fountain pens, mechanical pencils, hand and electrical razors, pocketknives, scissors, flashlights, wallets, and purses are to be repaired by the Economic and Administrative Main Office in special repair shops, cleaned, and evaluated; and have to be delivered quickly to frontline troops. Delivery to the troops is on a cash basis through the post exchanges. Three-fourth price grades are to be set and it has to be made sure that each officer and man cannot buy more than one watch. Exempt from sale are the gold watches, the utilization of which rests with me. The proceeds go to the Reich.

   d. Men's underwear and men's clothing including footwear has to be sorted and valued. After covering the needs of the concentration camp inmates and in exceptions for the troops they are to be handed over to the Volksdeutsche Mittelstelle. The proceeds go to the Reich in all cases.

e. Women's clothing and women's underwear, including footwear; children's clothing and children's underwear, including footwear, have to be handed over to the Volksdeutsche Mittelstelle against payment. Underwear of pure silk is to be handed over to the Reich Ministry of Economics according to orders by the SS Economic and Administrative Main Office. This order refers also to underwear.

f. Featherbeds, quilts, woollen blankets, cloth for suits, shawls, umbrellas, walking sticks, thermos flasks, ear flaps, baby carriages, combs, handbags, leather belts, shopping baskets, tobacco pipes, sun glasses, mirrors, table knives, forks and spoons, knapsacks, and suitcases made from leather or artificial material are to be delivered to the Volksdeutsche Mittelstelle. The question of payment will be decided later.

The needs in quilts, woollen blankets, thermos flasks, ear flaps, combs, table knives, forks and spoons, and knapsacks can be furnished from Lublin and Auschwitz from these stocks against payment from budget funds.

g. Linen, such as bed sheets, bed linen, pillows, towels, wiping cloths, and tablecloths are to be handed over to the Volksdeutsche Mittelstelle against payment. Bed sheets, bed linen, towels, wiping cloths, and table cloths can be furnished for the needs of troops from these stocks against payment from budget funds.

h. Spectacles and eyeglasses of every kind are to be handed in to the medical office for utilization. (Spectacles with golden frames have to be handed in without glasses together with the rare metals.) A settlement of accounts for the spectacles and eyeglasses need not take place with regard to their low value and their limited use.

i. Valuable furs of all kinds, raw and cured, are to be delivered to the SS WVHA.

j. Ordinary furs (lamb, hare, and rabbit skins) are to be reported to the SS WVHA, Amt B II, and are to be delivered to the clothing plant of the Waffen SS, Ravensbrück near Fuerstenbern (Mecklenburg).

k. All items mentioned under the letters d, e, and f, which have only one-fifth or two-fifths of the full value, or are useless altogether will be delivered via the SS WVHA to the Reich Ministry for Economics for utilization.

    For the decision on items which are not mentioned under the letters b-k, application for a decision as to their utilization should be made to the chief of the WVHA.

2   The SS WVHA will establish all prices under observation of the legally controlled prices. This estimation, however, can be made later on. Petty evaluations which only waste time and personnel may be eliminated. Average prices for single items have to be established in general. For instance, one pair of used men's trousers 3.00 RM, one woollen blanket 6.00 RM, etc. For the delivery of useless items to the Reich Ministry for Economics, average Kilo prices will have to be established.

It has to be strictly observed, that the Jewish Star is removed from all garments and outer garments which are to be delivered. Furthermore, items which are to be delivered have to be searched for hidden and sewed-in values; this should be carried out with the greatest possible care.

ACTING FOR

[Signed] FRANK

SS-Brigadeführer and Brigadier General of the Waffen-SS

SS Execution Squad in Action, Volhynia, Ukraine, 5 October 1942
HERMANN GRAEBE

Graebe was a manager with a German engineering firm Jung AG in occupied Ukraine, where he tried to prevent the deportation of Jewish workers from his factory. Below is his testimony, delivered to the post-War International Military Tribunal, concerning the round-up and execution of the Jews from the Röwne (Rovno) ghetto.

On the evening of this day, I drove to Röwne and posted myself with Fritz Einsporn in front of the house in the Bahnhofstrasse in which the Jewish workers of my firm slept.

    Shortly after 2200 the ghetto was encircled by a large SS detachment and about three times as many members of the Ukrainian militia. Then the electric arc-lights which had been erected in and around the ghetto were switched on.

SS and militia squads of four to six men entered or at least tried to enter the houses. Where the doors and windows were closed and the inhabitants did not open at the knocking, the SS men and militia broke the windows, forced the doors with beams and crowbars, and entered the houses.

The people living there were driven on the street just as they were, regardless of whether they were dressed or in bed. Since the Jews in most cases refused to leave their houses and resisted, the SS and militia applied force. They finally succeeded, with strokes of the whip, kicks and blows, and rifle-butts, in clearing the houses.

The people were driven out of their houses in such haste that small children in bed had been left behind in several instances. In the streets women cried out for their children and children for their parents.

That did not prevent the SS from driving the people along the road at running pace, and hitting them, until they reached a waiting freight train. Carriage after carriage was filled and the screaming of women and children and the cracking of whips and rifle shots resounded unceasingly.

Since several families or groups had barricaded themselves in especially strong buildings and the doors could not be forced with crowbars or beams, the doors were now blown open with hand grenades.

Since the ghetto was near the railroad tracks in Röwne, the younger people tried to get across the tracks and over a small river to get away from the ghetto area. As this stretch of country was beyond the range of the electric lights, it was illuminated by signal rockets. All through the night these beaten, hounded, and wounded people moved along the lighted streets. Women carried their dead children in their arms, children pulled and dragged their dead parents by their arms and legs down the road towards the train. Again and again the cries 'Open the door! Open the door!' echoed through the ghetto.

About 6 o'clock in the morning I went away for a moment, leaving behind Einsporn and several other German workers who had returned in the meantime. I thought the greatest danger was past and that I could risk it. Shortly after I left, Ukrainian militia men forced their way into 5 Bahnhofstrasse and brought seven Jews out and took them to a collecting point inside the ghetto. On my return I was able to prevent further Jews from being taken out. I went to the collecting point to save these seven men. I saw dozens of corpses of all ages and both sexes in the streets I had to walk along. The doors of the houses stood open, windows were smashed. Pieces of clothing, shoes, stockings, jackets, caps, hats, coats, etc., were lying in the street. At the corner of a house lay a baby, less than a year old with his skull crushed. Blood and brains were spattered over the house wall and covered the area immediately around the child. The child was dressed only in a little skirt.

* * *

On 5 October 1942, when I visited the building office at Dubno, my foreman told me that in the vicinity of the site Jews from Dubno had been shot in three large pits, each about thirty metres long and three metres deep. About 1,500 persons had been killed daily. All were liquidated. As the shootings had taken place in his presence he was still very upset.

Moennikes and I went straight to the pits. Nobody prevented us. I heard a quick succession of shots from behind one of the mounds of earth. The people who had got off the lorries – men, women and children of all ages – had to undress upon the order of an SS man, who carried a riding or a dog whip. They had to put their clothes on separate piles of shoes, top clothing, and underclothing.

I saw a heap of shoes that must have contained 800 to 1,000 pairs, great piles of clothes and undergarments. Without screaming or weeping these people undressed, stood in family groups, kissed each other, said their farewells, and waited for a sign from another SS man, who stood near the pit, also with a whip in his hand.

During the fifteen minutes that I stood near the pit, I did not hear anyone complain or beg for mercy. I watched a family of about eight, a man and a woman, both about fifty, with their children, aged about one, eight and ten, and two grown-up daughters of about twenty to twenty-four.

An old woman with snow-white hair was holding the one-year-old child in her arms, singing something to it and tickling it. The child was crowing with delight. The man and wife were looking on with tears in their eyes.

The father was holding the hand of a boy about ten, speaking to him softly. The boy was fighting back his tears. The father pointed to the sky, stroked the boy's head and seemed to explain something to him.

At that moment the SS man at the pit shouted something to his comrade, who separated off about twenty persons and ordered them to go behind the mound of earth. Among them was the family I have mentioned.

I still clearly remember a dark-haired, slim girl who pointed to herself as she passed close to me and said, 'Twenty-three.' I walked to the other side of the mound and found myself standing before an enormous grave. The people lay so closely packed, one on top of the other, that only their heads were visible.

Nearly all had blood running over their shoulders from their heads. Some of them were still moving. Some lifted an arm and turned a head to show that they were still alive.

The pit was already two-thirds full. I estimated that it already contained about 1,000 people. I looked round for the man who had shot them. He was an SS man who was sitting on the edge of the narrow end of the pit, his legs dangling into it. He had a sub-machine gun across his knees and was smoking a cigarette.

The people, completely naked, went down some steps which had been cut in the clay wall of the pit and climbed over the heads of those already lying there, to the place indicated by the SS man. They lay down in front of the dead or injured people. Some of them caressed those who were still alive and spoke to them softly.

Then I heard a series of shots. I looked into the pit and saw that the bodies were twitching or that the heads lay motionless on top of the bodies which lay before them. Blood was pouring from their necks.

I was surprised I was not ordered away, but saw there were also two or three uniformed policemen standing nearby. The next batch was already approaching. They climbed into the pit, lined up against the previous victims and were shot. When I walked back round the mound I noticed another lorry-load of people which had just arrived.

This time it included sick and infirm people. A very thin old woman, with terribly thin legs, was undressed by others who were already naked, while two people supported her. The woman appeared to be paralyzed. The naked people carried the woman around the mound. I left with Moennikes and drove back to Dubno in the car.

On the morning of the next day, when I visited the site, I saw about thirty naked people lying near the pit – about thirty to fifty metres away from it. Some of them were still alive; they looked straight in front of them with a fixed stare and seemed to notice neither the chilliness of the morning nor the workers of my firm who stood around.

A girl of about twenty spoke to me and asked me to give her clothes and help her escape. At that moment we heard a fast car approach and I noticed it was an SS detail. I moved away to my site. Ten minutes later we heard shots from the vicinity of the pit. Those Jews who were still alive had been ordered to throw the corpses into the pit, then they themselves had to lie down in the pit, to be shot in the neck.

Of the 7,000 Jews rounded up from the Röwne ghetto, 5,000 were shot by the SS.

Parents Ordered to Give Up Their Children, Zduńska Wola Ghetto, August 1942
RYVKA SALT

In August 1942 the real nightmare started when early one morning we were woken up with shouts, 'All Jews out! Into the streets!' We had to get dressed quickly. We heard rumours that old people and children were being killed, so we took our grandparents and one young cousin of three years and hid them in the attic, thinking we would be back. We went out into the streets which were already crowded with people and followed one another until we came to a very big field. When we were all there, they ordered us all to sit down. Then, again, through loud-speakers, they ordered parents to give up their children under the age of eighteen years. Anyone who didn't actually see the scene could not imagine the cries of the mothers, 'Almighty God, help us!' And you could see the little children running towards the officers, the bigger ones holding their little siblings in their hands. While all this was going on, my mother was trying to hide me on one side and my little sister on the other. Before long they got hold of my little sister and my mother got badly beaten up. My sister, then ten, said to the officer, 'Please don't hit her, that's not my mother.' And I was told that she was running away with tears running down her face.

When they had taken all the children, we were lined up in fives and taken to the local (Jewish) cemetery where there was a selection: right to live, left to be taken away. That went on until it was dark. We were left sitting on those graves for three days and three nights. They installed electric lights around the cemetery and continued to make selections. People tried to make me look older: someone gave me a scarf to wear and powder to make me look more mature. But just before we left, I was spotted by a German officer; he pointed at me and said, 'You, stand up! How old are you?' I was so nervous, I couldn't answer. My father said, 'Oh, she's eighteen, I know her.' The officer stood there looking at me – I was twelve and looked about eight – he looked me up and down and he could see that I wasn't eighteen years old. Finally, he said, 'She can sit down.' No one could believe it; it was God's will. When we left that cemetery, there were only three children left, I was one of the three. I can never forget it: the guilty feeling that they got hold of my sister and not of me.

'Like basalt pillars the dead stand inside, pressed together in the chambers': Gassing with Diesel Fumes, Belzec, 18 August 1942
SS-OBERSTURMFÜHRER KURT GERSTEIN

Gerstein was a First Lieutenant in the Waffen-SS. As Head of Technical Disinfection Services of the SS he witnessed one of the first gassings of the Jews at Belzec.

He was an unusual Nazi. A member of the NSDAP from 1933, he was imprisoned in a concentration camp by the self-same Party for circulating anti-Nazi pamphlets. (He was a committed Christian.) By his own account he joined the Waffen-SS to discover the truth about 'ovens and [gas] chambers', circulating his eye-witness account of gassing at Belzec to 'hundreds of personages', including the Papal Nuncio in Berlin. Gerstein's report was subsequently used in a number of high-profile war-crimes trials, including those of Göring and Eichmann.

When I heard about the beginning of the killing of mentally ill persons at Grafeneck and Hadamar and other sites, I decided to make every effort to look into the matter of these ovens and chambers in order to learn what happened there. This was all the more relevant as a sister-in-law by marriage – Bertha Ebeling – was compulsorily killed in Hadamar. With two references from Gestapo officers who had worked on my case, I easily succeeded in joining the SS. The gentlemen took the view that my idealism, which they probably admired, must be of advantage to the Nazi cause. On 10 March 1941 I joined the SS. I received my basic training in Hamburg-Langenhorn, in Arnhem (Holland), and in Oranienburg. In Holland I immediately contacted the Dutch resistance movement (graduate engineer Ubbink, Doesburg). Because of my dual studies I was soon taken over by the technical-medical service and allotted to the SS-Führungshauptamt, Amtsgruppe D, Sanitätswesen der Waffen-SS Abteilung Hygiene. I completed the training in a course together with forty physicians. At the Hygienedienst I could determine my activities for myself. I constructed mobile and stationary disinfection facilities for the troops, for prisoner-of-war camps, and concentration camps. With this I had great success and was from then on undeservedly considered as a kind of technical genius. Indeed it turned out well at least to some extent, by getting the horrible epidemic typhus wave in 1941 in the camps under control. Because of my successes I soon became Leutnant and then Oberleutnant.

At Christmas 1941 the court which had ordered my expulsion from the NSDAP was informed about my joining the SS in a leading position. The result was a severe witch hunt against me. But because of my great successes and my personality I was protected and kept in office. In January 1942 I became head of the Department of Health Engineering, and in addition in a double function for the same sector I was taken over by the Reichsarzt SS und Polizei. In this function I took over the whole technical disinfection service, including disinfection with highly toxic gases.

In this capacity I was visited on 8 June 1942 by the until then unknown to me SS-Sturmführer Günther from Reichssicherheitshauptamt Berlin, Kurfürstenstraße. Günther arrived in civil clothing. He gave me the order immediately to obtain 100 kilograms of prussic acid for a very secret Reichs order, and to drive with it by car to an undisclosed location which would be only known by the driver. Then some weeks later we drove to Prague. I understood little of the nature of the order but accepted it because here was an accidental opportunity to do something which I had longed for a long time – to be able to view inside these objects. In addition I was recognized as such an authority and considered so competent as an expert on prussic acid, that in every case it would have been very easy for me to declare on some pretext that the prussic acid was unsuitable – because of decomposition or the like – in order to prevent its use for the real killing purpose. Together with us travelled – merely by chance – Professor Dr med. Pfannenstiel, SS-Obersturmbannführer, full Professor of Hygienics at the University of Marburg/Lahn.

Then we drove by car to Lublin where SS-Gruppenführer Globocnik awaited us. In the factory in Collin I had intentionally intimated that the acid was destined for the killing of human beings. A man appeared in the afternoon who was very interested in the vehicle and, after being noticed, promptly fled at a breakneck tempo. Globocnik said: 'This whole affair is one of the most secret things of all in this time, one can say the most secret of all. Whoever talks about it will be shot on the spot. Only yesterday two blabbers had been shot.' Then he explains to us: 'Actually' – that was on 17 August 1942 – 'we are running three facilities', namely:

1. Belzec, at the country road and railway line Lublin–Lemberg, at the demarcation line with Russia. Maximum output 15,000 persons daily.
2. Treblinka, 120 kilometres north-east of Warsaw. Maximum output 25,000 persons daily.
3. Sobibór, also in Poland, I don't know exactly where. 20,000 persons maximum output daily.
4. Then in preparation – Majdanek near Lublin.

Belzec, Treblinka, and Majdanek I have visited personally in detail, together with the leader of these facilities, Polizeihauptmann Wirth.

Globocnik consulted me alone and said: 'It is your task in particular to disinfect the extensive amounts of textiles. The whole *Spinnstoffsammlung* [collection of spun material in Germany] has only been gathered in order to explain the origin of the clothing material for the *Ostarbeiter* [eastern workers] etc., and to present it as an offering of the German nation. In reality the yield of our facilities is ten to twenty times larger than that of the whole *Spinnstoffsammlung*.'

Thereafter I discussed with the most efficient companies the possibility of disinfecting such amounts of textiles – it consisted of an accumulated stock of approximately 40 million kilograms = sixty complete freight trains – in the existing laundries and disinfection facilities. However, it was absolutely impossible to place such huge orders. I used all these negotiations to make known in a skilful way, or at least to intimate, the fact of the killing of the Jews. In the end it was sufficient for Globocnik that everything was sprinkled with a bit of Detenolin so that it at least smelled of disinfection. That was then carried out.

'Your other and far more important task is the changeover of our gas-chambers which actually work with diesel exhaust fumes into a better and quicker system. I think especially of prussic acid. The day before yesterday the Führer and Himmler were here. On their order I have to personally take you there, I am not to issue written certificates and admittance cards to anybody!'

Then Pfannenstiel asked: 'What did the Führer say?' Glob.: 'Quicker, carry out the whole action quicker.' Pfannenstiel's attendant, Ministerialrat Dr Herbert Lindner, then asked: 'Mr Globocnik, do you think it is good and proper to bury all the corpses instead of cremating them? A generation could come after us which doesn't understand all this!'

Then Globocnik said: 'Gentlemen, if ever a generation will come after us which is so weak and soft-hearted that it doesn't understand our task, then indeed the whole of National Socialism has been in vain. To the contrary, in my opinion one should bury bronze plates on which it is recorded that we have had the courage to carry out this great and so necessary work.'

The Führer: 'Good, Globocnik, this is indeed also my opinion!'

Later the alternative option was accepted. Then the corpses were cremated on large grids, improvised from rails, with the aid of petrol and diesel oil.

The next day we drove to Belzec. A small special station had been created for this purpose at a hill hard north of the Lublin–Lemberg road, in the left angle of the demarcation line. South of the road [were] some houses with the inscription 'Sonderkommando Belzec der Waffen-SS'. Because the actual chief of the whole killing facilities, Polizeihauptmann Wirth, was not yet there, Globocnik introduced me to SS-Hauptsturmführer Obermeyer (from Pirmasens). That afternoon he let me see only that which he simply had to show me. That day I didn't see any corpses, just [noticed] the smell of the whole region. [It] was stinking to high heaven in a hot August, and millions of flies were everywhere.

Near to the small double-track station was a large barrack, the so-called 'cloakroom', with a large counter for valuables. Then followed the barber's room with approximately 100 chairs. Then an alley in the open air below birches, fenced in to the right and left by double barbed wire with inscriptions: 'To the inhalation- and bathrooms!' In front of us a sort of bath house with geraniums, then a small staircase, and then to the right and left three rooms, each 5 × 5 metres, 1.90 metres high, with wooden doors like garages. At the back wall, not quite visible in the dark, larger wooden ramp doors. On the roof as a 'clever, little joke' the Star of David. In front of the buildings an inscription: Hackenholt-Foundation. More I couldn't see that afternoon.

The next morning, shortly before 7 a.m., someone announced to me: 'In ten minutes the first transport will come!' In fact the first train arrived after some minutes, from the direction of Lemberg: 45 wagons with 6,700 people of whom 1,450 were already dead on arrival. Behind the barred hatches children as well as men and women looked out, terribly pale and nervous, their eyes full of the fear of death. The train comes in: 200 Ukrainians fling open the doors and whip the people out of the wagons with their leather whips. A large loudspeaker gives the further orders: 'Undress completely, also remove artificial limbs, spectacles, etc.' Handing over valuables at the counter, without receiving a voucher or a receipt. The shoes carefully bound together (to aid the *Spinnstoffsammlung*), because on the almost twenty-five-metre-high heap nobody would have been able to find the matching shoes again. Then the women and girls to the barber who, with two, three scissor strokes is cutting off all hair and collecting it in potato sacks. 'This is for special purposes in the submarines, for seals or the like!' the SS-Unterscharführer who is on duty there says to me.

Then the procession starts moving. In front a very lovely young girl; so all of them go along the alley, all naked, men, women, children, without artificial limbs. I myself stand together with Hauptmann Wirth on top of the ramp between the gas-chambers. Mothers with babies at their breast, they come onward, hesitate, enter the death chambers! At the corner a strong SS man stands who, with a voice like a pastor, says to the poor people: 'There is not the least chance that something will happen to you! You must only take a deep breath in the chamber, that widens the lungs; this inhalation is necessary because of the illnesses and epidemics.' On the question of what would happen to them, he answered: 'Yes, of course, the men have to work building houses and roads, but the women don't need to work. Only if they wish they can help in housekeeping or in the kitchen.'

For some of these poor people this gave a little glimmer of hope, enough to go the few steps to the chambers without resistance. The majority are aware, the smell tells them of their fate! So they climb the small staircase, and then they see everything. Mothers with little children at the breast, little naked children, adults, men, women, all naked – they hesitate but they enter the death chambers, pushed forward by those behind them or driven by the leather whips of the SS. The majority without saying a word. A Jewess of about forty years of age, with flaming eyes, calls down vengeance on the head of the murderers for the blood which is shed here. She gets five or six slashes with the riding crop into her face from Hauptmann Wirth personally, then she also disappears into the chamber. Many people pray. I pray with them, I press myself in a corner and shout loudly to my and their God. How gladly I would have entered the chamber together with them, how gladly I would have died the same death as them. Then they would have found a uniformed SS man in their chamber – the case would have been understood and treated as an accident, one man quietly missing. Still I am not allowed to do this. First I must tell what I am experiencing here!

The chambers fill. 'Pack well!' Hauptmann Wirth has ordered. The people stand on each other's feet: 700–800 on 25 square metres, in 45 cubic metres! The SS physically squeezes them together, as far as is possible.

The doors close. At the same time the others are waiting outside in the open air, naked. Someone tells me: 'The same in winter!' 'Yes, but they could catch their death of cold,' I say. 'Yes, exactly what they are here for!' says an SS man to me in his Low German. Now I finally understand why the whole installation is called the Hackenholt-Foundation. Hackenholt is the driver of the diesel engine, a little technician, also the builder of this facility. The people are brought to death with the diesel exhaust fumes. But the diesel doesn't work! Hauptmann Wirth comes. One can see that he feels embarrassed that that happens just today, when I am here. That's right, I see everything! And I wait. My stop watch has honestly registered everything: fifty minutes, seventy minutes [?] – the diesel doesn't start. The people are waiting in their gas-chambers. In vain! One can hear them crying, sobbing ... Hauptmann Wirth hits the Ukrainian who is helping Unterscharführer Hackenholt twelve, thirteen times in the face. After two hours and forty-nine minutes – the stop watch has registered everything well – the diesel starts. Until this moment the people live in these four chambers, four times 750 people in four times 45 cubic metres! Twenty-five minutes pass. Right, many are dead now. One can see that through the small window in which the electric light illuminates the chambers for a moment. After twenty-eight minutes only a few are still alive. Finally, after thirty-two minutes, everyone is dead!

From the other side men from the work command open the wooden doors. They have been promised – even Jews – freedom, and some one-thousandth of all valuables found, for their terrible service. Like basalt pillars the dead stand inside, pressed together in the chambers. In any event there was no space to fall down or even bend forward. Even in death one can still tell the families. They still hold hands, tensed in death, so that one can barely tear them apart in order to empty the chamber for the next batch. The corpses are thrown out, wet from sweat and urine, soiled by excrement, menstrual blood on their legs. Children's corpses fly through the air. There is no time. The riding crops of the Ukrainians lash down on the work commands. Two dozen dentists open mouths with hooks and look for gold. Gold to the left, without gold to the right. Other dentists break gold teeth and crowns out of jaws with pliers and hammers.

Among all this Hauptmann Wirth is running around. He is in his element. Some workers search the genitals and anuses of the corpses for gold, diamonds, and valuables. Wirth calls me to him: 'Lift this can full of gold teeth, that is only from yesterday and the day before yesterday!' In an incredibly vulgar and incorrect diction he said to me: 'You won't believe what we find in gold and diamonds every day' – he pronounced it (in German *Brillanten*) with two Ls – 'and in dollars. But see for yourself!' And now he led me to a jeweller who managed all these treasures, and let me see all this. Then someone showed me a former head of the Kaufhaus des Westens in Berlin, and a violinist: 'That was a Hauptmann of the Austrian Army, knight of the Iron Cross 1st Class, who is now camp elder of the Jewish work command!'

The naked corpses were carried on wooden stretchers to pits only a few metres away, measuring 100 x 20 x 12 metres. After a few days the corpses welled up and a short time later they collapsed, so that one could throw a new layer of bodies upon them. Then ten centimetres of sand were spread over the pit, so that a few heads and arms still rose from it here and there. At such a place I saw Jews climbing over the corpses and working. One told me that by mistake those who arrived dead had not been stripped. Of course this has to be done later because of the *Spinnstoffsammlung* and valuables which otherwise they would take with them into the grave.

Neither in Belzec nor in Treblinka was any trouble taken over registering or counting the dead. The numbers were only estimates of a wagon's content ... Hauptmann Wirth asked me not to propose changes in Berlin re his facilities, and to let it remain as it is, being well established and well tried. I supervised the burial of the prussic acid because it allegedly had decomposed.

The next day – 19 August 1942 – we drove in the car of Hauptmann Wirth to Treblinka, 120 kilometres north-north-east of Warsaw. The equipment was nearly the same as, but much larger than, in Belzec. Eight gas chambers and real mountains of suitcases, textiles, and clothes. In our honour a banquet was given in old German style in the communal room. The meal was simple but everything was available in sufficient quantity. Himmler himself had ordered that the men of these commandos received as much meat, butter and other things, especially alcohol, as they wanted.

Then we drove in the car to Warsaw. I met the secretary of the Swedish legation in Berlin, Baron von Otter, in the train when I tried in vain to get a bed in a sleeping car. Still under the immediate impression of the terrible events, I told him everything with the entreaty to inform his government and the Allies of all of this immediately because each day's delay must cost the lives of further thousands and tens of thousands. He asked me for a reference, as to which I specified Generalsuperintendent Dr Otto Dibelius, Berlin, Brüderweg 2, Lichterfelde-West, an intimate friend of the pastor Martin Niemöller and member of the church resistance movement against Nazism. I met Mr von Otter twice again in the Swedish legation. Meanwhile he had reported to Stockholm and informed me that this report has had considerable influence on Swedish-German relations. At the same time I tried to report to the Papal Nuncio in Berlin. There I was asked if I am a soldier. Then any further conversation with me was refused and I was asked to leave the embassy of His Holiness. While leaving the embassy, I was shadowed by a policeman on a bicycle who shortly passed me, got off, and then absolutely incomprehensibly, let me go. Then I reported all this to hundreds of personages, among others the company lawyer of the Catholic bishop of Berlin, Dr Winter, with the special entreaty to forward it to the Holy See. I must also add that SS-Sturmbannführer Günther from the Reichssicherheitshauptamt – I think he is the son of the Race-Günther – again demanded from me very large amounts of prussic acid in early 1944 for a very sinister purpose. On the Kurfürsten-Street in Berlin he showed me a shed in which he intended to store the prussic acid. I consequently explained to him that I cannot take sole responsibility. It was approximately several wagon loads, enough to kill millions of people. He told me that he himself doesn't know whether the poison would still be needed; when, for whom, in which way, etc. But it has to be permanently kept available.

Later I often thought about the words of Goebbels. I can believe that they wanted to kill a majority of the German nation, surely including the clergy or the unpopular officers. It should happen in [places resembling] reading rooms or club rooms, so far as I gathered from the questions re the technical realization that Günther asked me. It could also be that he intended to kill the foreign workers or prisoners-of-war – I don't know. In every case I managed to ensure that the prussic acid disappeared for some purpose of disinfection after arrival in the two concentration camps, Oranienburg and Auschwitz.

That was somewhat dangerous for me but I could easily have said that the poison had already been in a dangerous condition of decomposition. I am sure that Günther tried to get the poison in order to probably kill millions of persons. It was sufficient for approximately 8 million people: 8,500 kilograms. I have authorized invoices for 2,175 kilograms. I always allowed the invoices to be authorized in my name, allegedly for the sake of discretion, but in truth because of being free to dispose of the poison and being able to allow it to disappear. Above all I avoided presentation of invoices again and again, delaying payment and putting off companies until later.

As for the rest I avoided appearing in concentration camps too often because it was sometimes usual to hang people or to carry out executions in honour of the visitors.

All my statements are true, word-for-word. I am fully aware of the extraordinary tragedy of my record before God and the whole of mankind, and take it on my oath that nothing of all this that I have registered has been made up or invented but everything is exactly the truth.

On the Run, Poland, 1944
CHAIM PRINZENTHAL

Below is an extract from a farewell letter from Chaim Prinzenthal to his children, who had found refuge in Palestine.

I am alone now in my misfortune, my comrade in distress was caught by the murderers on the second day of Rosh Hashana [the Jewish New Year], in full daylight; he had not been cautious enough. They tortured and then shot him. They searched for me, too, they even trod on me in the stack of straw where I was hiding. Yet, for the time being, they have not succeeded. Since then I have been wandering alone at night from village to village, from tent to tent, from forest to forest. But the forest, unfortunately, has started balding, and I also am naked and barefoot, hungry and sleepy. I am walking like a sleepwalker without seeing my own shadow, I am wandering – where to, I myself do not know. Shall I succeed in staying alive? I am not at all sure, it is very improbable.

The fate of Prinzenthal is unknown. Poland was one of Eastern Europe's most anti-Semitic countries. Even so some Gentile Poles offered refuge. From December 1942 a secret Council for Assistance to the Jews in Warsaw did whatever it could to help Semitic Poles, although everyone knew that any Pole caught helping Jews would be tortured and executed. At Szczebrzeszyn a Polish peasant who hid six Jews in his barn was shot to death – as were his wife and two children, a six-year-old girl and a three-year-old boy.

Theresienstadt: The Children's Quarters,
September 1942–May 1944
RUTH KLUGER

Approximately 140,000 Jews were deported to the Theresienstadt (Terezín) ghetto. Usually 40,000–50,000 were imprisoned at any one time in a fortress intended to hold, at most, 3,500. Fifteen thousand children passed through Theresienstadt. Although forbidden by the SS to do so, they continued their education there.

The children's barracks were the former officers' quarters – two large yellow buildings flanking the church, which was closed in our time. They had numbers: L410 and L414. The Jews who ran the camp had put the Czech children into the first building and the German-speaking children into the second. I came to live in L414, in a room for the youngest group of girls. L414 is the only one of my many addresses which I have never forgotten. We were assured that I had been lucky to get in, because there wasn't enough space for all the eligible children.

At first, however, I didn't feel all that lucky. We were thirty girls in a room where two or three would have been comfortable. This wasn't our dormitory, it was our home, the only place we had. We even washed there with cold water which we fetched from the hallway in basins. Soap was scarce and treasured. In cold weather our teeth chattered in concert. There was a warm shower in the basement, and every two weeks we could use it. The hot water would barely come on before it would go off again. You had to be on the ball to make use of it. We slept in three-tiered bunks on straw mattresses, one or two girls per berth, depending on the width of the bed. Those were my first weeks of protracted hunger; in Vienna I had had enough to eat. There is little to say about chronic hunger: it's always there and is boring to talk about. Hunger gnaws at and weakens you. It takes up mental space which could otherwise be used for thinking. What can you do with your food ration to stretch it? We acted as if the skim milk we were rationed was whipping cream and beat it into a foam, a popular pastime. (I think of this pastime dreamily when I order latte.) It could take hours, because it's difficult to make skim milk foam with a fork. We were not sorry for ourselves: we laughed a lot, we were noisy and full of beans, like other children our age, and we thought we were stronger than the 'pampered' free kids.

There was always a long line in front of the toilets, for there were only two on each floor, in a building that held hundreds of children. I tried to figure out when there was the least traffic, but the problem – everyone's perennial problem – was diarrhoea. During the first weeks I was the outsider, the newcomer who had few social skills. I was stupid and clumsy, and the other girls laughed at me. I don't know which of my reclusive habits made me the butt of their jokes, for who know how she appears to others? I must have seemed peculiar, coming out of my enforced company with hospital patients, nurses, and the grown-ups who shared our apartment. I was used to amusing myself, mostly with books, and mostly adult books at that. I wasn't used to adapting to a group of peers and coevals, and at first I just wanted to go back to my mother. When she came to visit, I ran after her and desperately begged her to take me along. But she simply left, very quickly, without explanation or advice, leaving me to cope as best I could with my disappointment.

So I turned to the group, and soon I learned to become part of it. At bottom I wasn't too unhappy to escape from my mother's contradictory demands, and it soon dawned on me that it might be easier to live with other kids. I observed the behaviour of the girls around me and saw that it wouldn't be too hard to please them. In the end I developed a gift for friendship, which I believe I still have …

The administration of L414 was in the hands of youngsters who employed other youngsters. A sixteen-year-old was in charge of our room. These half-grown children made a point of creating some group spirit and turned our forced community into part of the youth movement, be it Socialist or Zionist. Either one was an antidote to fascism, but Zionism was the be-all and end-all of our political awareness, and I was swept up in it, because it simply made sense. It was the way out of an unendurable diaspora, it had to work, and besides, my father had been a member of a Zionist youth organization back in Vienna when he was a student. A land without a people for a people without a land – a catchy motto. Turning Jew boys into young Jews – a phrase from our prophet, Theodor Herzl, who was not above using the derogatory lingo of our enemies, if it served his cause. To till the soil and become a beacon for mankind. Show the world an example of a just commonwealth. We learned all we could about the history of Zionism and about the land of Palestine, which we called Eretz Israel. We sang Zionist songs and danced the hora for hours on end in the barracks yard. Our elders (by a few years) addressed us as *haverim* and *haverot* (comrades, male and female) and when going to bed we didn't wish each other *Gute Nacht*, but *Leila tov*, one of the few Hebrew tags we had learned.

Because we lived in this children's home and had ideas about the future, we thought of ourselves as an elite. We formed haughty groups and were proud of our commitment to each other and our ideals. And yet I have largely forgotten my *haverot*. Sometimes a name floats to the surface from the depths of forgetfulness where my roommates lie buried: there was a German girl, Renate, and I learned that the name means born again, and that she owed the name to a sister who had died as an infant. She was dark and tall. Another girl from Germany was petite and delicate and knew how to step dance. She was as sweet as her name, Melissa.

Of course I haven't forgotten Hanna, who lives today in Australia. She was from Vienna and we became best friends. Her father was a mathematician, had wild hair, and was the author of unpublished mythological stories. Hanna showed me one of them about an earth goddess, Hertha. I was impressed by his ability to write so many pages in a rather impenetrable language, and by the fact that he was both a scientist and a writer. I envied Hanna for having a father.

It was common for two girls to bond and share everything. Food was precious, and bread was therefore a kind of currency. Sometimes in a supermarket I have a flashback and marvel that bread is so cheap. My mother traded her wedding ring, soon and without much ado, for bread. She has never been sentimental, except to impress an audience, not when it really mattered. (She was so right: it was the murder of a husband, not the loss of a ring, that ended her marriage. And at least she got something for it before the Nazis took it.) Once she brought me some extra food, and I shared it with Hanna. When she found out, she was angry: she had saved it from her own ration. 'It was for you, just for you.' 'But you told me that it was extra.' 'I said that only so you would take it.' Once again, a guilt-producing double blind. I had not only eaten my mother's food, which she needed as much as everyone else, but I had spread it around and felt good about it. Again, an insoluble dilemma: what belongs to you absolutely, so that you can give it away, and what is yours with strings attached? Such questions change in quality, not just quantitatively, where no one has much to give. Gift giving is a human impulse, generosity a function of social behaviour which doesn't disappear when you have virtually nothing to give. My mother knew this, she liked to give, and she was actually quite fond of this girl. She helped her after the war and wrote to her as long as she was still able to write letters.

We stored our few belongings either in our bunks or in small, open pigeonholes. Theft was virtually unheard of. We were far too well socialized, and besides, it could get you expelled from L414. In which case you would have had to move in with your parents, a depressing prospect, given how the parents lived. You could also get expelled for drinking the contaminated water from the pump in the yard, but I did just that a few times when I was thirsty, and was more afraid of being caught than of getting sick. Later in life, nothing offended me more than the generalization that the camps turned us all into brutal egotists, and whoever survived them must be morally defective. Again, the blithe refusal to look closely, to make distinctions, to reflect a little.

The Jewish camp administrations are today a bone of contention among historians and others. Was it necessary that the prisoners help the Germans maintain order, or wasn't it collaboration with the enemy? From my child's perspective, I saw, 'What would have happened to us if the Jews had done nothing to reduce the chaos, if there hadn't been these children's homes which they organized and ran within the purview of Nazi directives?' At the same time, I add that Jewish criticism of the forced community at Theresienstadt is nothing new and began in the ghetto itself. The outsider's tendency, presumed innate to Jews, to judge, to question, to uncover hidden motives, which has been a thorn in the side of gentiles for centuries, not because it is immoral (the Nazis called it degenerate and corrupting), but because it is irritating, was as present in the ghetto as discontent with the Chosen People is present in the books of the Biblical prophets. You can bring up children to develop the critical spirit, which is how I was educated. Very early in my childhood there were some brothers and friends of my father who would come in the door and immediately provoke me with jokes and comments just barely comprehensible to a child. These guys didn't expect me to be a good, shy little girl, they expected me to answer with quick repartee. If I succeeded, they would give me credit with some brief phrase, like 'just so'. Licence to be impertinent, or education for egalitarian thought? Take your pick. In Theresienstadt criticism was not only permitted but a matter of course. So I was not surprised that there were critical voices about the children's homes. Some said our games were too similar to the games of the Hitler Youth. You had to ponder this disturbing charge, and you might not come to any conclusion, but it kept you awake and alert. There were stormy open discussions, a boiling kettle without a lid.

Looking back, the treatment of the children in Theresienstadt seems to me to have been exemplary, with one exception. That was the separation of the Czech children from the German speakers. The Czechs in L410 looked down on us because we spoke the enemy's language. Besides, they really were the elite, because they were in their own country, and many Czechs had connections to the outside, which we didn't have. I know some Czech survivors who claim they were never hungry in Theresienstadt, while I never got enough to eat. I think the young Jews in charge should have made an effort to reduce the hostility of one group of Jewish kids towards another.

Approximately 90 per cent of the children who passed through Theresienstadt perished, either from disease and malnutrition in the ghetto, or from gassing in an extermination camp. Ruth Kluger survived both Theresienstadt and Auschwitz.

Escape from a Train Bound for the Camps, Franco-German Border, 7 November 1942
LEO BRETHOLZ

Leo Bretholz was one of the many Austrian and German Jews who fled the Reich westwards, to the Low Countries and then France, to find that everywhere he went the German Army followed. He crossed into Switzerland in September 1942, only to be expelled. On being sent back into France, Bretholz was held initially at Drancy, the infamous transit camp outside Paris, before being put on a train to a camp in the East.

The moans of the elderly, the screams of the children, the 'Sha! Sha!' 'Hush! Hush!' plea of a mother to her infant, were being drowned by the clatter of the death train as it moved through the French countryside of contrasting bucolic beauty and serenity.

My thoughts flashed back to my childhood. Then, the sound of a train had that soothing, even romantic, quality – and it made me dream of faraway places I would have liked to visit. At this time, however, it was striking a note of fateful doom and finality. The gamut of emotions accompanying the rattle of the train ranged from hysterical cries of despair by many, to absolute silence of fatalistic resignation by others.

The scenes were unbearable to the witness, who had all intentions to keep a clear mind and a cool grasp of the situation. We needed to keep our senses intact, as our decision was made to escape before the train would reach the devil's enclave, Nazi Germany itself.

Two parallel iron bars in the rectangular opening in the corner of the cattle car represented the only obvious obstacle to our escape. We had to go to work immediately. The mood of the occupants provided the impetus, and set the stage. Many among them shouted words of encouragement. Our decision would give them some measure of hope, if only symbolically.

We took off our sweaters, soaked them in human waste, wrung them out, thereby giving the fabric greater tensile strength. We then wrapped them around the iron bars, tourniquet-style. Working feverishly, we applied that twisting method until the bars showed some inward bending. Relaxing the tourniquet, we tried with our hands to bend the bars in the other – outward – direction. The bars began to give.

We repeated that process for several hours, until the bars were loose enough in the frame, we were able to bend them at will. Having achieved this, we put the bars back into their normal position. All we had to do now was to wait for darkness to provide the cover for our escape. It was now early afternoon, and our attempt was only a matter of a few hours away.

By evening, the din which had emanated from the ghost-like forms in the car throughout the day had somewhat died down. We were now six or seven hours into our journey to oblivion, and many had dozed off, collapsed from exhaustion or fainted. An old lady on crutches – one of her legs had been amputated below the knee – pointed a crutch towards us, faintly uttering the French words: '*Courrez, courrez et que Dieu vous garde!*' 'Run and may God watch over you!' This woman's gesture of encouragement keeps flashing back to me through the veil of time. I shall never forget her words, or her face ...

It was a dreary, raw and cold November evening. My body was shivering, my mouth was dry, my cheeks felt feverish ...

We chose the moment of escape very carefully. It had to come at a time when the train would slow down for a curve. It also had to be timed correctly to avoid the floodlights which the guards were aiming over the entire length of the concave curvature of the train during the period of reduced speed.

At the propitious moment we bent the bars into the spread-apart position. I lifted myself, rump first, out of the opening, holding on to the ledge above it on the outside. The rest of my body followed. My right leg, testingly, reached around the corner for the coupling which joined our car with the next. I found it and was safely standing on it, holding on to one of the rungs of the iron steps leading to the roof of the car.

My friend followed, using the same method. The train, at that point, was going full speed as the two of us were standing on the couplings between cars. Something had held up our friend who was part of the escape plan, for it took him some time to lift himself on to the opening. As he appeared to have reached the outside, the train went into a slight curve, slowing down as we had expected.

At this split second, we had to take our chances and leap before the beams of the floodlights would fall upon us. We jumped. We tumbled into a ravine and held our breath for what seemed like an eternity. Our friend never joined us. He must have been frightened or he had been caught in the glare of the lights and discovered.

The Hoefle Telegram, 11 January 1943
SS-STURMBANNFÜHRER HERMANN HOEFLE

This message was an intercepted 'Enigma' signal, decoded by British analysts at Bletchley Park. The bare figures and letters do not do justice to its implications; it records the arrivals of Jews over the previous fortnight, together with a cumulative total, for five camps in Action Reinhard, the Nazis' programme for the extermination of Polish Jewry following the assassination of Reinhard Heydrich. 'L' is Lublin Majdanek, 'B' is Belzec, 'S' is Sobibór, and 'T' is Treblinka.

State secret! From the Reich Security Main Office, for the attention of SS-Obersturmbannführer EICHMANN, BERLIN

13/15. OLQ de OMQ 10005 83 234 250

State secret! To the commander of the Security Police, for the attention of SS-Obersturmbannführer HEIM, KRAKOW. Re 14-day report REINHARD. Reference: radio telegram from there Recorded arrivals until 31 December 42, L 12761, B 0, S 515, T 10335 totalling 23611. Situation [gap] 31 December 42, L 24733, B 434508, S 101370, T 71355, totalling 1274166

SS and police leader of Lublin, HOEFLE, Sturmbannführer

The Warsaw Ghetto Uprising, April 1943
SAMUEL ZYLBERSZTEJN

From the outset, there was resistance by Europe's Jews to Nazi terror. This resistance increased with the knowledge that the Third Reich had unambiguously determined on the destruction of the Jewish race within its sphere of influence. Underground resistance groups, usually led by Bundists or left-wing Zionists, formed in most ghettos, but with few arms they had little real chance of stopping deportations; their intention was more, as one Jewish resistance fighter put it, 'to bring down as many Germans as possible'. By dying fighting, the resistance gave heart to Jews throughout Europe.

Of all the ghetto revolts, that in Warsaw over April–May 1943 is most famous. When the liquidation of the ghetto began on 19 April 1943, some 750 Jewish men and women of the Jewish Fighting Organization rose up against 2,000 Waffen-SS and their Ukrainian auxiliaries.

Finally the Nazis decided Warsaw must be *Judenrein*; all Jews had to leave. They devised a perfidiously clever tactic of murder, securing the help of the shop owners. The slave dealer Schultz went from house to house delivering his pre-planned 'sermons'. 'My workers! Come out to the country with me and we'll work there. I will take care of you. From now on you will no longer be considered Jews but workers in a German armament plant. Stick with me and you'll survive the war.'

His colleague Többens gave a solemn speech at 72 Leszno Street: 'Workers! I swear by the life of my child, who is very dear to me, that if you go with me to Poniatów you will not be going to your deaths. You will be leaving to work there and to live. I want it inscribed in your history that my Jews survived this terrible war by staying with me.' His partner – who happened to be his brother-in-law – picked up where his accomplice in murder left off. 'We have also set up a nursery school for your children who have survived and hired teachers to look after them.' He further promised to organize an orchestra.

Next they took Jewish envoys to Poniatów and Trawniki to verify the Nazi promises. The Nazis were overjoyed when the envoys came back and made speeches in the workshops, pitching their propaganda to the more naïve and simpleminded among the slaves: 'Let us leave, let us leave to live and to work.' But all these agitators who called on people to leave for Poniatów had long before secured a hiding place on the Polish side, where their families were waiting for them. Every one of them knew when he had to disappear. *Jews, let us leave* – indeed!

At tremendous risk, Jewish resistance groups tore down the SS posters calling on Jews to leave and distributed flyers to the shop workers: 'To those of our brothers still alive! We warn you, do not deliver yourselves into the hands of the murderers! Do not offer yourselves voluntarily to the Nazis. Do not believe the slave-trader accomplices of the SS.' A genuine debate commenced on the walls between the SS appeals and the Jewish flyers.

Meanwhile the round-up was beginning in the Többens factories on Leszno Street and inside the little ghetto. At that point the majority of workers were still being sent to Poniatów instead of to Treblinka. The murderers weighed their options: 'How long will we have to deal with the Jews before they're all deported? There's still plenty of time. They're caught in a net and will fall into our hands sooner or later. First we should delude as many as we can, then move in and sweep up any trash left behind.'

Until then Jews had been prohibited, under pain of death, from sending letters outside or receiving them, but now the Nazis Steinmann and Bauch brought letters – unstamped, at that – from Poniatów into the Warsaw Ghetto. The people from Poniatów wrote that they were in paradise. Unfortunately, this convinced most of the Jews still alive to leave for Poniatów and Trawniki. And so every few days a new group was sent to be 'taken care of'. They were given special permission to take their belongings with them, and packed up the little they had. Others would say to themselves, 'Those people are leaving in order to live,' and join the transport.

My comrades and I, on the other hand, decided not to leave under any circumstances. We preferred to die fighting in the ghetto, armed with a few revolvers, than fall victim to Nazi sadism in Poniatów. Since we felt the decisive day was drawing close, we began to prepare for armed resistance. First I made my way to the brushmakers' shop on Świętojerska Street to say farewell to my family and friends. I wanted to see my sister's wonderful little boy, five-year-old Mietek, one last time. On 7 September, his father had saved him by hiding him in a sack and carrying him out of a group already selected for deportation. My heart ached as I looked at him, a child who at the age of five was as mature as a thirty-year-old man. 'What can I do with my papa?' he asked me. 'He thinks we should both go to Poniatów. But they'll just shoot us there. They promise Mama work there too. And she rode right off to the gas, my beautiful dear mama. Why was I even born!' I hugged and caressed the little boy and said to him, 'You'll see, it'll all end well.' The child started crying, 'No, no!' When I kissed him for the last time, his eyes were flooded with tears. I closed the door behind me.

The next morning I went to work. An hour after I arrived, the factory was blocked off by a detachment of SS. The work that day turned out to be a little different. Instead of overseeing production, they compiled lists of people who could stay and those who had to leave. They announced the order of transport for all the workers on the second floor; I'm safe for the moment. So I decided to save my comrades who were already lined up in the factory courtyard. I quickly threw on a Werkschutz uniform and ran to the comrades at 76 Leszno Street. There I managed to obtain four additional uniforms for men from the Schultz factory. Unfortunately, I couldn't get hold of any more.

The definitive order came on 19 April 1943. In every shop, the Werkschutz men were told to order all workers to report – with baggage – at 72 Leszno Street by 9 a.m. for the final transport. Whoever failed to appear on time would be shot. A few prominent figures and shop managers were allowed to stay behind for several days to dismantle the factories. The news spread like lightning. The next day everyone ran with their bundles to Leszno Street. They arrived punctually at nine o'clock. God forbid they should be late.

Our group consisted of seventeen men; we had seven revolvers and four grenades. We stationed ourselves in three separate hiding places. All was quiet once everyone had left. Just before sunrise, Czarny had come to deliver the news: 'Get ready, comrades! This is where it's going to start – here, in our building, with us! It's going to start with us! Rufinow is still inside the factory; he has a permit from the SS.' I ran up to the attic where I could watch. I had to be there, I had to witness the Jewish fighters avenging their nation, avenging the blood that had been shed.

I wait at my post anxiously, but not for long. I cock my ears and hear the heavy tread of the uniformed killers. A detachment of murderers is marching down Żelazna towards Leszno, into the ghetto: one-two, one-two, more blood, more blood. But then comes the most beautiful moment in my life. A tremendous explosion rends the air. *Crash!* They're falling to the ground. Again, *crash!* All of a sudden the Ukrainians are rolling in puddles of blood. Blood for blood! The murderers disperse in a wild panic, seeking shelter in the entranceways. Shots and flames, on the right and on the left, start spewing from buildings on both sides of the street, Aryan as well as Jewish. Bullets go whizzing over my head. I have to retreat. I race through the secret attic corridor that runs from house to house down the entire length of the street, an emergency lane for saving Jewish lives. I want to make it back to the shelter, but the stairs seem to snake on a long way ahead of me. More bullets whiz by. I feel hot, my leg is bleeding, I have been wounded.

At last I make it to the darkness of a bunker, then cross to the Aryan side of Leszno, where I manage to stay for several days. I telephone my comrade at the brush factory to learn what's going on there. He yells into the telephone, 'It's horrible!'

They're fighting in the ghetto; our boys are fighting like heroes. The area around Muranowski Square has become a fortress that the Waffen-SS can't take. And two flags are flying over the building at number 19, one blue and white, the other white and red.

'I can't go on any longer. Our building's on fire. My apartment's going up in flames. There are SS men outside with their rifles trained on the exits, shooting the Jews as they run from the building. I can't go on!' he shouts. His voice is filled with horror. 'The door's caught fire. I'm going to stay here in the flames. Take care, farewell.'

I took one more look outside. There, next to the building at 76 Leszno, the bodies of my murdered comrades were lying in their blood. Over the city I saw a sea of fire. The Jewish ghetto was burning, and with it the heroes of my nation.

'For Your Freedom and Ours':
A Resistance Communiqué, Warsaw, 23 April 1943
JEWISH COMBAT ORGANIZATION

FOR YOUR FREEDOM AND OURS
Warsaw Ghetto: 23 April 1943

Poles, citizens, freedom fighters!

From out of the roar of the cannon with which the German Army is battering our homes, the dwellings of our mothers, children, and wives;

From out of the reports of machine guns which we have captured from the cowardly police and SS men;

From out of the smoke of fires and the blood of the murdered Warsaw Ghetto, we – imprisoned in the ghetto – send you our heartful fraternal greetings. We know that you watch with pain and compassionate tears, with admiration and alarm, the outcome of this war which we have been waging for many days with the cruel occupant.

Let it be known that every threshold in the ghetto has been and will continue to be a fortress; that we may all perish in this struggle, but we will not surrender; that, like you, we breathe with desire for revenge for all the crimes of our common foe.

A battle is being waged for your freedom as well as ours.

For your and our human, civic, and national honour and dignity.

We shall avenge the crimes of Auschwitz, Treblinka, Belzec, Majdanek!

Long live the brotherhood of arms and blood of fighting Poland!

Long live freedom!

Death to the hangmen and torturers!

Long live the struggle for life and death against the occupant.

Jewish Combat Organization

The Destruction of the Warsaw Ghetto:
The Report of the SS Commander, 16 May 1943
SS BRIGADEFÜHRER JURGEN STROOP

Stroop was sent to Warsaw on 17 April 1943 as a replacement for SS-Oberführer Ferdinand von Sammern-Frankenegg, following the latter's failure to suppress the uprising in the city. Stroop had his report – which he entitled 'The Jewish Quarter of Warsaw is no more!' concerning his successful destruction of the ghetto – bound in black leather. It was later used as evidence in the Nuremberg trials. For his part in the Warsaw 'action' Stroop was awarded the Iron Cross 1st Class. Seven thousand Jews were shot during the revolt, and 56,000 captured and sent to the camps.

THE WARSAW JEWISH QUARTER IS NO MORE!

I
For the Führer
and for their country

the following were killed in action during the destruction of Jews and bandits in the former Jewish quarter in Warsaw [15 names with date of birth and rank, arranged by date of death]. In addition, the Polish Police Sergeant Julian Zieliński, born 13 November 1891, 14th Commissariat, was killed on 19 April 1943, while carrying out his duties.

They ventured their utmost, their lives. We shall never forget them …

Units Used in the Action	Average Number of Personnel Used per Day
SS Staff and Police Leaders	6/5
Waffen-SS	
SS Armoured Grenadier Training and Reserve Battalion No. 3, Warsaw	4/440
SS Cavalry Training and Reserve Unit, Warsaw	5/381

Police

SS Police Regiment 22, 1st Battalion	3/94
3rd Battalion	3/134
Engineering Emergency Service	1/6
Polish Police	4/363
Polish Fire Brigade	166
Security Police	3/32

Army

Light Anti-Aircraft Alarm Battery III/8, Warsaw	2/22
Engineers Detachment of Railway Armoured Trains Reserve Unit, Rembertow	2/42
Engineers Reserve Battalion 14, Gora-Kalwaria	1/34

Foreign Guard Units

1 Battalion Trawniki men	2/335

II

... Security considerations made it necessary to remove the Jews entirely from the city of Warsaw. The first large resettlement action took place in the period from 22 July to 3 October 1942. In this action 310,322 Jews were removed for resettlement. In January 1943, a second resettlement action was carried out, comprising 6,500 Jews in all.

In January 1943, the Reichsführer SS, on the occasion of his visit to Warsaw, ordered the SS and Police Leader in the District of Warsaw *to transfer to Lublin the armament factories and other enterprises of military importance installed within the ghetto, including their personnel and machines.* The execution of this order proved to be quite difficult, since both the managers and the Jews resisted the transfer in every conceivable way. The SS and Police Leader therefore decided to effect the transfer of the enterprises by force, in a large-scale action to be carried out in three days. My predecessor had attended to the preparation and orders for this large-scale action. I myself arrived in Warsaw on 17 April 1943, at 0800 hours, the action itself having started the same day at 0600 hours.

Before this large-scale action began, the boundaries of the former Jewish quarter had been blocked by an exterior cordon to prevent the Jews from breaking out. This cordon was continually maintained from the start to the end of the action and was especially reinforced at night.

When the ghetto was first invaded, the Jews and the Polish bandits, by a well-prepared concentration of fire, succeeded in repelling the participating units, including tanks and armoured cars. In the second attack, at about 0800 hours, I deployed the forces separately through previously defined fighting zones, so as to have the whole ghetto combed out by the different units. Although the firing was repeated, the blocks were now successfully combed out according to plan. The enemy was forced to retreat from roofs and elevated bases to basements, bunkers, and sewers. To prevent escapes into the sewers, the sewer system beneath the Jewish quarter was promptly closed off and filled with water, but this move was for the most part frustrated by the Jews, who blew up the turn-off valves. Late the first day, rather heavy resistance was encountered, but was quickly broken by a specially assigned raiding party. Further operations succeeded in expelling the Jews from their prepared resistance bases, sniper holes, etc., and, during 20 and 21 April, in gaining control of most of the so-called residual ghetto, to the extent that resistance within these blocks could no longer be called major or considerable.

The main Jewish fighting group, which was mixed with Polish bandits, retreated as early as the first and second day to the so-called Muranowski Square. There it had been reinforced by a considerable number of Polish bandits. Its plan was to maintain itself in the ghetto by every means in order to prevent us from invading it. Jewish and Polish flags were hoisted on top of a concrete building as a call to arms against us. These two flags, however, were captured as early as the second day of the action by a special raiding party. In this skirmish with the bandits, SS Untersturmführer Dehmke was killed when a grenade he was holding in his hand was hit by the enemy and exploded, injuring him fatally.

After the first few days, I realized that the original plan had no prospect of success, unless the armament factories and other enterprises of military importance scattered throughout the ghetto were dissolved. It was therefore necessary to require these enterprises to evacuate their quarters and move immediately, within an appropriate deadline. One enterprise after another was dealt with in this way, and thus in minimal time the Jews and bandits were deprived of the opportunity to take refuge, again and again, in these enterprises, which were under the supervision of the Army. Thorough inspections were necessary to decide in what length of time these enterprises could be evacuated. The conditions observed in the course of these inspections are indescribable. I cannot imagine that greater chaos could have existed anywhere than existed in the Warsaw Ghetto. The Jews had control of everything, from chemical substances for manufacturing explosives to Army clothing and equipment. The managers knew so little of their own enterprises that the Jews were able to produce arms of every kind, especially hand grenades, Molotov cocktails, etc., inside these shops.

Moreover, the Jews had managed to set up resistance bases in these enterprises. One such resistance base, in an enterprise serving the Army Quartermaster's Office, had to be combated as early as the second day by deploying an engineers' unit with flame throwers and by artillery fire. The Jews had installed themselves so firmly in this enterprise that it proved impossible to induce them to leave the shop voluntarily. I therefore resolved to destroy the enterprise by fire on the next day.

The managers of these enterprises, even though usually supervised by an Army officer, were in nearly all cases unable to provide concrete information about their stocks of the locations where stocks were stored. The statements they made as to the number of Jews employed by them did not check out in a single case. Again and again it was found that rich Jews, under cover as 'armament workers', had found accommodations for themselves and their families in the labyrinths of buildings attached to the armament concerns as residential blocks, and were leading cushy lives there. Despite all orders to make the Jews leave those enterprises, it was repeatedly found that managers shut the Jews in, expecting that the action would last only a few days and that they then would go on working with the Jews remaining to them. According to statements by arrested Jews, owners of businesses arranged drinking parties with Jews. In these, women were said to have played a prominent part. The Jews reportedly endeavoured to maintain good relations with Army officers and men. Carousals are said to have been frequent; and, in their course, business deals allegedly were concluded between Germans and Jews.

The number of Jews taken out of the houses and apprehended during the first few days was relatively small. It turned out that the Jews were hiding in the sewers and in specially constructed bunkers. Whereas it had been assumed during the first days that there were only isolated bunkers, it appeared in the course of the large-scale action that the whole ghetto had been systematically equipped with cellars, bunkers, and passageways. In every case these passageways and bunkers had access to the sewer system. Thus, undisturbed subterranean traffic among the Jews was possible. The Jews also used this sewer network to escape underground into the Aryan part of the city of Warsaw. Continually, reports were received of Jews attempting to escape through the sewer holes. Under the pretext of building air-raid shelters, the bunkers had been constructed in this former Jewish quarter since the late autumn of 1942. They were intended to house all Jews during the new resettlement action, which had long been expected, and the resistance against the task forces was to be organized from here. Through posters, handbills, and whispering campaigns, the Communist resistance movement in the former Jewish quarter had in fact managed to have the bunkers occupied as soon as the new large-scale action started. How far the Jews' precautions went was demonstrated by many instances of bunkers skilfully laid out with accommodation for entire families, washing and bathing facilities, toilets, arms and munition-storage bins, and ample food supplies for several months.

... To discover the individual bunkers was extremely difficult for the task forces, due to camouflage, and in many cases was possible only through betrayal on the part of the Jews.

After only a few days it was clear that the Jews no longer had any intention to resettle voluntarily, but were determined to fight back by every means and with the weapons at their disposal. Under Polish Bolshevik leadership, so-called combat groups had been formed; they were armed and paid any price asked for available arms.

During the large-scale action it was possible to capture some Jews who had already been evacuated to Lublin or Treblinka, but had broken out from there and returned to the ghetto, equipped with arms and ammunition. Time and again Polish bandits found refuge in the ghetto and remained there virtually undisturbed, since no forces were on hand to penetrate this maze. Whereas at first it had been possible to capture the Jews, who normally are cowards, in considerable numbers, apprehending bandits and Jews became increasingly difficult during the second half of the large-scale action. Again and again, battle groups of twenty to thirty or more Jewish youths, eighteen to twenty-five years of age, accompanied by corresponding numbers of females, kindled new resistance. These battle groups were under orders to put up armed resistance to the last and, if necessary, to escape capture by suicide.

One such battle group managed to climb from a sewer basin in the so-called Prosta on to a truck and to escape with it (about thirty to thirty-five). One bandit, who had arrived with this truck, exploded two hand grenades, which was the signal for the bandits waiting in the sewer to climb out of the basin. The bandits and Jews – there frequently were Polish bandits among them, armed with carbines, small arms, and one with a light machine gun – climbed on the truck and drove away in an unknown direction. The last member of this gang, who was on guard in the sewer and was assigned to close the sewer-hole cover, was captured. He gave the above information. The search for the truck unfortunately provide fruitless.

During the armed resistance, the females belonging to the battle groups were armed in the same way as the men; some were members of the *halutzim* movement. Not infrequently, these females fired pistols with both hands. Time and again it happened that they kept pistols and hand grenades (Polish 'pineapple' hand grenades) concealed in their drawers up to the last moment, to use them against the men of the Waffen-SS, Police, or Army.

The resistance put up by the Jews and bandits could be broken only through energetic, indefatigable deployment of the patrols day and night. *On 23 April 1943, through the Higher SS and Police Leader for the East, at Cracow, the Reichsführer SS issued an order to effect the combing of the ghetto in Warsaw with the greatest severity and ruthless tenacity.* I therefore decided to carry out the total destruction of the Jewish quarter by burning down all residential blocks, including the blocks attached to the armament factories. One enterprise after the other was systematically evacuated and immediately destroyed by fire. Nearly always the Jews then came out of their hiding places and bunkers. Not infrequently, the Jews stayed in the burning houses until, because of the heat and fear of being burned to death, they chose to jump from the upper floors after having thrown mattresses and other upholstered articles from the burning houses into the street. With bones broken, they still would try to crawl across the street into blocks of houses which were not yet in flames, or only partly so. Often, too, Jews changed their hiding places during the night, by moving into the ruins of buildings already burned out and taking refuge there until they were found by the individual patrols. Their stay in the sewers also ceased to be pleasant after the first week. Frequently, loud voices, coming through the sewer shafts, could be heard in the street. The men of the Waffen-SS or Police or Army engineers would then courageously climb down the shafts to bring out the Jews, and not infrequently they stumbled over Jews already dead, or were shot at. It was always necessary to use smoke candles to drive out the Jews. Thus, one day 193 sewer entrance holes were opened and at a fixed time smoke candles were lowered into them, with the result that the bandits, fleeing from what they believed to be gas, assembled in the centre of the former Jewish quarter and could be pulled out of the sewer holes there. Numerous Jews, who could not be counted, were taken care of by explosions in sewers and bunkers.

The longer the resistance lasted, the tougher the men of the Waffen-SS, Police, and Army became; here as always, they tackled their duties indefatigably, in faithful comradeship, and constantly held their own in model, exemplary fashion. Their duty often lasted from early morning until late at night. At night, search patrols with rags wound around their feet remained at the heels of the Jews and kept up the pressure on them without interruption. Not infrequently, Jews who used the night for supplementing their stores of victuals from abandoned bunkers or for making contact or exchanging information with neighbouring groups were apprehended and taken care of.

Considering that the men of the Waffen-SS for the most part had had only three to four weeks' training before being assigned to this action, the mettle, courage, and devotion to duty which they showed deserves special recognition. It may be stated that the Army engineers, too, executed their work of blowing up bunkers, sewers, and concrete buildings with indefatigable devotion to duty. Officers and men of the Police, a large part of whom already had front-line experience, again proved themselves through exemplary daring.

Only the continuous and untiring deployment of all forces made it possible to apprehend or verifiably destroy a total of 56,065 Jews.

To this figure should be added those Jews who lost their lives in explosions, fires, etc., but whose numbers could not be ascertained.

Even while the large-scale action was going on, the Aryan population was informed by posters that entering the former Jewish quarter was strictly forbidden, and that anybody found in the former Jewish quarter without a valid permit would be shot. At the same time, the Aryan population was once more instructed by these posters that anybody who knowingly gave refuge to a Jew, especially anyone who housed, fed, or concealed a Jew outside the Jewish quarter, would be punished by death.

The Polish police were authorized to turn over to any Polish policeman who arrested a Jew in the Aryan part of the city of Warsaw one-third of the Jew's cash property. This measure has already produced results.

The Polish population by and large welcomed the measures taken against the Jews. Towards the end of the large-scale action, the Governor addressed a special proclamation, which was submitted to the undersigned for approval before publication, to the Polish population, enlightening the Poles about the reasons for destroying the former Jewish quarter and calling them to battle against Communist agents, with reference to the assassinations lately carried out in the territory of the city of Warsaw and to the mass graves in Katyn.

The large-scale action was terminated on 16 May 1943, with the blowing up of the Warsaw synagogue at 2015 hours.

At this time, there no longer are any industrial enterprises in the former Jewish quarter. All objects of value, raw materials, and machines there have been moved and stored elsewhere. Whatever buildings, etc., existed have been destroyed. The only exception is the so-called Dzielna Prison of the Security Police, which was exempted from destruction.

III

Inasmuch as one must reckon with the possibility, even after completion of the large-scale action, that a few Jews still remain among the ruins of the former Jewish quarter, this area must remain firmly shut off from the Aryan quarter during the near future, and must be guarded. Police Battalion III/23 has been assigned to this duty. This Police Battalion has instructions to keep watch over the former Jewish quarter, particularly to see that no one enters the former ghetto, and immediately to shoot anybody found there without authorization. The Commander of the Police Battalion will continue to receive further instructions directly from the SS and Police Leader. In this way, the small remnants of Jews, if any, must be kept under constant pressure and destroyed. By the destruction of all buildings and hiding places and the cutting off of the water supply, the remaining Jews and bandits must be deprived of any further chance of existence.

It is suggested that the Dzielna Prison be made into a concentration camp and that the inmates be used to salvage the millions of bricks, scrap iron, and other materials, collect them and make them available for reuse.

IV

Of the total of 56,065 Jews apprehended, about 7,000 were destroyed within the former ghetto in the course of the large-scale action, and 6,929 by transporting them to T. II, which means that altogether 14,000 Jews were destroyed. Beyond the number of 56,065 Jews, an estimated 5,000 to 6,000 were killed by explosions or in fires.

The number of destroyed bunkers amounts to 631.

BOOTY:

7 Polish rifles, 1 Russian rifle, 1 German rifle
59 pistols of various calibres
Several hundred hand grenades, including Polish and homemade ones
Several hundred incendiary bottles
Homemade explosives
Infernal machines with fuses
A large amount of explosives, ammunition for weapons of all calibres, including some machine-gun ammunition

Regarding the booty of arms, it must be taken into consideration that the arms themselves could in most cases not be captured, as the bandits and Jews would, before being arrested, throw them into hiding places or holes which could not be ascertained or discovered. The smoking out of the bunkers by our men also often made the search for arms impossible. As the bunkers had to be blown up at once, a search later on was out of the question.

The captured hand grenades, ammunition, and incendiary bottles were at once reused by use against the bandits.

FURTHER BOOTY TAKEN:
1,240 used military tunics (part of them with medal ribbons – Iron Cross and East Medal)
600 pairs of used trousers
Other equipment and German steel helmets
108 horses, 4 of them still in the former ghetto (hearse)

Up to 23 May [*sic*] 1943, we had counted:
4.4 million złotys; furthermore, about 5–6 million złotys not yet counted, a large amount of foreign currency, among others, $14,300 in paper money and $9,200 in gold, besides jewellery (rings, necklaces, watches, etc.) in large quantities.

State of the ghetto at the termination of the large-scale action:

Apart from eight buildings (police barracks, hospital, and accommodation for housing the factory police), the former ghetto is completely destroyed. Only fireproof walls are left standing where no explosions were carried out. But the ruins still contain a vast amount of stones and scrap material which could be used.

Warsaw: 16 May 1943

The SS and Police Leader in the District of Warsaw
[Signed] *Stroop*
SS Brigadeführer and Major General of Police

'The Jews tried to avoid evacuation by all possible means': Report on the Solution of the Jewish Question, Galicia, 30 June 1943
SS-GRUPPENFÜHRER FRITZ KATZMANN

Katzmann was Commander of the German SS and Police in the District of Galicia; the report below, entitled 'The Solution of the Jewish Question in the District of Galicia', was submitted to SS and police chief Friedrich Kruger.

Reich Secret Document
The SS and Police Leader (SS-und Polizeiführer) in the District of
Galicia Lvov, 30 June 1943
Re: Solution of the Jewish Question in Galicia
Reference: Attached Report
Enclosure: 1 Report (3 copies)
1 Copy (bound)
To the
Higher SS and Police Leader East
SS Obergruppenführer and General of the Police
Kruger
Kraków

Enclosed I forward the first copy of the final report on the Solution
of the Jewish Question in the District of Galicia, and request that you
may acknowledge it.

Katzmann
SS-Gruppenführer
And Generalleutnant of Police

Solution of the Jewish Problem in the District of Galicia

Owing to the phrase 'Galician Jew', Galicia was probably the
small corner on earth most known and most frequently mentioned
in connection with the Jews. Here they lived in great, compact
multitudes, forming a world of their own, from which the rest of
world Jewry renewed its population continuously. Jews were to be
met with in their hundreds of thousands in all parts of Galicia.

According to old statistics dating back to 1931, there were then
about 502,000 Jews. This number is unlikely to have diminished in the
period between 1931 and the summer of 1941. There are no precise
figures for the number of Jews present when the German troops
marched into Galicia. The figure of 350,000 was given by the *Judenrat*
of Galicia for the end of the year 1941. That this figure was incorrect
can be seen from the records concerning evacuation appended to
this report. The city of Lvov alone housed about 160,000 Jews in the
months of July–August 1941 ...

Our first measure was to identify every Jew by means of a white armlet with the blue Star of David. In accordance with a decree issued by the Governor General, the Interior Administration was responsible for the identifying and registration of the Jews, as well as setting up the *Judenrat*. Our task as police was first of all to fight effectively against the immense black market operated by the Jews all over the District. Energetic measures also had to be taken against idlers loafing around and against do-nothings.

The best means for this was the establishment of Forced Labour Camps by the SS and Police Leader. There was, first of all, work on the urgently needed reconstruction of [highway] Dg. 4, which was extremely important for the entire southern section of the Front and which was in catastrophically bad condition. On 15 October 1941, a start was made on the building of camps along the railroad tracks, and after a few weeks, despite considerable difficulties, seven camps had been put up, containing 4,000 Jews. More camps soon followed, so that in a very short period of time the completion of fifteen camps could be reported to the Higher SS and Police Leader. About 20,000 Jewish labourers passed through these camps in the course of time. Despite all conceivable difficulties that turned up on this project, about 160 kilometres have now been completed.

At the same time all other Jews who were fit for work were registered by the Labour Offices and directed to useful work. Both when the Jews were identified with the Star of David and when they were registered by the Labour Offices, the first indications were noted that the Jews were trying to evade the orders issued by the Authorities. The control measures carried out as a result led to thousands of arrests. It became increasingly apparent that the Civil Administration was not in a position to move the Jewish problem to an even reasonably satisfactory solution. Because repeated attempts of the City Administration of Lvov, for instance, to move the Jews into a Jewish quarter, failed, this question, too, was solved by the SS and Police Leader and his organizations. This measure had become all the more urgent because in the winter of 1941 centres of typhus infection had appeared all over the city, endangering not only the local population but, even more, the German troops either stationed in the city or passing through ...

Owing to the peculiarity that almost 90 per cent of the artisans in Galicia consisted of Jews, the problem to be solved could only be carried out gradually, as an immediate removal of the Jews would not have been in the interest of the war economy. Not that one could observe that those Jews who were working made any special contribution by their work. Their place of work was often only a means to an end for them: firstly, to escape the sharper measures taken against the Jews; and, secondly, to be able to carry out their black-market dealings without interruption. Only continuous police intervention could prevent these activities. Draconic measures had to be introduced by us after it was noted in increasing numbers of cases that the Jews had succeeded in making themselves indispensable to their employers by providing goods in short supply, etc. It is very sad to have to note that the wildest black-market deals with the Jews were made by Germans who were brought here, and in particular those in the so-called 'operating firms' (*Einsatzfirmen*) or the 'ill-reputed trustees' (*beruchtigte Treuhander*), both of which operated Jewish firms taken from their owners. Cases were known where Jews seeking to obtain some kind of working certificate not only did not ask for pay from their employers but paid regularly themselves. In addition, Jewish 'organizing' on behalf of their 'employers' reached such catastrophic dimensions that energetic action had to be taken in the interest of the reputation of the German people.

As the Administration was not in the position to overcome this chaos, and proved weak, the whole issue of Jewish Labour was simply taken over by the SS and Police Leader. The existing Jewish Labour Offices, which were staffed by hundreds of Jews, were dissolved. All work certificates issued by firms and official employers were declared invalid, and the cards given to Jews by the Labour Offices revalidated by the Police.

In the course of this *Aktion* thousands of Jews were again caught in possession of forged certificates or labour certificates obtained fraudulently by means of all kinds of excuses. These Jews were also sent for special treatment (*Sonderbehandlung*). The Wehrmacht authorities in particular aided the Jewish parasites by issuing special certificates without proper control … There were cases where Jews were caught with from ten to twenty such certificates. When Jews were arrested in the course of further checks, most of the employers felt obliged to attempt to intervene in favour of the Jews. This was often done in a manner that can only be described as deeply shameful …

Despite all these measures for the regulation of Jewish labour, a start was made in April 1942 on the evacuation of Jews from the District of Galicia, and this was carried out steadily.

When the Higher SS and Police Leader again intervened in the Jewish question in general on 10 November 1942, and a Police Order was issued for the formation of Jewish quarters, 254,989 Jews had already been evacuated or resettled. Since the Higher SS and Police Leader gave further instructions to accelerate the total evacuation of the Jews, further considerable work was necessary in order to catch those Jews who were, for the time being, to be left in the armaments factories. These remaining Jews were declared labour prisoners of the Higher SS and Police Leader and held either in the factories themselves or in camps erected for this purpose. For Lvov itself a large camp was erected on the outskirts, which holds 8,000 Jewish labour prisoners at the present time. The agreement made with the Wehrmacht concerning employment and treatment of the labour prisoners was set down in writing ...

In the meantime further evacuation was carried out vigorously, with the result that by 23 June 1943 all Jewish quarters could be dissolved. Apart from the Jews in camps under the control of the SS and Police Leader, the District of Galicia is thus free of Jews (*Judenfrei*).

Individual Jews occasionally picked up by the Order Police or the Gendarmerie were sent for special treatment. Altogether, 434,329 Jews had been evacuated up to June 27, 1943 ... [This is followed by a list of 21 camps in which there were still 21,156 Jews.]

Together with the evacuation *Aktionen* Jewish property was collected. Valuables were secured and handed over to the Special Staff 'Reinhard'. Apart from furniture and large quantities of textiles, etc., the following were confiscated and delivered to Special Staff 'Reinhard':

As of 30 June 1943:

25,580 kg. copper coins
53,190 nickel coins
97,581 gold coins
82,600 silver chains
6,640 chains, gold
4,326,780 broken silver
167,740 silver coins

18,490 iron coins
20,050 brass coins
20,952 wedding rings gold
22,740 pearls
11,730 gold teeth bridges
28,200 powder compacts silver or other metal
44,655 broken gold
482,900 silver flatware
343,100 cigarette cases silver and other metal
20,880 kg rings, gold, with stones
39,917 brooches, earrings, etc.
1,802 rings, silver
6,166 pocket watches, various
3,133 pocket watches, silver
1,256 wrist watches gold
2,892 pocket watches gold
68 cameras
98 binoculars
7 stamp collections complete
5 travel baskets of loose stamps
3 sacks of rings, jewellery not genuine
1 box corals
1 case corals
1 case corals
1 suitcase of fountain pens and propelling pencils
1 travel basket of fountain pens and propelling pencils
1 suitcase of cigarette lighters
1 suitcase of pocket knives
1 trunk of watch parts
Currency: Bank Notes and Metal

There were also other immense difficulties during the *Aktionen* as the Jews tried to avoid evacuation by all possible means. They not only tried to escape, and concealed themselves in the most improbable places, drainage canals, chimneys, even in sewage pits, etc. They barricaded themselves in catacombs of passages, in cellars made into bunkers, in holes in the earth, in cunningly contrived hiding places, in attics and sheds, inside furniture, etc.

As the number of Jews still remaining decreased, their resistance became the greater. They used weapons of all types for their defence, and in particular those of Italian origin. The Jews bought these Italian weapons from Italian soldiers stationed in the district in exchange for large sums in złotys ...

Subterranean bunkers were discovered which had cleverly concealed entrances, some in the flats, and some out of doors. In most cases the entrance to the bunker was only just large enough for one person to slip through. The entrances to the bunkers were so well hidden that they could not be found if one did not know where to look ...

Owing to increasingly grave reports of the growing arming of the Jews, the sharpest possible measures were taken for the elimination of Jewish banditry in all parts of the District of Galicia in the last two weeks of June 1943. Special measures were needed for the breaking up of the Jewish quarter in Lvov, where the bunkers described above had been installed. In order to avoid losses to German forces, brutal measures had to be taken from the outset; several houses were blown up or destroyed by fire. The astonishing result was that in place of the 12,000 Jews registered a total of 20,000 were caught ...

Song of the Bialystok Ghetto, Poland, circa 1943
ANONYMOUS

The Jewish Ghetto in Bialystok, Poland, was established following the German takeover of Russian-occupied Poland in 1941. Upwards of 60,000 Jews were herded into a small quarter of the city astride the Biala river, many of them forced to labour in armaments and textile factories overseen by the *Judenrat*.

In the ghetto factories we slave,
We make shoes and we produce,
We knit and sew and weave.
And for that we earn a pass
For a ride to Treblinka, alas.

Alas, how bitter are the times,
But deliverance is on its way;

It's not so far away.
The Red Army will come to free us,
It's not so far away.

The Jews of Bialystok staged a failed uprising in August 1943 against deportations to Treblinka. Some fighters, however, managed to escape the ghetto cordon to join the Polish partisans. Of the surrendered Jews, almost all were murdered or died of starvation and disease.

'A page of glory never mentioned and never to be mentioned': The Posen Speeches, 4–6 October 1943
REICHSFÜHRER-SS HEINRICH HIMMLER

The speeches delivered by Himmler to assembled SS officers, Reichsleiters and Gauleiters in Posen (Poznań) in occupied Poland are one of the few occasions on which the Nazi leaders did not use euphemisms when referring to the events of the Holocaust. The speeches also clearly show Himmler's role as architect of the 'Final Solution'.

I also want to mention a very difficult subject before you here, completely openly. It should be discussed amongst us, and yet, nevertheless, we will never speak about it in public.

Just as we did not hesitate on 30 June to carry out our duty, as ordered, and stand comrades who had failed against the wall and shoot them. About which we have never spoken, and never will speak.

That was, thank God, a kind of tact natural to us, a foregone conclusion of that tact, that we have never conversed about it amongst ourselves, never spoken about it; everyone shuddered, and everyone was clear that the next time, he would do the same thing again, if it were commanded and necessary.

I am talking about the 'Jewish evacuation': the extermination of the Jewish people.

It is one of those things that is easily said. 'The Jewish people is being exterminated,' every party member will tell you, 'perfectly clear, it's part of our plans, we're eliminating the Jews, exterminating them. Ha! A small matter.'

And then along they all come, all the 80 million upright Germans, and each one has his decent Jew. They say: All the others are swine, but here is a first-class Jew.

And none of them has seen it, has endured it. Most of you will know what it means when 100 bodies lie together, when there are 500, or when there are 1,000. And to have seen this through, and – with the exception of human weaknesses – to have remained decent, has made us hard and is a page of glory never mentioned and never to be mentioned.

Because we know how difficult things would be, if today in every city during the bomb attacks, the burdens of war and the privations, we still had Jews as secret saboteurs, agitators and instigators. We would probably be at the same stage as 1916–17, if the Jews still resided in the body of the German people.

We have taken away the riches that they had, and I have given a strict order, which Obergruppenführer Pohl has carried out, we have delivered these riches completely to the Reich, to the State. We have taken nothing from them for ourselves. A few, who have offended against this, will be [judged] in accordance with an order, that I have at the beginning: He who takes even one mark of this is a dead man.

A number of SS men have offended against this order. There are not very many, and they will be dead men – WITHOUT MERCY! We have the moral right, we had the duty to our people to do it, to kill this people who wanted to kill us. But we do not have the right to enrich ourselves with even one fur, with one mark, with one cigarette, with one watch, with anything. That we do not have. Because at the end of this, we don't want, because we exterminated the bacillus, to become sick and die from the same bacillus.

I will never see it happen, that even one bit of putrefaction comes in contact with us, or takes root in us. On the contrary, where it might try to take root, we will burn it out together. But altogether we can say: We have carried out this most difficult task for the love of our people. And we have taken no defect within us, in our soul, or in our character.

[…]

I ask of you that which I say to you in this circle be really only heard and not ever discussed. We were faced with the question: what about the women and children? I decided to find a clear solution to this problem too. I did not consider myself justified to exterminate the men – in other words, to kill them or have them killed – and allow the avengers of our sons and grandsons in the form of their children to grow up. The difficult decision had to be made to have this people disappear from the earth. For the organization which had to execute this task, it was the most difficult which we had ever had … I felt obliged to you, as the most senior dignitary, as the most superior dignitary of the party, this political order, this political instrument of the Führer, to also speak about this question quite openly and to say how it has been. The Jewish question in the countries that we occupy will be solved by the end of this year. Only remainders of odd Jews that managed to find hiding places will be left over.

The Posen speech of 6 October seemingly implicates Albert Speer in the Final Solution, as Himmler directly addresses him in the course of his peroration on the Warsaw Ghetto uprising of April–May 1943:

This entire ghetto was producing fur coats, dresses, and the like. Whenever we tried to get at it in the past we were told: Stop! Armaments factory! Of course, this has nothing to do with Party Comrade Speer. It wasn't your doing. It is this portion of alleged armaments factories that Party Comrade Speer and I intend to clear out in the next few weeks.

Speer, Reich Minister for Armaments and War Production, maintained after 1945 that he left the town hall in Posen before Himmler made his speech, and was ignorant of the Holocaust.

'Tell our brothers … we went to meet our death in full consciousness and with pride': A Young Polish Girl Shouts Her Defiance, Auschwitz-Birkenau, 17 November 1943
ANONYMOUS

The girl who made the 'very short but fiery speech' described below was part of an underground Jewish group.

A certain young Polish woman made a very short but fiery speech in the gas-chamber, addressing all who were present, stripped to their skins. She condemned the Nazi crimes and oppression and ended with the words, 'We shall not die now. The history of our nation shall immortalize us, our initiative and our spirit are alive and flourishing, the German nation shall as dearly pay for our blood as we possibly can imagine. Down with savagery in the guise of Hitler's Germany! Long live Poland!'

Then she turned to the Jews from the Sonderkommando. 'Remember that it is incumbent on you to follow your sacred duty of revenging us, the guiltless. Tell our brothers, our nation, that we went to meet our death in full consciousness and with pride.'

Then the Poles kneeled on the ground and solemnly said a certain prayer, in a posture that made an immense impression, then they arose and all together in chorus sang the Polish anthem; the Jews sang the *Hatikvah*.

The cruel common fate in this accursed spot merged the lyric tones of these diverse anthems into one whole. They expressed in this way their last feelings with a deeply moving warmth and their hope for, and belief in, the future of their nation. Then they sang the 'Internationale'.

One of the Sonderkommandos in the gas-chamber did follow the 'sacred duty' incumbent upon him; he made a detailed manuscript of the events he had witnessed – including the girls' defiance as described above – and buried it for later finding. Other Sonderkommandos secreted their testimonies, among them Salmen Gradowski, who hid his notes in a pit of ash, rightly deducing that one day 'people will certainly dig to find traces of millions of men who were exterminated'. He wrote in his covering letter:

Dear finder, search everywhere, in every inch of soil. Tens of documents are buried under it, mine, and those of other persons, which will throw light on everything that was happening here ... We ourselves have lost hope of being able to live to see the moment of liberation.

A Performance of Verdi's Requiem, *Theresienstadt, circa 1944*
ANNA BERGMAN

Despite deportations, hunger and disease, the Theresienstadt ghetto developed a rich cultural life: Designed to house privileged Jews, Theresienstadt's inmates included world-famous artists, musicians and writers. At least four concert orchestras were established in the camp, while the lending library held 60,000 volumes.

There was a performance of Verdi's *Requiem*, the first public-performance with all the trimmings, and the Germans came to listen to what the Jews could do. This was performed with all the hidden meanings stressed. Well, they finished and waited and waited, and the conductor turned round, and everyone waited: to applaud or not? And then the Germans started to applaud. You can't imagine the *irony*, the absolute stupidity: the Germans came to the performance, they applauded and they left. And the Jews applauded, everyone was in tears. It was *magnificent*.

Pretending to be Aryan, Kraków, Poland, c. 1944
LEAH HAMMERSTEIN SILVERSTEIN

Born in Praga, Poland, Leah Hammerstein Silverstein worked under a false non-Jewish identity in the German-run hospital in Kraków.

At another time I was sitting in front of a big basket with vegetables, cleaning it, and the sun rays came on my head and one of the girls said, 'Look, her hair is reddish like a Jewess.' And everybody laughed, and I laughed most hilariously, you know, but inside, you know, the fear was gnawing on my insides … At another time the kitchen chef grabbed me and put my head on the table. He was preparing the sausage for the evening supper.

And he put this long knife to my neck and said, 'You see, if you were Jewish, I would cut off your head.' Big laughter in the room, and I laughed most hilariously, of course. But you know what it does to a psyche of a young girl in her formative years? Can you imagine? With nobody to console you, with nobody to tell you it's okay, it'll be better, hold on. Total isolation, total loneliness. It's a terrible feeling. You know, you are among people and you are like on an island all alone. There is nobody you can go to [to] ask for help. You can ask nobody for advice. You had to make life-threatening decisions all by yourself in a very short time, and you never knew whether your decision will be beneficial to you or detrimental to your existence. It was like playing Russian roulette with your life. And it was not only one incident. It was this way from the moment I came on the Aryan side.

Auschwitz Observed, April 1942–April 1944
RUDOLF VRBA AND ALFRED WETZLER

Vrba and Wetzler were two Slovak Jews who escaped from Auschwitz; their report on conditions inside the camp, transcribed by Dr Oscar Krasniansky of the Slovak *Judenrat*, was the first eyewitness account of Auschwitz, together with an attempted estimate of numbers murdered. The 'Vrba-Wetzler report' is also known as 'The Auschwitz Protocols'.

On 13 April 1942, our group of 1,000 men was loaded on to railway carriages at the assembly camp at Sered'. The doors were sealed, so that nothing would reveal the direction of the journey. When they were opened after a long while, we realized that we had crossed the Slovak frontier and were in Zwardoń. Until then the train had been guarded by Hlinka men, but it was not taken over by SS guards. After a few carriages had been uncoupled from our convoy, we continued on our way, arriving at night at Auschwitz, where we stopped at a siding … Upon arrival, we were counted off in rows of five. There were 643 of us. After a walk of about twenty minutes with our heavy packs – we had left Slovakia well equipped – we reached the concentration camp of Auschwitz.

We were led at once into a huge barracks, where we had to deposit all our luggage on one side and on the other undress completely, leaving our clothes and valuables behind. Naked, we then proceeded to an adjoining barracks, where our heads and bodies were shaved and disinfected. At the exit, every man was given a number, beginning with 28,600. With this number in hand, we were then herded to a third barracks, where so-called registration took place. Here the numbers we received in the second barracks were tattooed on the left side of our chests. The extreme brutality with which this was done made many of us faint. The particulars of our identity were also recorded. Then we were led by hundreds into a cellar and later to a barracks, where we were issued striped prisoners' clothes and wooden clogs. This lasted until 10 a.m. In the afternoon our prisoners' outfits were taken away from us and replaced by the ragged and dirty remains of Russian uniforms. Thus equipped, we were marched off the Birkenau.

Auschwitz is a concentration camp for political prisoners under so-called 'protective custody'. At the time of my arrival, that is, April 1942, about 15,000 prisoners were in the camp, the majority Poles, Germans, and civilian Russians under protective custody. A small number of prisoners came under the categories of criminals and 'work-shirkers'.

Auschwitz camp headquarters also controls the labour camp of Birkenau as well as the farm-labour camp of Harmense. All the prisoners arrive first at Auschwitz, where they are provided with prisoners' registration numbers and then are kept there, or are sent either to Birkenau or, in very small numbers, to Harmense ...

There are several factories on the grounds of the camp of Auschwitz: a war production plant of *Deutsche Ausrüstungswerke* (DAW [an SS enterprise founded in 1939]), a factory belonging to the Krupp works, and one to the Siemens concern. Outside the camp's boundary is a tremendous plant covering several square kilometres named Buna. The prisoners work in all the aforementioned factories.

The prisoners' actual living quarters, if such a term is at all appropriate, covers an area approximately 500 by 300 metres, surrounded by a double row of concrete posts about three metres high, interconnected, inside and out, by a dense netting of high-tension wires fixed into the posts by insulators. Between these two rows of posts, at intervals of 150 metres, there are five-metre-high watchtowers, equipped with machine guns and searchlights. The inner high-tension ring is encircled by an ordinary wire fence. Merely to touch this fence is to draw a stream of bullets from the watchtowers. This system is called the 'small' or 'inner ring of sentry posts'.

The camp itself is composed of three rows of houses. The camp thoroughfare lies between the first and second row. A wall used to stand between the second and third row. Up to mid-August 1942, the over 7,000 Jewish girls deported from Slovakia in March and April 1942, lived in the houses separated by this wall. After these girls had been removed to Birkenau, the wall was removed. The road into the camp bisects the row of houses. Over the entrance gate, always, of course, heavily guarded, stands the ironic inscription: 'Work brings freedom'.

At a radius of some 2,000 metres, the whole camp is encircled by a second ring called the 'big' or 'outer ring of sentry posts', also with watchtowers every 150 metres. Between the inner- and outer-ring sentry posts are the factories and other workshops. The towers of the inner ring are manned only at night when the high-tension current is switched into the double row of wires. During the day the garrison of the inner-ring sentry posts is withdrawn, and the men take up duty in the outer ring. Escape – and many attempts have been made – through these sentry posts is practically impossible. Getting through the inner-ring posts at night is completely impossible, and the towers of the outer ring are so close to one another that it is out of the question to pass unnoticed. The guards shoot without warning. The garrison of the outer ring is withdrawn at twilight, but only after all the prisoners have been ascertained to be within the inner ring. If the roll call uncovers a missing prisoner, sirens immediately sound the alarm.

The men in the outer ring remain in their towers on the lookout, the inner ring is manned, and hundreds of SS guards and bloodhounds begin a systematic search. The siren brings the whole surrounding countryside to a state of alarm, so that if by miracle the escaping man has succeeded in getting through the outer ring, he is almost certain to be caught by one of the numerous German police and SS patrols. The escapee is furthermore handicapped by his clean-shaven head, his striped prisoner's outfit or red patches sewn on his clothing, and the passiveness of the thoroughly intimidated population. The mere failure to give information on the whereabouts of a prisoner, not to speak of extending help, is punished by death. If the prisoner has not been caught sooner, the garrison of the outer-ring sentry posts remains on the watch for three days and nights, after which it is presumed that the fugitive succeeded in breaking through the double ring. The following night the outer guard is withdrawn. If the fugitive is caught alive, he is hanged in the presence of the whole camp. If he is found dead, his body – wherever it may have been located – is returned to camp (it is easily identifiable by the tattooed number) and seated at the entrance gate, a small notice clasped in his hands, reading: 'Here

I am'. During our two years' imprisonment, many attempts at escape were made, but except for two or three, all were brought back dead or alive. It is not known whether those two or three actually managed to get away. It can, however, be asserted that among the Jews who were deported from Slovakia to Auschwitz or Birkenau, we are the only two who were lucky enough to save ourselves.

As stated previously, we were transferred from Auschwitz to Birkenau on the day of our arrival. Actually there is no such district as Birkenau. Even the word Birkenau is new in that it has been adapted from the nearby Brzezinki. The existing camp centre of Birkenau lies four kilometres from Auschwitz, though the outer borders of Birkenau and Auschwitz adjoin ...

When we arrived in Birkenau, we found only one huge kitchen there for 15,000 people and three stone buildings, two already completed and one under construction. The buildings were encircled by an ordinary barbed-wire fence. The prisoners were housed in these buildings and in others later constructed ... All are built according to a standard model. Each house is about thirty metres long and eight to ten metres wide [divided into tiny cubicles] ... too narrow for a man to lie stretched out and not high enough for him to sit upright. There is no question of having enough space to stand upright. Thus, some 400–500 people are accommodated in one house or 'block' ...

After three days I was ordered, together with 200 other Slovak Jews, to work in the German armament factories at Auschwitz, but we continued to be housed in Birkenau. We left early in the morning, returning at night, and worked in the carpentry shop as well as on road construction. Our food consisted of one litre of turnip soup at midday and 300 grams of bad bread in the evening. Working conditions were inconceivably hard, so that the majority of us, weakened by starvation and the inedible food, could not endure. The mortality was so high that our group of 200 had thirty to thirty-five dead every day. Many were simply beaten to death by the overseers – the Kapos – during work, without the slightest provocation. The gaps in our ranks caused by these deaths were replaced daily by prisoners from Birkenau. Our return at night was extremely painful and dangerous, as we had to drag, over a distance of five kilometres, our tools, firewood, heavy cauldrons, and the bodies of those who had died or had been killed during the working day. With these heavy loads we had to maintain a brisk pace, and anyone incurring the displeasure of one of the Kapos was cruelly knocked down, if not beaten to death. Until the arrival of the second group of Slovak men some fourteen days later, our original number had dwindled to 150. At night we were counted, the bodies of the dead were piled up on flat, narrow-gauge cars or in a truck and brought to Brzezinki, where they were burned in a trench several metres deep and about fifteen metres long …

Until the middle of May 1942, a total of four convoys of Jewish men from Slovakia arrived at Birkenau and all were given treatment similar to ours.

From the first two transports 120 men – ninety Slovak and thirty French Jews – were chosen, including myself, and placed at the disposal of the administration of the camp of Auschwitz, which needed doctors, dentists, intellectuals, and clerks. As I had in the meantime managed to work my way up to a good position in Birkenau – being in command of a group of fifty men, which had brought me considerable advantage – I at first felt reluctant to leave for Auschwitz. However, I was finally persuaded to go. After eight days, eighteen doctors and attendants as well as three other persons were selected from this group of 120. The doctors were used in the so-called *Krankenbau* ('patients' building' infirmary) at Auschwitz … The remaining ninety-nine persons were sent to work in the gravel pits where they all died within a short time.

Shortly thereafter a *Krankenbau* was set up. It was destined to become the much dreaded Block 7, where I was first chief attendant and later administrator. The 'infirmary' chief was a Pole. This building actually was nothing but an assembly centre of candidates for death. All prisoners incapable of working were sent there. There was no question of any medical attention or care. We had some 150 dead daily and their bodies were sent for cremation to Auschwitz.

At the same time, the so-called 'selections' were introduced. Twice-weekly, Mondays and Thursdays, the camp doctor indicated the number of prisoners who were to be gassed and then burned. Those selected were loaded on to trucks and brought to Brzezinki. Those still alive upon arrival were gassed in a big barracks erected near the trench used for burning the bodies. The weekly contingent of dead from Block 7 was about 2,000, 1,200 of whom died a 'natural death' and about 800 by 'selection'. For those who had not been 'selected', a death certificate was issued and sent to the central administration at Oranienburg, whereas a special list was kept of the 'selectees' with the indication 'S.B.' (*Sonderbehandlung* – special treatment). Until 15 January 1943, up to which time I was administrator of Block 7 and therefore in a position directly to observe the events, some 50,000 prisoners died of 'natural death' or by 'selection'.

As previously described, the prisoners were numbered consecutively, so that we can reconstruct fairly clearly their order of succession and the fate which befell each individual convoy on arrival.

The first transport of Jewish men reaching Auschwitz for Birkenau was composed, as mentioned, of 1,320 naturalized French Jews bearing approximately the following numbers: 27,400–28,000

28,600–29,600	In April 1942 the first convoy of Slovak Jews (our convoy).
29,600–29,700	100 men (Aryans) from various concentration camps.
29,700–32,700	3 complete convoys of Slovak Jews.
32,700–33,100	400 professional criminals (Aryans) from Warsaw prisons.
33,100–35,000	1,900 Jews from Kraków.
35,000–36,000	1,000 Poles (Aryans) – political prisoners.
36,000–37,300	In May 1942 – 1,300 Slovak Jews from Lublin-Majdanek.
37,300–37,900	600 Poles (Aryans) from Radom, a few Jews among them.
37,900–38,000	100 Poles from the concentration camp of Dachau.
38,000–38,400	400 naturalized French Jews with their families.

This whole convoy consisted of about 1,600 individuals, of whom approximately 200 girls and 400 men were admitted to the camp, while the remaining 1,000 persons (women, old people, children, as well as men) were sent without further procedure from the railway siding directly to Brzezinki, and there gassed and burned. From this moment on, all Jewish convoys were dealt with in the same way. Approximately 10 per cent of the men and 5 per cent of the women were assigned to the camps and remaining members were immediately gassed. This process of annihilation had already been applied earlier to the Polish Jews. During long months, without interruption, trucks brought thousands of Jews from the various ghettos directly to the pit in Birkenwald …

48,300–48,620	320 Jews from Slovakia. About 70 girls were transferred to the women's camp, the remainder, some 650 people, gassed in Birkenwald. This convoy included about 80 people who had been transferred by the Hungarian police to the camp at Sered' …
49,000–64,800	15,000 naturalized French, Belgian, and Dutch Jews. This figure certainly represents less than 10 per cent of the total convoy. This was between 1 July and 15 September 1942. Large family convoys arrived from various European countries and were at once directed to Birkenwald. The Sonderkommando, employed for gassing and burning, worked day and night shifts. Hundreds of thousands of Jews were gassed during this period.
64,800–65,000	200 Slovak Jews. Of this transport, about 100 women were admitted to the camp, the rest were gassed and burned …
65,000–68,000	Naturalized French, Belgian, and Dutch Jews. Not more than 1,000 women were 'selected' and sent to the camp. The others, 30,000 at the least, were gassed.
71,000–80,000	Naturalized French, Belgian, and Dutch Jews. The prisoners brought to the camp hardly represented 10 per cent of the total transport. A conservative estimate would be that approximately 65,000 to 70,000 persons were gassed …

Number 80,000 marks the beginning of the systematic annihilation of the Polish ghettos.

80,000–85,000	Approximately 5,000 Jews from various ghettos in Mlawa, Maków, Ciechanów, Lomża, Grodno, Bialystok. For fully thirty days truck convoys arrived without interruption. Only 5,000 persons were sent to the concentration camp; all the others were gassed at once. The Sonderkommando worked in two shifts, twenty-four hours daily, and was scarcely able to cope with the gassing and burning. Without exaggeration, it may be said that some 80,000–90,000 of these convoys received *Sonderbehandlung*. These transports also brought in a considerable amount of money, valuables, and precious stones.
85,000–92,000	6,000 Jews from Grodno, Bialystok, and Kraków, as well as 1,000 Aryan Poles. The majority of the Jewish convoys were directly gassed and about 4,000 Jews daily were driven into the gas-chambers. During mid-January 1943, three convoys of 2,000 persons each arrived from Theresienstadt … Only 600 men and 300 women of these 6,000 persons were admitted to the camp. The remainder were gassed.
99,000–100,000	End of January 1943, large convoys of French and Dutch Jews arrived; only a small proportion reached the camp.
100,000–102,000	In February 1943, 2,000 Aryan Poles, mostly intellectuals.
102,000–103,000	700 Czech Aryans. Later, those still alive were sent to Buchenwald.
103,000–108,000	3,000 French and Dutch Jews and 2,000 Poles (Aryans). During the month of February 1943, two contingents arrived daily. They included Polish, French, and Dutch Jews who, in the main, were sent to the gas-chambers. The number gassed during this month can be estimated at no smaller than 90,000.

At the end of February 1943, a new modern crematorium and gassing plant were inaugurated at Birkenau. The gassing and burning of the bodies in Birkenwald were discontinued, the whole job being taken over by the four specially built crematoria. The large ditch was filled in, the ground levelled, and the ashes used, as before, for fertilizer at the farm labour camp of Harmense, so that today it is almost impossible to find traces of the dreadful mass murder which took place.

At present four crematoria are in operation at Birkenau, two large ones, I and II, and two smaller ones, III and IV. Those of type I and II consist of three parts, i.e.: the furnace room, the large hall, and the gas chamber. A huge chimney rises from the furnace room around which are grouped nine furnaces, each having four openings. Each opening can take three normal corpses at once, after an hour and a half the bodies are completely burned. Thus, the daily capacity is about 2,000 bodies. A large 'reception hall' adjoins, so as to give the impression of the antechamber of a bathing establishment. It holds 2,000 people and apparently there is a similar waiting room on the floor below. From there, a door and a few stairs lead down into the very long and narrow gas-chamber. The walls of this chamber are also camouflaged with simulated entries to shower rooms in order to mislead the victims. The roof is fitted with three traps which can be hermetically closed from the outside. A track leads from the gas-chamber to the furnace room.

The gassing takes place as follows: the unfortunate victims are brought into the reception hall where they are told to undress. To complete the fiction that they are going to bathe, each person receives a towel and a small piece of soap issued by two men in white coats. Then they are crowded into the gas-chamber in such numbers that there is, of course, only standing room. To compress this crowd into the narrow space, shots are often fired to induce those already at the far end to huddle still closer together. When everybody is inside, the heavy doors are closed. Then there is a short pause, presumably to allow the room temperature to rise to a certain level, after which SS men with gas-masks climb on the roof, open the traps, and shake down a preparation in powder from out of tin cans labelled 'Zyklon – For use against vermin', manufactured by a Hamburg concern. It is presumed that this is a cyanide mixture of some sort which turns into gas at a certain temperature. After three minutes everyone in the chamber is dead. No one is known to have survived this ordeal, although it was not uncommon to discover signs of life after the primitive measures employed in Birkenwald. The chamber is then opened, aired, and the Sonderkommando carts the bodies on flat trucks to the furnace rooms where the burning takes place. Crematoria III and IV work on nearly the same principle, but their capacity is only half as large. Thus the total capacity of the four gassing and cremating plants at Birkenau amounts to about 6,000 daily.

On principle only Jews are gassed; Aryans very seldom, as they are usually given *Sonderbehandlung* by shooting. Before the crematoria were put into service, the shooting took place in Birkenwald and the bodies were burned in the long trench; later, however, executions took place in the large hall of one of the crematoria which has been provided with a special installation for this purpose.

Prominent guests from Berlin were present at the inauguration of the first crematorium in March 1943. The 'programme' consisted of the gassing and burning of 8,000 Kraków Jews. The guests, both officers and civilians, were extremely satisfied with the results and the special peephole fitted into the door of the gas-chamber was in constant use. They were lavish in their praise of this newly erected installation.

At the beginning of 1943, the political section of Auschwitz received 500,000 discharge certificates. We thought, with ill-concealed joy, that at least a few of us would be liberated. But the forms were simply filled out with the names of those gassed and filed away in the archives ...

Cautious estimate of the number of Jews gassed in Birkenau between April 1942 and April 1944, by country of origin

Poland (transported by truck)	ca.	300,000
Poland (transported by train)	ca.	600,000
Holland	ca.	100,000
Greece	ca.	45,000
France	ca.	150,000
Belgium	ca.	50,000
Germany	ca.	60,000
Yugoslavia, Italy, and Norway	ca.	50,000
Lithuania	ca.	50,000
Bohemia, Moravia, and Austria	ca.	30,000
Slovakia	ca.	30,000
Various camps for foreign Jews in Poland	ca.	300,000
Total	ca.	1,765,000

Train Journey to Auschwitz, May 1944
ELIE WIESEL

Wiesel was born in 1928 in Sighet, in Transylvania, a territory later transferred to Hungary. Between 14 May and 8 July 1944, 437,402 Hungarian Jews, among them Wiesel and his family, were deported to Auschwitz in forty-eight trains – the largest mass deportation of the Holocaust. Although by 1944 the Reich was being daily pushed back by the Soviets – and the first labour camps liberated – the Nazis did not slacken the pace of their slaughter.

Wiesel himself survived to become a Nobel Prize-winning writer. This is an extract from his memoir, *Night*:

Lying down was out of the question, and we were only able to sit by deciding to take turns. There was very little air. The lucky ones who happened to be near a window could see the blossoming countryside roll by.

After two days of travelling, we began to be tortured by thirst. Then the heat became unbearable.

Free from all social constraint, the young people gave way openly to instinct, taking advantage of the darkness to copulate in our midst, without caring about anyone else, as though they were alone in the world. The rest pretended not to notice anything.

We still had a few provisions left. But we never ate enough to satisfy our hunger. To save was our rule; to save up for tomorrow. Tomorrow might be worse.

The train stopped at Kaschau, a little town on the Czechoslovak frontier. We realized then that we were not going to stay in Hungary. Our eyes were opened, but too late.

The door of the car slid open. A German officer, accompanied by a Hungarian lieutenant-interpreter, came up and introduced himself.

'From this moment, you come under the authority of the German Army. Those of you who still have gold, silver, or watches in your possession must give them up now. Anyone who is later found to have kept anything will be shot on the spot. Secondly, anyone who feels ill may go to the hospital car. That's all.'

The Hungarian lieutenant went among us with a basket and collected the last possessions from those who no longer wished to taste the bitterness of terror.

'There are eighty of you in the wagon,' added the German officer. 'If anyone is missing, you'll all be shot, like dogs ...'

They disappeared. The doors were closed. We were caught in a trap, right up to our necks. The doors were nailed up; the way back was finally cut off. The world was a cattle wagon hermetically sealed.

We had a woman with us named Madame Schächter. She was about fifty; her ten-year-old son was with her, crouched in a corner. Her husband and two eldest sons had been deported with the first transport by mistake. The separation had completely broken her.

I knew her well. A quiet woman with tense, burning eyes, she had often been to our house. Her husband, who was a pious man, spent his days and nights in study, and it was she who worked to support the family.

Madame Schächter had gone out of her mind. On the first day of the journey she had already begun to moan and to keep asking why she had been separated from her family. As time went on, her cries grew hysterical.

On the third night, while we slept, some of us sitting one against the other and some standing, a piercing cry split the silence:

'Fire! I can see a fire! I can see a fire!'

There was a moment's panic. Who was it who had cried out? It was Madame Schächter. Standing in the middle of the wagon, in the pale light from the windows, she looked like a withered tree in a cornfield. She pointed her arm toward the window, screaming:

'Look! Look at it! Fire! A terrible fire! Mercy! *Oh, that fire!*'

Some of the men pressed up against the bars. There was nothing there; only the darkness.

The shock of this terrible awakening stayed with us for a long time. We still trembled from it. With every groan of the wheels on the rail, we felt that an abyss was about to open beneath our bodies. Powerless to still our own anguish, we tried to console ourselves:

'She's mad, poor soul ...'

Someone had put a damp cloth on her brow, to calm her, but still her screams went on:

'Fire! Fire!'

Her little boy was crying, hanging on to her skirt, trying to take hold of her hands. 'It's all right, Mummy! There's nothing there ... Sit down ...' This shook me even more than his mother's screams had done.

Some women tried to calm her. 'You'll find your husband and your sons again ... in a few days ...'

She continued to scream, breathless, her voice broken by sobs. 'Jews, listen to me! I can see a fire! There are huge flames! It is a furnace!'

It was as though she were possessed by an evil spirit which spoke from the depths of her being.

We tried to explain it away, more to calm ourselves and to recover our own breath than to comfort her. 'She must be very thirsty, poor thing! That's why she keeps talking about a fire devouring her.'

But it was in vain. Our terror was about to burst the sides of the train. Our nerves were at breaking point. Our flesh was creeping. It was as though madness were taking possession of us all. We could stand it no longer. Some of the young men forced her to sit down, tied her up, and put a gag in her mouth.

Silence again. The little boy sat down by his mother, crying. I had begun to breathe normally again. We could hear the wheels churning out that monotonous rhythm of a train travelling through the night. We could begin to doze, to rest, to dream …

An hour or two went by like this. Then another scream took our breath away. The woman had broken loose from her bonds and was crying out more loudly than ever:

'Look at the fire! Flames, flames everywhere …'

Once more the young men tied her up and gagged her. They even struck her. People encouraged them:

'Make her be quiet! She's mad! Shut her up! She's not the only one. She can keep her mouth shut …'

They struck her several times on the head – blows that might have killed her. Her little boy clung to her; he did not cry out; he did not say a word. He was not even weeping now.

An endless night. Towards dawn, Madame Schächter calmed down. Crouched in her corner, her bewildered gaze scouring the emptiness, she could no longer see us.

She stayed like that all through the day, dumb, absent, isolated among us. As soon as night fell, she began to scream: 'There's a fire over there!' She would point at a spot in space, always the same one. They were tired of hitting her. The heat, the thirst, the pestilential stench, the suffocating lack of air – these were as nothing compared with these screams which tore us to shreds. A few days more and we should all have started to scream too.

But we had reached a station. Those who were next to the windows told us its name:

'Auschwitz.'

The Jews of Hungary would see, even in the context of the Holocaust, the best and worst of humanity. Thousands were saved by the efforts of Swedish diplomat Raoul Wallenberg and the Swiss Consul, Charles Lutz, who issued passports and put Budapest buildings under diplomatic protection. On the other hand, after the forced resignation of the Regent, Admiral Horthy, Hungary's Jews were left in the hands of Adolf Eichmann and the native fascist groups, the Arrow Cross and the Nyilas. Jews not deported to the extermination camps died in casual acts of terror, or on marches westward to become forced labourers on behalf of the Reich.

Arrival at Auschwitz, 1944
HUGO GRYN

I got out, and that was the point where my whole life was saved. There were these peculiar-looking people in striped uniforms. I made the assumption that they were inhabitants of the local lunatic asylum. They were moving up and down, their job was to clear the trains, but one of them, as he passed me, he's muttering in Yiddish, 'You're eighteen and you've got a trade, you're eighteen and you've got a trade.' And my father says to me, 'If they ask you anything, you're nineteen and you are a *Tischler und Zimmermann* – a joiner and carpenter. Gabriel, my brother, was eleven – extraordinarily lovely, a very, very bright boy; we came to the head of the line, they ask how old I am, I say nineteen.

'*Betreibst Du in Handwerk?*' 'Are you skilled in a trade.?'

'*Ja, Tischler und Zimmermann.*' 'Yes, a joiner and carpenter.'

They don't even ask my brother and he is sent one way with my grandfather and grandmother, and my father and I another, my mother in roughly the same direction. My mother is not going to let my brother go without her, and the last I saw of her was her being pulled back roughly and sent in our direction, although the men and women were separated there.

Later, in the barracks, I asked what happened about family reunions – you know: when are we going to meet the women and the others? How does it work? This man, who had been there some time, said, 'You'll never see them again.'

I said, 'Why not?'

He says, 'Well, by now they're dead.'

'What do you mean, "they're dead"? Look, I'm so scared, don't make bad jokes.' Will you believe it, I didn't believe it, I didn't believe what was happening there for at least twenty-four hours.

The Angel of Death: Dr Mengele on the Ramp at Auschwitz, 1944
ZDENKA EHRLICH

SS physician Dr Josef Mengele supervised the initial selection of new arrivals as they detrained on the ramp at Auschwitz-Birkenau. Those he sent to the left, between 20–30 per cent, had their lives spared, at least for a while. Those sent to the right entered the queue for the gas-chamber.

Zdenka Ehrlich was a young Czech deportee.

When we all jumped out of the wagons we were put into a long, long column and told to march forward. It was not a station, no platforms, just these barracks, the barbed wire, nowhere else to go – it really was the end of the line. On the right were these creatures in rags, and naked women, I thought: What are they doing here? I will never be like them. Then I saw some men on the other side in striped gear. And in between, all you tried to do was avoid the guards, the sticks and the dogs. So you kept inside the column and marched. You were carried like a flood, it must have been for a mile. Then, three men in uniform; the uniforms were spotless, the boots were gleaming like mirrors. I'll never forget the impression of the man in the middle, Dr Mengele, I just glanced at him; he was very good-looking. Not a menacing face at all, rather ... not benevolent, but not menacing. I remember his boots were so shiny, he was absolutely immaculate. He had white gloves on, not exactly like a traffic policeman, but a sign of distinction and importance. He lifted his hand as he looked at everybody who marched past him and just made a very slow gesture, a very light gesture, and said 'right, left, left, left, right, left, right ...'

They put us in a huge room to count – five, five, five. Straight afterwards a woman with a whip chased us into the next room. There were mountains, but *mountains* of rags. Clothing that you had never seen, not even in theatrical wardrobes – Fellini would be pleased to have the imagination to put together the things that we saw. Behind each mountain of these rags was a guard, a woman guard, always with a whip. We had to run in front of it, she grabbed something and threw it at you. The next pile were shoes, men's, women's, everything together. A pair was grabbed and flung at you. So what I finished up with was the most extraordinary outfit you can imagine: I got an olive green ball gown of light material with pearls on it and an irregular hemline – it was like something from a Chekhov or Dostoyevsky play – and a short coat which had probably belonged to a ten-year-old girl, and shoes which saved my life.

Mengele also committed horrific experiments on Auschwitz inmates, including live vivisection. His 'speciality' was operations on twins.

Punishment ... and Kindness, Auschwitz, May 1944
GIULIANA TEDESCHI

Fascist Italy had been largely uninterested in anti-Semitism and not until 1938 did Mussolini, by now under the spell of Hitler, implement the 'Manifesto of Race' and Jews in Italy begin to suffer persecution. Even so, Fascist Italy resisted deportations, leaving Goebbels to complain to his diary:

> *The Italians are extremely lax in the treatment of the Jews. They protect the Italian Jews both in Tunis and in occupied France and will not permit their being drafted for work or compelled to wear the Star of David ... Everywhere, even among our allies, the Jews have friends to help them.*

It was only with the fall of Mussolini and the German takeover of Northern Italy that Italian Jews were rounded up and sent to the camps. Tedeschi, a young Jewish woman from Turin, was deported to Auschwitz-Birkenau in April 1944.

Shoved violently out of the block, I fell to my knees on the bare earth. Thinner than ever, in the white nightshirt that left arms and neck exposed, my curly hair cut short, I looked like an adolescent. Around me was the vastness of the night: I buried myself in it, I took refuge in it. The starry sky was close; it was a friend. So cold and so foreign by day when it was almost always covered by big stormclouds, tonight that Polish sky had something mysterious and familiar about it, something of the sky of my home country far away. With joy I recognized the Great Bear, as if it were an old family friend, then the polestar, Venus with its three stars in line, all the same.

At that hour of the night the camp looked sinister, with its interminable rows of dark silent blocks, the barbed-wire boundary fence lit by powerful lamps all around, and the ghostly white path of the searchlight ruthlessly coming on and off as it hunted down your humiliated individuality in the general misery. Inside the huts, huddled bodies vainly sought some rest after the daily toils, some respite from desperation. Everybody's sleep was disturbed, populated by ghosts; among the frequent cries and groans, the word 'mama' could be heard coming like some distressed plea from the lips of the young sleepers.

In a silence and darkness deprived of the relaxation that night should bring, the stars seemed to belong to a different world, where our infinite misery was unknown. And in the abandon of the sleeping camp you saw that misery more clearly and sharply than during the gigantic struggle for existence that went on in the light of day.

I had violent pains in one wrist and down one side where the *bloccova*'s club had beat me just a few minutes ago to remind me not to break the *Lagerruhe*, the strict silence that must be kept after eight in the evening. There would have been no point in trying to explain that I hadn't slept for three nights, that I was literally suffocating, crammed and crushed between eight other prisoners, that a Belgian was stealing my place, that …

The ground was hard, and clods and pebbles pressed into my flesh. I clutched my arms to my breasts and shivered in that May night, frosty as an Italian night in February. Never before had I had such a strong feeling of being a grain of sand lost in the infinity of the universe. I was seized by dismay and desperation. In front of me the block windows reflected the light of a fire, and the same red flame flickered across a hundred other windows. The whole camp seemed to be on fire. That flame … I tried to find some way not to see it but couldn't. High up, over the chimney of the crematorium, commanding the scene, it had reddened a corner of the sky. It burned night and day.

I heard the confused sounds of people who had got off the train and were heading, unawares, to the doors of the mysterious building. I didn't dare turn around, that glow paralyzed me, and in my state of spiritual prostration an overwhelming desperation took hold of me.

Something appalling had happened before my eyes, something which so far I had sought at all costs to avoid and which tormented me far more than the pain in my wrist and knees. I had been shaken to the core, my human dignity had been violated, violated by an abject being who knew nothing of me or the world. I threw myself face-down on the ground and wept and suffered terribly at the thought that I had a husband and children. I wanted to be alone, to be the only one who need think about my destiny.

From a lookout post came the sound of an accordion accompanied by a grating male voice: the guard *Posten*, who watched over all this misery in the constant presence of that flame, had found a way to pass the time and relieve the boredom of his watch.

Two delicate hands laid a smock on my shoulders, and a voice I didn't know muttered something. I recognized her in the glow from the flame: a Frenchwoman, quite old, who worked in the Schuhkommando, one of those dull creatures, without life or intelligence, who in normal circumstances barely manage to get by, and who in the camps seemed mad and moronic.

I threw my arms around the neck of this companion in punishment, while to console me she whispered: '*Ça va finir, mon petit, ça va finir; bientôt!*'

A Girl is Found Alive in the Gas-chamber, Auschwitz-Birkenau, 1944
MIKLOS NYISZLI

Nyiszli was a Jew and a medical doctor; he was spared the gas-chamber in order that he might help the SS medical staff perform 'scientific' experiments on inmates.

In number one crematorium's gas-chamber 3,000 dead bodies were piled up. The Sonderkommando had already begun to untangle the lattice of flesh ... the chief of the gas-chamber commando almost tore the hinges off the door to my room as he arrived out of breath, his eyes wide with fear or surprise. 'Doctor,' he said, 'come quickly. We just found a girl alive at the bottom of a pile of corpses.'

I grabbed my instrument case, which was always ready, and dashed to the gas-chamber. Against the wall, near the entrance to the immense room, half covered with bodies, I saw a girl in the throes of a death rattle, her body seized with convulsions. The gas commando men around me were in a state of panic. Nothing like this had ever happened in the course of their horrible career.

We moved the still-living body from the corpses pressing against it. I gathered the tiny adolescent body into my arms and carried it back to the room adjoining the gas-chamber ... I laid the body on a bench. A frail young girl, almost a child, she could have been no more than fifteen.

I took out my syringe and, taking her arm – she had not yet recovered consciousness and was breathing with difficulty – I administered three intravenous injections. My companions covered her body, which was as cold as ice, with a heavy overcoat. One ran to the kitchen to fetch some tea and warm broth. Everybody wanted to help as if she were his own child.

The reaction was swift. The child was seized by a fit of coughing which brought up a thick globule of phlegm from her lungs. She opened her eyes and looked fixedly at the ceiling. I kept a close watch for every sign of life. Her breathing became deeper and more and more regular. Her lungs, tortured by the gas, inhaled the fresh air avidly. Her pulse became perceptible, the result of the injections. I waited impatiently. I saw that within a few minutes she was going to regain consciousness: her circulation began to bring colour back into her cheeks, and her delicate face became human again.

I made a sign for my companions to withdraw. I was going to attempt something I knew without saying was doomed to failure ... From our numerous contacts, I had been able to ascertain that Mussfeld had a high esteem for the medical expert's professional qualities ... And this was the man I had to deal with, the man I had to talk into allowing a single life to be spared.

I calmly related the terrible case we found ourselves confronted with. I described for his benefit what pains the child must have suffered in the undressing room, and the horrible scenes that preceded death in the gas-chamber. When the room had been plunged into darkness, she had breathed in a few lungfuls of Zyklon gas. Only a few, though, for her fragile body had given way under the pushing and shoving of the mass as they fought against death. By chances she had fallen with her face against the wet concrete floor. That bit of humidity had kept her from being asphyxiated, for Zyklon gas does not react under humid conditions.

These were my arguments, and I asked him to do something for the child. He listened to me attentively then asked me exactly what I proposed doing. I saw by his expression that I had put him face to face with a practically impossible problem.

'There's no way of getting round it,' he said, 'the child will have to die.' Half an hour later the young girl was led, or rather carried, into the furnace room hallway, and there Mussfeld sent another in his place to do the job. A bullet in the back of the neck.

Mala Zimetbaum, July 1944
RAYA KAGAN

A Belgian Jew of Polish descent, Mala Zimetbaum escaped from Auschwitz with the aid of her boyfriend and fellow inmate, Edward Galinek. After two weeks of freedom, the couple were recaptured. Nonetheless her escape and her bravery at her public execution made her a heroine, among her peers and subsequent generations. Raya Kagan, Auschwitz prisoner, made the following testimony during the trial of Adolf Eichmann in Israel in 1961:

Q. What happened to Mala Zimetbaum?

A. I had known Mala Zimetbaum since the summer of 1942. At that time, she became a *Laeuferin* – a messenger between blocks and a liaison between the Blockführerstube, the Kapo and the prisoners. She was a young girl, of Polish origin, but she had been living in Belgium and arrived with the Belgian transport. She was very decent. She was known throughout the camp, since she helped everybody. And her opportunities and the power, as it were, that she possessed were never wrongfully exploited by her, as was often done by the Kapos. She suffered like everybody else. However, she had better conditions – she was able to take a shower in Birkenau.

And suddenly, in the summer of 1944, I heard – I was sitting in the room of my superior – there was a telephone call – and suddenly, I heard them ringing and alerting all the Kripo and the Stapoleitstelle, all stations of the gendarmerie, and I heard the name of the prisoner,

Mala Zimetbaum. She had escaped. The escape was organized. She fled in the uniform of the SS, of an *Aufseherin* (supervisor). The escape occurred on a Saturday afternoon when there was a reduced camp guard. Another Pole escaped with her. They met beyond the camp, on their way to Slovakia. We hoped – we had great hopes – every morning when we got up, that possibly she would succeed.

It is important to note that Mala had many opportunities – she had access to the documents. And it was said that she had stolen documents from the Blockführerstube relating to the SD, and that she wanted to publish them abroad. I must remark here that her courage was well known, but there was also a legend about Mala, and I am not sure whether it is correct that she managed to steal the documents, but it was said of her that she was capable of doing so. A fortnight later, we learned that they had been captured; they were caught in a very foolish way, right on the border, by customs officials. Apparently, they had lost their way and asked which way to go. There they had to cross mountains, to pass through the Carpathians. That was when they were captured. It seemed strange to the customs officers that a couple ...

Q. At any rate, she was sent back to Auschwitz?

A. She was returned to Auschwitz. This Polish man was interrogated in our block, and not only in our block. Our hut, in which we worked, was close to the small crematorium which was already out of action, but it was a favourite place for our interrogators, mainly for Wilhelm Burger, who had invented his own forms of torture. There was a torture instrument there called a see-saw. That was where he took this Pole. We saw him there, passing by after terrible tortures. He was hanged in the Auschwitz camp. Mala was taken to Birkenau. Interrogations took place once again in Auschwitz, and we saw her.

Q. Did you speak to her?

A. Yes, I asked her how she was.

Q. You went in to her?

A. No. She was in a small hut – that was where people waited to be interrogated.

Q. What did she do?

A. Serenely and heroically, she said, somewhat ironically: 'I am always well.'

Presiding Judge: In what language did she say this?

Witness Kagan: In German.

Q. What did she say?

A. *'Mir geht e simmer wohl'*

Q. What happened to her in the end?

A. Eventually they brought her to Birkenau. They held a major roll-call, and Mandel, the Schutzlagerführerin (leader of the protective camp), Marie Mandel, made a speech and demanded a spectacular and exemplary punishment for her. Mala had succeeded in placing a razor blade in her sleeve and, at the time of the roll-call, she cut open her veins. The SS man went up to her and began mocking and cursing her. Then, with a hand covered in blood, she slapped his cheek and – again, this may be a legend – she said to him: 'I shall die as a heroine, and you will die like a dog.' After that, she was taken, in this very terrible state, to the *Revier*, and in the evening she was put on a cart and taken to the crematorium.

Portrait of a *Muselmann, Auschwitz, 1944*
AHARON BEILIN

'Muselmann' was ironic camp slang for an inmate who was near-dead from starvation and overwork. Beilin was a Jewish doctor incarcerated in Auschwitz-Birkenau.

They began speaking about food. Usually this was a taboo. Two things were taboo – crematoria and food. Food – that was a reflex, a conditioned reflex; because whenever people spoke about food the secretion of digestive acids would increase, and people tried not to speak about food. As soon as a person lost that self-control and began remembering the good food which he used to have at home in the good old times, such a talk was called a '*muselmann* conversation'.

That was the first stage, and we knew that within a day or two, he would enter the second stage. There was not such a rigorous division, but he would stop taking an interest in his surroundings and would also cease reacting to orders, and his motions would become very slow, his face frozen like a mask. He would no longer have control over his bowels. He would relieve himself where he was. He was not even turning over when he lay down.

And thus he entered the '*muselmannship*'. It was a skeleton with bloated legs. And these people, because they wanted to drag them from the blocks to the roll-call, they were placed forcibly next to the wall with their hands above their heads, their face to the wall for support, and it was a skeleton with grey face that would lean against the wall, swaying back and forth. They had no sense of balance. That was the typical *muselmann*, who would be taken afterwards by the 'skeleton' Kommando with the real bodies.

A Day in the Life of a Prisoner, Bergen-Belsen, 13 September 1944
ABEL J. HERZBERG

The Dutch lawyer Herzberg was a so-called 'privileged Jew', one kept alive by the Nazis for possible use as a bargaining counter with the Allies.

13 September, A day in B-B. Yesterday: roll-call 6.15 a.m. Roll-call 9.00 a.m. Roll-call does not tally. Kept standing till 11.00 a.m. Air-raid alert. Roll-call still does not tally. Roll-call adjourned. 12.30 p.m. duty roll-call. 1.30 p.m. Roll-call for all the women. 3.00 p.m. Roll-call. Roll-call does not tally. 5.00 p.m. Roll-call tallies. Air-raid alert. 7.10 p.m. Roll-call. It gets dark. Roll-call does not tally. 9.10 p.m. Roll-call tallies. We stood for hours, hours and hours. The French women are diametrically opposed to Prussian discipline. They never forget their lipstick and speak Yiddish. Their parents fled Poland because of the Russians and the children were deported from Paris by the Germans and wherever they were, they were nationalists. What will happen to the grandchildren? They are remarkable women these Polish-French Jewesses. Returning from work on the fourteenth of July, they marched through the gate singing the *Marseillaise*. The Germans threatened collective punishment if they did it again.

The Great Selection in Auschwitz, October 1944
PRIMO LEVI

Levi was born into a middle-class Jewish family in Italy in 1919. His early life was little troubled by anti-Semitism, and he even joined the Fascist youth movement. This youthful indiscretion behind him, he joined the Giustizia e Libertà partisan movement and, following his capture by the Fascist authorities was sent to Auschwitz, arriving in February 1944. Prisoner No. 174,517 spent eleven months in the camp before its liberation by the Red Army in January 1945, the period described in his famous memoirs *If This is a Man* and *Survival in Auschwitz*.

We fought with all our strength to prevent the arrival of winter. We clung to all the warm hours, at every dusk we tried to keep the sun in the sky for a little longer, but it was all in vain. Yesterday evening the sun went down irrevocably behind a confusion of dirty clouds, chimney stacks and wires, and today it is winter.

We know what it means because we were here last winter; and the others will soon learn. It means that in the course of these months, from October till April, seven out of ten of us will die. Whoever does not die will suffer minute by minute, all day, every day: from the morning before dawn until the distribution of the evening soup we will have to keep our muscles continually tensed, dance from foot to foot, beat our arms under our shoulders against the cold. We will have to spend bread to acquire gloves, and lose hours of sleep to repair them when they become unstitched. As it will no longer be possible to eat in the open, we will have to eat our meals in the hut, on our feet, everyone will be assigned an area of floor as large as a hand, as it is forbidden to rest against the bunks. Wounds will open on everyone's hands, and to be given a bandage will mean waiting every evening for hours on one's feet in the snow and wind.

Just as our hunger is not that feeling of missing a meal, so our way of being cold has need of a new word. We say 'hunger', we say 'tiredness', 'fear', 'pain', we say 'winter' and they are different things. They are free words, created and used by free men who lived in comfort and suffering in their homes. If the Lagers had lasted longer a new, harsh language would have been born; and only this language could express what it means to toil the whole day in the wind, with the temperature below freezing, wearing only a shirt, underpants, cloth jacket and trousers, and in one's body nothing but weakness, hunger and knowledge of the end drawing nearer.

In the same way in which one sees a hope end, winter arrived this morning. We realized it when we left the hut to go and wash: there were no stars, the dark grey of dawn, when we assembled for work, no one spoke. When we saw the first flakes of snow, we thought that if at the same time last year they had told us that we would have seen another winter in the Lager, we would have gone and touched the electric wire-fence; and that even now we would go if we were logical, were it not for this last senseless crazy residue of unavoidable hope.

Because 'winter' means yet another thing.

Last spring the Germans had constructed huge tents in an open space in the Lager. For the whole of the good season each of them had catered for over a thousand men: now the tents had been taken down, and an excess two thousand guests crowded our huts. We old prisoners knew that the Germans did not like these irregularities and that something would soon happen to reduce our number.

One feels the selections arriving. '*Selekcja*': the hybrid Latin and Polish word is heard once, twice, many times, interpolated in foreign conversations; at first we cannot distinguish it, then it forces itself on our attention, and in the end it persecutes us.

This morning the Poles had said '*Selekcja*'. The Poles are the first to find out the news, and they generally try not to let it spread around, because to know something which the others still do not know can always be useful. By the time that everyone realizes that a selection is imminent, the few possibilities of evading it (corrupting some doctor or some prominent with bread or tobacco; leaving the hut for Ka-Be or vice-versa at the right moment so as to cross with the commission) are already their monopoly.

In the days which follow, the atmosphere of the Lager and the yard is filled with '*Selekcja*': nobody knows anything definite, but all speak about it, even the Polish, Italian, French civilian workers whom we secretly see in the yard. Yet the result is hardly a wave of despondency: our collective morale is too inarticulate and flat to be unstable. The fight against hunger, cold and work leaves little margin for thought, even for this thought. Everybody reacts in his own way, but hardly anyone with those attitudes which would seem the most plausible as the most realistic, that is with resignation or despair.

All those able to find a way out, try to take it; but they are the minority because it is very difficult to escape from a selection. The Germans apply themselves to these things with great skill and diligence.

Whoever is unable to prepare for it materially, seeks defence elsewhere. In the latrines, in the washroom, we show each other our chests, our buttocks, our thighs, and our comrades reassure us: 'You are all right, it will certainly not be your turn this time ... *du bist kein* Muselmann ... more probably mine ...' and they undo their braces in turn and pull up their shirts.

Nobody refuses this charity to another: nobody is so sure of his own lot [as] to be able to condemn others. I brazenly lied to old Wertheimer; I told him that if they questioned him, he should reply that he was forty-five, and he should not forget to have a shave the evening before, even if it cost him a quarter-ration of bread; apart from that he need have no fears, and in any case it was by no means certain that it was a selection for the gas-chamber; had he not heard the *Blockältester* say that those chosen would go to Jaworszno, to a convalescent camp?

It is absurd of Wertheimer to hope: he looks sixty, he has enormous varicose veins, he hardly even notices the hunger any more. But he lies down on his bed, serene and quiet, and replies to someone who asks with my own words; they are the command-words in the camp these days: I myself repeated them just as – apart from details – Chajim told them to me, Chajim, who has been in the Lager for three years, and being strong and robust is wonderfully sure of himself; and I believed them.

On this slender basis I also lived through the great selection of October 1944 with inconceivable tranquillity. I was tranquil because I managed to lie to myself sufficiently. The fact that I was not selected depended above all on chance and does not prove that my faith was well-founded.

Monsieur Pinkert is also, *a priori*, condemned: it is enough to look at his eyes. He calls me over with a sign, and with a confidential air tells me that he has been informed – he cannot tell me the source of information – that this time there is really something new: the Holy See, by means of the International Red Cross ... in short, he personally guarantees both for himself and for me, in the most absolute manner, that every danger is ruled out; as a civilian he was, as is well known, attaché to the Belgian Embassy at Warsaw.

Thus in various ways, even those days of vigil, which in the telling seem as if they ought to have passed every limit of human torment, went by not very differently from other days.

The discipline in both the Lager and Buna is in no way relaxed: the work, cold and hunger are sufficient to fill up every thinking moment.

Today is working Sunday, *Arbeitssonntag*: we work until 1 p.m., then we return to camp for the shower, shave and general control for skin diseases and lice. And in the yards, everyone knew mysteriously that the selection would be today.

The news arrived, as always surrounded by a halo of contradictory or suspect details: the selection in the infirmary took place this morning; the percentage was 7 per cent of the whole camp, 30, 50 per cent of the patients. At Birkenau, the crematorium chimney has been smoking for ten days. Room has to be made for an enormous convoy arriving from the Poznań ghetto. The young tell the young that all the old ones will be chosen. The healthy tell the healthy that only the ill will be chosen. Specialists will be excluded. German Jews will be excluded. Low Numbers will be excluded. You will be chosen. I will be excluded.

At 1 p.m. exactly the yard empties in orderly fashion and for two hours the grey unending army files past the two control stations where, as on every day, we are counted and recounted, and past the military band which for two hours without interruptions plays, as on every day, those marches to which we must synchronize our steps at our entrance and our exit.

It seems like every day, the kitchen chimney smokes as usual, the distribution of the soup is already beginning. But then the bell is heard, and at the moment we realize that we have arrived.

Because this bell always sounds at dawn, when it means the reveille; but if it sounds during the day, it means *Blocksperre*, enclosure in huts, and this happens when there is a selection to prevent anyone avoiding it, or when those selected for the gas, to prevent anyone seeing them leave.

Our *Blockältester* knows his business. He has made sure that we have all entered, he has the door locked, he has given everyone his card with his number, name, profession, age and nationality and he has ordered everyone to undress completely, except for shoes. We wait like this, naked, with the card in our hands, for the commission to reach our hut. We are hut 48, but one can never tell if they are going to begin at hut 1 or hut 60. At any rate, we can rest quietly at least for an hour, and there is no reason why we should not get under the blankets on the bunk and keep warm.

Many are already drowsing when a barrage of orders, oaths and blows proclaims the imminent arrival of the commission. The *Blockältester* and his helpers, starting at the end of the dormitory, drive the crowd of frightened, naked people in front of them and cram them in the *Tagesraum* which is the Quartermaster's office. The *Tagesraum* is a room seven yards by four: when the drive is over, a warm and compact human mass is jammed into the *Tagesraum*, perfectly filling all the corners, exercising such a pressure on the wooden walls as to make them creak.

Now we are all in the *Tagesraum*, and besides there being no time, there is not even any room in which to be afraid. The feeling of the warm flesh pressing all around is unusual and not unpleasant. One has to take care to hold one's nose so as to breathe, and not to crumple or lose the card in one's hand.

The *Blockältester* has closed the connecting door and has opened the other two which lead from the dormitory and the *Tagesraum* outside. Here, in front of the two doors, stands the arbiter of our fate, an SS subaltern. On his right is the *Blockältester*, on his left, the quartermaster of the hut. Each one of us, as he comes naked out of the *Tagesraum* into the cold October air, has to run the few steps between the two doors, give the card to the SS man and enter the dormitory door. The important thing for the Lager is not that the most useless prisoners be eliminated, but that free posts be quickly created, according to a certain percentage previously fixed.

The selection is now over in our hut, but it continues in the others, so that we are still locked in. But as the soup-pots have arrived in the meantime, the *Blockältester* decides to proceed with the distribution at once. A double ration will be given to those selected. I have never discovered if this was a ridiculously charitable initiative of the *Blockältester*, or an explicit disposition of the SS, but in fact, in the interval of two or three days (sometimes even much longer) between the selection and the departure, the victims at Monowitz-Auschwitz enjoyed this privilege.

Ziegler holds out his bowl, collects his normal ration and then waits there expectantly. 'What do you want?' ask the *Blockältester*: according to him, Ziegler is entitled to no supplement, and he drives him away, but Ziegler returns and humbly persists. He was on the left, everybody saw it, let the *Blockältester* check the cards; he has the right to a double ration. When he is given it, he goes quietly to his bunk to eat.

Now everyone is busy scraping the bottom of his bowl with his spoon so as not to waste the last drops of the soup; a confused, metallic clatter, signifying the end of the day. Silence slowly prevails and then, from my bunk on the top row, I see and hear old Kuhn praying aloud, with his beret on his head, swaying backward and forward violently. Kuhn is thanking God because he has not been chosen.

Kuhn is out of his senses. Does he not see Beppo the Greek in the bunk next to him, Beppo who is twenty years old and is going to the gas-chamber the day after tomorrow and knows it and lies there looking fixedly at the light without saying anything and without even thinking any more? Can Kuhn fail to realize that next time it will be his turn? Does Kuhn not understand that what has happened today is an abomination, which no propitiatory prayer, no pardon, no expiation by the guilty, which nothing at all in the power of man can ever clean again?

If I were God, I would spit at Kuhn's prayer.

The exact number of Jews who died at Auschwitz is unknown, but the figure is generally thought to be between 1.1 and 1.5 million. The last gassings took place in November 1944, by which time the SS were blowing up the camp in an attempt to destroy the evidence of what had occurred there.

'Deaths, deaths, deaths': A Day in the Life of a Prisoner, Bergen-Belsen, 13 January 1945
ABEL J. HERZBERG

13 January 1945 Yesterday marked our first year here. It has been a terrible year, far from home, from the children, without news from them, a year of disappointment. The transport to Palestine, the peace that did not come, a year of hunger, cold, hounding, persecution and humiliation. Fortunately, though, apart from a few bouts of dysentery, we have not been seriously ill.

The food is getting worse and worse. At midday, swede soup, every day without a single potato. The 'extra' food is distributed centrally now. Every day there are genuine punch-ups over a ticket. Some are given to the *Dienstbereiche* and some to the doctor for the weak and the sick. Recriminations about favouritism, at every attempt, of course, to be as fair as possible.

The extra food is distributed outdoors by a Kapo, accompanied by the inevitable blows with the ladle in every direction.

The Kapo system has existed for three weeks now. Its characteristics are: hounding with truncheons and sticks when there is work to be done.

Postcards dated early November have reached us from Amsterdam. Everything I had feared seems true. No gas, no electricity, two hundred grams of bread a day. Hunger and shortage. I fear it may be as bad as here. The game is lasting too long. Probably in Holland there will also be large numbers of deaths.

Here it is increasing all the while. Today J. H. Yesterday O. S., Dr C., dentist F., et cetera, et cetera, et cetera. Young B., nineteen years old, Ant. B., who therefore also did not help with preventing the hiring out of a camp blanket.

There is no news. No parcels either. We have reached the bottom, and are therefore facing the worst hunger again.

T. is bearing up extremely well. She keeps herself going and is full of courage. It is mostly men who die. If it carries on like this it will be a matter of a few months – then no one will be left.

People look pitiful. Literally living corpses. They are dropping with tiredness and wretchedness.

The Stubbenkommando is dreadful [work]. Although they get extra rations, they also get extra beatings. Yesterday afternoon, another court case. A large quantity of semolina had been stolen, a bag containing ten to fifteen kilos that one of the Hungarians was keeping for a group of Hungarians. The accused were a Greek woman and her brother, who confessed. The woman we sentenced to five days' bunker and the man to eight (three days on bread and water), and assignment to the Stubbenkommando. The Commandant changed this to: one month's assignment to the Stubbenkommando, *without any extra allocation*. If, after one month, he has behaved himself, the bunker sentence will be quashed.

This is all but the death penalty. At this time of the year Stubbenkommando without extra food is impossible. *Stubben* are tree stumps that must be dug up and dispatched.

The court sittings have become onerous. The Kapos enter with their truncheons and sticks and stay to observe. One can imagine what remains of the independence of the bench and the rights of the accused. It is all unimaginably bad. Oh Holland, oh poor humanity! From time to time there is no bread at all here – from time to time (tonight, for example) we are not allowed to use the toilet. Those who have diarrhoea must go outdoors. We have procured some buckets for ourselves, discarded jam buckets.

This morning, my neighbour had to resort to them.

This morning his bunkmate discovered to his horror that his shoes were full. The other had soiled himself twice during the night.

We are living amid the lice. For months I have not been able to change into clean underwear, nor had a shower. Naturally there is also no heating here, we suffer terribly from the cold in the huts, which are draughty and where the door is never shut.

Deaths, deaths, deaths.

For how long?

Apparently, Westerbork was still in existence at the beginning of November. The persecution of the Jews continues. Nevertheless we are a year nearer to peace than on 13 January 1944.

The Death March from Auschwitz, January 1945
JOHN FINK

In the autumn and winter of 1944–5 the SS did more than destroy the evidence of their extermination camps; they removed the inmates by forced marches westwards to labour camps and factories. It was a last cruelty visited on Europe's Jews. With little food or clothing, tens of thousands perished, or were shot by SS guards.

When we were marched out of Auschwitz-Birkenau on 18 January 1945, we didn't know where we were going. The only ones left behind were the sick prisoners, about 8–9,000 of them, including Primo Levi; we thought they would all get killed because we couldn't imagine that they would let anybody live.

So we marched. Well, the weather was terrible and anybody who dropped back was shot in the back by the SS; so many. They were just left lying there, and there were already dead people lying there who had marched before us. These were the people who really couldn't do it because most people didn't even have shoes; they only had those wooden clogs and you couldn't march in those in that terrible frost and snow. I had a pair of shoes, but the right and left weren't the same. When you could keep your feet in order you had a chance of life; so many died because of their feet, many got water in their knees and the pus would come out of their bodies.

Anyway, we marched during the night and in the morning they put us in an empty tyre factory. We rested there for a while, then we were ordered to march again. In the afternoon we must have reached the former German border. We marched through the streets of Gleiwitz, there were trams running and civilians about. The SS weren't around us there and we were so desperate for food that we asked people where there was a concentration camp – can you imagine the mentality! We stayed two days in an overcrowded camp; no order there, nothing.

After a day or two we were ordered to the railway yards. We were put on an open train: every carriage was filled with prisoners, you couldn't sit down. We went on through the days and nights, the train would stop every so often because of the bombings. People died. We would just throw the dead out of the cattle trucks to make room to finally sit down. We came through Czechoslovakia and at the railway stations we would have to take the sick out and leave them on the platforms where the Gestapo would kill them in front of the civilians of those towns in Czechoslovakia and Austria. Then they took us to Mauthausen. By then the camp was so overcrowded that its *Kommandant* refused our unloading, so the train went on and on.

Suddenly we came to Berlin. I knew Berlin, I saw the famous radio tower – that was 28 January 1945. We were unloaded in the big, old concentration camp of Sachsenhausen. Then back on the train again to Flossenburg, another overcrowded camp. Since the Americans were coming from one side, the Russians from another, and the British from up north, the noose was tightened. But they never got rid of the prisoners for some reason, except those who got killed or died on the way. Then I was loaded on another train and now we were sitting on the dead. We weren't human any more, we weren't supposed to *be* human anyway; that's how I came to Belsen around 8 March 1945.

The Death March from Auschwitz II, January 1945
GIULIANA TEDESCHI

Tedeschi ended up at Leipzig via Ravensbrück, with some of the journey undertaken in overcrowded cattle trucks, not a jot different from those that had taken her to Auschwitz originally.

The column is getting longer; there are other women marching behind the Auschwitz group. The Birkenau women, 13–14,000 of us on the road in all.

Will those we left behind be among them? Natalia, Dina, Ruth, and all the others? No, many women were sent by train to other work camps in Germany months ago. Then Dina and Ruth ... we must consider them lost; they have watched the others leave – everybody who could stand on their feet, that is – with indifferent, almost extinguished eyes. Now they are lying on their mattresses amid the empty bunks in the disorder of the hospital block that still shows all the signs of flight and evacuation. They expect nothing.

The women have been marching since dawn. They have to stay in line to one side of the road; to the left, at regular intervals, are the *Posten* with their rifles slung across their backs, and a few *Aufseherin*; there are some women from the *Polizei* too with revolvers in their belts. Some have already overtaken the column on a wobbly cart, apparently looking to escape amid the general flight.

We have done twenty miles and the sun is nearly down. The landscape remains stubbornly the same – a flat plain stretching endlessly away under the opaque whiteness of sky and snow, deadening the already exhausted senses. The Germans accelerate their pace, not allowing us any more stops. Perhaps there is some goal to reach? How many miles away, when? Or perhaps this march is to be infinite, without a break, without a goal? By now our legs move only from the force of momentum. The road is littered with blankets, since many women, exhausted by the effort, have decided to abandon them. You're unable to lift your eyes to the sky; they remain stubbornly fixed on the ground, fascinated by the movement of the legs in the row before you, all advancing with the same rhythm – feet in clogs, feet wrapped in rags and strips of blankets, feet poking wretchedly out of torn shoes.

Earlier on, in the sunshine, everybody had tried to keep their eyes on the progress of their friends. Some had pressed ahead to the front of the column, others had lost ground, and Violette, her nose even purpler than usual, eyes swollen with tears, could scarcely move her swollen legs.

I said something to her as she walked alongside me; when I looked for her a few moments later, she was gone. The road had swallowed her up. In the morning five pairs of hands would reach out to help anybody who slipped on the ice; in the evening those who slipped lay where they fell. No one had the strength to do anything but push their legs forward, and even this was automatic, not willed. You stepped slightly to one side so as not to trample on the body you found beneath your feet, and you went on without looking.

The moon came up, the landscape became ghostly. The wind howled in the dense pine woods; it slashed your face, cut through your thin clothes and into your bones.

Came the echo of the first rifle shots fading away in the silent trees. We stopped, hesitant, listening, then, as if spurred on, dragged ourselves forward.

'Olga … Vicky … Giuliana …' Every so often we would call to each other in the dark, check that everybody was there; God help us if the bond of resistance that united us were to snap!

By now Violette, the mother of a small French girl, and others likewise who hadn't been able to keep the pace, were lying on their backs on the ground, black shapes in the whiteness, a small stream of blood trickling away in the snow.

Liberation: A Jewess Meets a GI, April 1945
GERDA WEISSMANN KLEIN

Gerda Weissmann Klein was transported from the Bielsko Ghetto to the labour camp at Gross-Rosen in June 1942. She was liberated after the death march.

All of a sudden I saw a strange car coming down the hill, no longer green, not bearing the swastika, but a white star. It was a sort of mud-splattered vehicle but I've never seen a brighter star in my life. And two men sort of jumped out, came running towards us, and one came towards where I stood. He was wearing battle gear ... he was wearing dark glasses and he spoke to me in German. And he said, 'Does anybody here speak German or English?' And I said, 'I speak German.' And I felt I had to tell him we are Jewish, and I didn't know if he would know what the star means or anything ... and I looked at him. I was a little afraid to tell him that but I said to him, 'We're Jewish, you know.' He didn't answer me for quite a while. And then his own voice sort of betrayed his own emotion and he said, 'So am I.' I would say it was the greatest hour of my life. And then he asked an incredible question. He said, 'May I see the other ladies?' ... what we had been addressed as for six years and then to hear this man [call us that]. He looked to me like a young god ... I weighed sixty-eight pounds. My hair was white ... I hadn't had a bath in years. And this creature asked for 'the other ladies'. And I told him that most of the other girls were inside ... They were too ill to walk, and he said, 'Won't you come with me?' And I said, 'Sure.' ... He held the door open for me to precede him and in that gesture restored me to humanity. And that young American today is my husband.

The Liberation of Buchenwald:
The Prisoner's View, 5–10 April 1945
ELIE WIESEL

Liberation was not necessarily salvation. The richness of the food offered by Allied troops – tinned meat, dried milk, oats, chocolate – caused many inmates to die.

On 5 April, the wheel of history turned.

It was late in the afternoon. We were standing in the block, waiting for an SS man to come and count us. He was late in coming. Such a delay was unknown till then in the history of Buchenwald. Something must have happened.

Two hours later the loudspeakers sent out an order from the head of the camp: all the Jews must come to the assembly place.

This was the end! Hitler was going to keep his promise.

The children in our block went towards the place. There was nothing else we could do. Gustav, the head of the block, made this clear to us with his truncheon. But on the way we met some prisoners who whispered to us:

'Go back to your block. The Germans are going to shoot you. Go back to your block, and don't move.'

We went back to our block. We learned on the way that the camp resistance organization had decided not to abandon the Jews and was going to prevent their being liquidated.

As it was late and there was great upheaval – innumerable Jews had passed themselves off as non-Jews – the head of the camp decided that a general roll-call would take place the following day. Everybody would have to be present.

The roll-call took place. The head of the camp announced that Buchenwald was to be liquidated. Then blocks of deportees would be evacuated each day. From this moment, there would be no further distribution of bread and soup. And the evacuation began. Every day, several thousand prisoners went through the camp gate and never came back.

On 10 April, there were still about twenty thousand of us in the camp, including several hundred children. They decided to evacuate us all at once, right on until the evening. Afterwards, they were going to blow up the camp.

So we were massed in the huge assembly square, in rows of five, waiting to see the gate open. Suddenly, the sirens began to wail. An alert! We went back to the blocks. It was too late to evacuate us that evening. The evacuation was postponed again to the following day.

We were tormented with hunger. We had eaten nothing for six days, except a bit of grass or some potato peelings round near the kitchens.

At ten o'clock in the morning the SS scattered through the camp, moving the last victims towards the assembly place.

Then the resistance movement decided to act. Armed men suddenly rose up everywhere. Bursts of firing. Grenades exploding. We children stayed flat on the ground in the block.

The battle did not last long. Towards noon everything was quiet again. The SS had fled and the resistance had taken charge of the running of the camp.

At about six o'clock in the evening, the first American tank stood at the gates of Buchenwald.

Our first act as free men was to throw ourselves on to the provisions. We thought only of that. Not of revenge, not of our families. Nothing but bread.

And even when we were no longer hungry, there was still no one who thought of revenge. On the following day, some of the young men went to Weimar to get some potatoes and clothes – and to sleep with girls. But of revenge, not a sign.

Three days after the liberation of Buchenwald I became very ill with food poisoning. I was transferred to the hospital and spent two weeks between life and death.

One day I was able to get up, after gathering all my strength. I wanted to see myself in the mirror hanging on the opposite wall. I had not seen myself since the ghetto.

From the depths of the mirror, a corpse gazed back at me.

The look in his eyes, as they stared into mine, has never left me.

A BBC Reporter Visits Belsen, 20 April 1945
P. GORDON WALKER

From Gordon Walker's private diary:

Friday 20 April 1945
Got to Belsen. It was a vast area surrounded by barbed wire. The whole thing was being guarded by armed Hungarian guards. They had been in the German Army and are now, immediately and without hesitation, serving us. They are saving us a large number of men for the time being. Outside the camp which is amidst bushes, pines and

heath – all fairly recently planted – were great notices in red letters: 'DANGER TYPHUS'. We drove into what turned out to be a great training camp – a sort of Aldershot. Fine two-storey buildings – brick – with asphalt road – Adolf Hitler Strasse, Rommel Strasse, Fredericus Rex Strasse, etc. A fine officers' house at the end to which we drove and where we found officers of the Oxfordshire yeomanry. Colonel Taylor in command was a pupil (a very idle one) of mine at Oxford. They made princie and made me welcome and we had a drink with them.

They began to tell us about the concentration camp. It lies south of the training area: it is behind its own barbed wire. The Wehrmacht was not allowed near it. It was guarded entirely by SS men and women.

This is what I discovered about the relief of the camp – which happened on the 15th. I got this story from Derek Sington, from officers and men of the Oxfordshire Yeomanry.

Typhus broke out in the camp and a truce was arranged so that we could take the camp over. The Germans originally proposed that we should by-pass the camp. In the meanwhile thousands and thousands of people would have died and been shot. We refused these terms and demanded the withdrawal of the Germans and the disarmament of the SS guards.

Some dozen SS men and women were left behind under the command of Hauptsturmführer Kramer – who had been at Auschwitz. Apparently they had been told all sorts of fairy-tales about the truce – that they could go on guarding – that we would let them free, etc. In fact all that had been agreed was that the camp should for a few days be a neutral zone so that we could take over and prevent the inmates breaking out and spreading typhus.

Sington (who has done a magnificent job of work) arrived with a few trucks – and was met by Kramer who showed them round the camp. There were volleys of cheers all the way – people broke out of the compounds to greet the British spearhead.

Kramer seemed to expect us to accept his attitude as quite normal. He did not expect us to be shocked by the things we saw. He had been the man who stood by the ovens at Auschwitz and picked out those to be burned at once. He described the inmates of the camp as asocial – anti-social, useless people. He clearly regarded them as cattle. As we drove in the SS opened fire from their towers on people who broke out of a compound to get at a potato field. This was stopped quickly.

We only had a handful of men so far and the SS stayed there that night. The first night of liberty, many hundreds of people died of joy.

Next day some men of the Oxfordshire Yeomanry arrived. People crowded round them kissing their hands and feet and dying from weakness. Corpses in every stage of decay were lying around, piled up on top of each other in heaps. There were corpses in the compounds, in the blocks. People were falling dead all around – people who were walking skeletons. One woman came up to the soldier who was guarding the milk-store and doling milk out to children and begged for milk for her baby. The man took the baby and saw it had been dead for days – black in the face and shrivelled up. The mother went on begging for milk – so he poured some into its dead lips. The mother then gibbered and crooned with joy – and carried the baby off in triumph. She stumbled and fell dead in a few yards. I have this story and some others on records spoken by the men who saw them. On the 16th Kramer and the SS were arrested and were very heavily beaten up by our men with boots and rifle-butts. Kramer was taken off and kept in the ice box (with some stinking fish) of the officers' home. He has now gone back to rear. The rest, men and women, were kept under guard (to save them from the inmates). The men were set to work shovelling up the corpses into lorries. Thirty-five thousand reckoned, more actually than the living – about 30,000.

The SS men were driven and pushed along and made to ride on top of the loaded corpses and then shovel them into the great mass open graves. They were so tired and beaten up that they fell exhausted amongst the corpses. Jeering crowds collected around them and they had to be kept under strong guard. Two men committed suicide in their cells. Two jumped off the lorries and tried to run away and get lost in the crowds. They were shot down. One jumped into a concrete pool of water and was riddled with bullets. The other was brought to the ground with a shot in the belly and was then finished off with a sten-gun.

The SS women are made to cook and carry heavy loads. One of them tried to commit suicide. The inmates say that they were more cruel and brutal than the men. They are all young – in their twenties. One SS woman tried to hide, disguised as a prisoner. She was denounced and arrested.

The camp was so full because people had been brought here from East and West. Some people were brought from Nordhausen – 5 days' journey without food. Many had marched for two to three days. There was no food at all in the camp. A few piles of mangoldwurzols [sic] amidst the piles of dead bodies. Some of the dead bodies were of people so hungry that, though the mangoldwurzels were guarded by SS men, they had tried to storm them and been shot down then and there. There was no water. Nothing but these wurzols [sic] and some boiled stinking carrots – enough for a few hundred people. Men and women had fought for raw mangoldwurzols. Dead bodies – black and blue and bloated – and skeletons had been used as pillows by sick people.

The day after we tood [sic] over seven *Blockleiters*, mostly Poles, were murdered by the inmates. Some were still beating the people. We arrested one woman who had beaten another with a board. She admitted quite frankly to the offence. We are arresting these people.

An enormous buried dump of personal jewellery and belongings was discovered – in suitcases.

When I went into the camp five days after its liberation there were still bodies all around. I saw about a thousand. In one place hundreds had been shovelled into a mass grave by bulldozers. In another Hungarian soldiers were putting corpses into a grave that was sixty feet by sixty and thirty feet deep. It was almost half-full. Other and similar pits were being dug. Five thousand people had died since we got into the camp. People died before my eyes – scarcely human moaning skeletons, many of them gone mad. Bodies were just piled up – higgledy-piggledy in piles. Many had gashed wounds and bullet marks and terrible sores. One Englishman (who had lived in Ostend) was picked up half-dead. It was found that he had a great bullet wound in his back. He could just speak. He had no idea when he had been shot. He must have been lying half-conscious when some SS men shot him as he was crawling about. This was quite normal.

I walked all round the camp. Everywhere the smell and odour of death. After a few hours you get used to it and don't notice it any more. People have typhus and dysentry. In one compound I went into I saw women standing up quite naked washing themselves: nearby were piles of corpses. Other women, suffering from dysentry, were defecating in the open and then staggering back, half-dead, to their blocks. Some were lying groaning on the ground. Life has reverted to the absolute primitive.

A great job has been done in getting water into the camp. It has been pumped in from outside and carried by hoses all over the camp

– with frequent outlet points. There are taps of fresh clean water everywhere. Carts with water move around. The RASC has also done a great job in getting food in.

I went into the typhus ward – packed thick with people lying in dirty rags and blankets on the floor, groaning and moaning. By the door sat an English Tommy, talking to the people and cheering them up – though they couldn't understand what he said – and ladling milk out of a cauldron.

I collected together some women who could speak English and German – and began to make records. An amazing thing is the number who have managed to keep themselves clean and neat. All of them said that in a day or two more they would have gone under from hunger and weakness. There are three main classes in the camp. The healthy who have managed to keep themselves decent – nearly all have had typhus. Then there are the sick. Who are more or less cared for by their friends. Then there is the vast underworld that has lost all self-respect, crawling around in rags, living in abominable squalor, defecating in the compounds, often mad or half-mad. By the other prisoners they are called the *Muselmann*. It is those who are still dying like flies. They can hardly walk on their legs. Thousands still of these cannot be saved – and, if they were, would be useless lunatic invalids for the short remainder of their pitiful lives.

There are a very large number of girls in the camp – mostly Jewesses from Auschwitz. They have to be healthy to have survived. Over and over again I was told the same story. The parades at which people were picked out arbitrarily for the gas-chambers and the crematoriums, where many were burned alive. Only a person in perfect health survived. Life and death was a question of pure chance. I talked to two pretty sisters – Anita and Renate LASKER, nieces of Lasker the chess-player. Renate had nearly died of typhus at Auschwitz. The inspection was made. Everyone was told to stand up – those who could not were written down on the death list. Renate could not stand. Her name was written down. She said, 'I'm the sister of one of the girls who plays in the Orchestra.' 'Oh, that's all right then.' And her name was crossed off. Otherwise she would have been dead in an hour. Only those who played in the Orchestra or did some similar work had some chance to survive.

At Auschwitz the band was made to play at the station as the new batches of inmates arrived and during the parades when those to be gassed and burned were picked out. At Auschwitz there was a horrible luxury. Rich Jews arrived with their belongings and were able to keep some. There was soap and perfume and fountain pens and watches. All amidst the chance of sudden arbitrary death; amidst work-commandos from which the people returned so dead beat that, if they lived, they were sure to be picked for the gas-chamber at the next parade. All amidst the most horrible death, filth and squalor that could be imagined. People at Auschwitz were saved by being moved away to do work in towns like Hamburg and were then moved back to Belsen as we advanced.

At Auschwitz every woman had her hair shaved absolutely bald – many twice. I met pretty young girls whose hair was one inch long. They all had their numbers tattooed on their left arm. A mark of honour they will wear all their lives.

One of the most extraordinary things was the women and men (there are only a few) who have kept themselves decent and clean. On the fifth day many had on powder and lipstick. The SS stores had been looted – and boots and clothes had been found.

Hundreds of people came up to me with letters which I have taken and am sending back to London to be posted all over the world. Many have lost all their relatives. 'My father and mother were burned.' 'My sister was burned.' This is what you hear all the time. The British Army is doing what it can. Units are voluntarily giving up blankets – 50,000 arrived while I was there and are being laundered. Sweets, chocolate and cigarette rations are being voluntarily given. While I was there a long convoy of 240,000 hard rations arrived from Military Government – four days' reserve of biscuit, chocolate, tinned meats, etc.

This first day I recorded the Lasker sisters. They both helped French soldiers over the frontier. I also recorded Charlotte GRUND, a Berlin woman and a Dutchman.

I met the Jewish Padre with the 2nd Army and we recorded the first eve of the Sabbath service held in the camp.

That evening I went back to the camp with Derek Sington, the political officer. He took me to the women's block at the end of the camp. We talked for a while to a group of Polish women. They wanted to know about Yalta and the Lublin Committee. They all want to go to Palestine.

We then talked with a pretty Frenchwoman of twenty-four. She had been beaten by the Gestapo and had spent several years in concentration camps. She had done resistance work. We talked in the open compound. In the middle was a pile of old papers and skeletons. Around us were bodies of people who had died in the last three days. There were groaning and raving women lying around. And every few minutes, some women groaning with typhus would stagger out and defecate there in the open. Where the Frenchwoman slept there were ten healthy people and fifty sick and dying. She told us how she had seen corpses dragged off, under German command, by the still-living – on ropes along the ground. Their heads were open where people had cut out the brains to eat. There had been cannibalism in the camp. The flesh, brains and livers of people who had died of typhus were eaten.

I gave this woman the good Luftwaffe watch I had been given at Brunswick.

The female SS officer who tried to escape in civilian dress was the infamous Irma Grese.

The Arrest of Irma Grese, Bergen-Belsen, 20 April 1945
CHARLES SALT, BRITISH MILITARY POLICE

Irma Grese, an SS officer, came from Auschwitz with Kramer, the Camp *Kommandant* and somehow, when Kramer was taken, she escaped the net.

One day, I was in the information post when a woman inmate came in and said, 'There's an SS officer going out of the camp wearing civilian clothes.'

I said, 'What's she done?'

'She used to make the selections at Auschwitz and would beat up people.'

I said, 'Did you see her do this? I need witnesses otherwise it won't stand up in a court of law.'

She got down on her knees and said, 'I beg you as one Jew to another.'

So I told a chap standing there to take a jeep with an armed escort and bring her in.

He said, 'There's no point. If you bring her in and you've no witnesses, she goes scot-free and can't be charged again.'

But I insisted, thinking there must be *someone* there who saw her do these things. They brought her in: smartly dressed, very young. She showed me her pass which the British Camp Commandant had given her to travel to Celle, and her SS pass. I told the woman to go and find witnesses, that we could only hold her for forty-eight hours. First day went past, nothing happened; second day, nothing.

I said to the Sergeant, 'We'll hold her for another day. If no one comes for her by 4.30pm, that's it.'

I was going off duty at 5 p.m. that day. By then she had been let out of the bunker; because no one had come forward she was betting on a safe wicket and had stayed behind talking with some of the fellows and having tea. She felt they had no witnesses against her.

About 4.55 p.m. two sisters who spoke good English came in to discuss something with me, and I took them upstairs to the dining room to have some tea. The only empty place to sit was near where Irma Grese was sitting. So I indicated to go over there but one of them said, 'No, we don't want to sit there.'

I said, 'Look, I can't offer you the services of the Hotel Adlon!'

She said, 'But you don't expect us to sit next to an SS officer, do you?'

I explained that I knew about her, but we had no witnesses, and one of them said, 'Well *I* saw her do it. I used to play in the Orchestra in Auschwitz and saw what she did.'

In the twilight hours of the Reich, the SS, the Gestapo and other Nazis continued to kill Jews. At Stutthof on 25 April 1945, 200 Jewish women were shot. Probably the last atrocity came on 2 May when 500 Jews were shot at Lübeck. They joined the 5,999,500 other Jews murdered by the Nazis. Six days later the 'Thousand Year Reich' surrendered.

ENVOI:
The Nuremberg Trials

Sentence Day in the Great Trial at Nuremberg, 1 October 1946
MAURICE FAGENCE

The leaders of Nazi Germany who were tried by the International Military Tribunal at Nuremberg were accused of four different classes of crime:

i)   crimes against humanity, that is persecution, enslavement or extermination on religious or political grounds;
ii)   conspiring or having a common plan to commit crimes against peace;
iii) committing specific crimes against peace by planning or initiating wars of aggression;
iv)   crimes against the laws and customs of war.

Maurice Fagence was a reporter for the British newspaper, the *Daily Herald*.

NUREMBERG, Tuesday

When Goering [Göring] came into court to hear the sentence – he was first – he play-acted in the most terrible few minutes of his life.

Maybe he meant to show the judges how superhumanly uninterested he was in anything they did to him.

Whatever the reason, this is the scene as we saw it. The judges had been the last people to take their seats in the packed court. Before a sliding walnut panel that serves as a door to the dock a teashop-size table had been placed. On it was a pair of earphones plugged to the wall near the floor.

Every guard in court, we noticed, including the two in the dock, appeared without a revolver for the first time.

Even Colonel Andrus, Court Marshal, had discarded his. The astonishing security proceedings had reached the point at which no risk was being taken of a condemned man seizing a gun from a soldier's holster.

I thought the court was without a gun till I saw one young officer with his hand firmly on a Colt in his belt, as he lurked in an alcove near the dock.

Noiselessly the panel slid aside at the touch of a remote electrical button. Two unarmed soldiers stepped through, and a second later, to stand between them at the table – Goering.

He had donned his lavender-coloured Air Marshal's uniform, discarded three months ago, for this occasion. No insignia on it now. There was not even room on the breast of this thinner Goering for the medals he used to wear.

His rarely still face was now almost cheekily composed. He donned the headphones casually as if testing somebody's set, stood at attention. When the words of Lord Justice Lawrence reached him 'The tribunal sentence you', he waved the judge into silence.

By actions he conveyed to the judges that no sound was coming through.

What followed was unforgettable. Goering himself took turns at bending to the plug at floor level to see if there was good contact, always finishing by conveying that the earphones were not working.

Guards who had tested the earpieces and expressed themselves satisfied rushed into the dock. One vaulted a prisoner's seat. Goering handed them the earphones in turn, but although they were satisfied everything was working, he denied it with a faint smile.

They took turns at another pair of earphones, and Goering tested the floor contact again. And after two minutes he agreed all was well.

Lord Justice Lawrence read the sentence again – right up to 'death by hanging'. Goering, the man who ordered the bombing of London, and who now himself had to die, flashed a look of contempt on the court, turned ponderously on his heel and walked through the panel.

The guards maintain that never while they were listening through those two sets of earpieces did they fail to work.

We always knew Goering would take his sentence bravely. Did he prefer bravado?

Two minutes' hush – for each prisoner had to be brought up separately by lift from the prison tunnel – and Hess appeared.

With a savage swing of his arm he knocked down the earphones offered him, and faced the bench with legs far astride and hands clenched before him.

Imprisonment for life. He licked his lips and half goose-stepped out noisily in the boots he wore when he parachuted into Scotland.

Next Ribbentrop, pale and stooping when he appeared, but shaking himself into some sort of composure.

Death by hanging. He sagged, patted into place a bundle of papers that threatened to slide from under his arm, tried to walk out bravely, but drooped again as he reached the panel.

Then Keitel – rigid, erect, soldierly as he entered. A quick turn on his heels and he was out again.

Kaltenbrunner, the Gestapo chief who killed in hundreds of thousands. Tall and impeccable in a new blue suit, with shirt and collar to match, he bowed on entering, bowed acceptance of those words, *'Death by hanging'*, and bowed himself out again. A brave show, but the muscles of that face were twitching and the eyes were haunted by fear.

Of the first five sentences four were death. Murmurs were breaking the silence of the court. Judge Biddle silenced a tittering woman with a glare.

Philosopher Rosenberg, the man who would have had us believe he was nothing more. *Death by hanging.* The small plumpish scholar recoils as if not expecting it, sways slightly and walks out, head bent.

Bald-headed Frank, who wiped out whole villages and is now a convert to Roman Catholicism. 'Thank you' he says to the guards who turn him to face the judges. 'Thank you', to the judge who says: *Death by hanging.* And a final polite 'Thank you' to the men who escorted him through the panel.

Frick, racy in a heavy tweed sports coat. *Death by hanging.* He continues to listen as if expecting more will follow. Guards turn him and he walks out uncomprehendingly.

Jew-baiter Streicher, the pervert whose pornographic library here in Nuremburg has been burned by official order – whose eyes have never left a woman in his ten months in the dock. *Death by hanging.* He flung his earphones on the table with a crash, strutted out in a blaze of temper.

Funk, financial journalist turned fat banker, who stored the gold teeth of murdered millions in his vaults. *Imprisonment for life.* His eyes look slowly along the line of judges and he walks out, shaking his head.

Doenitz. *Ten years.* He walks out, as if still on the quarter deck.

Fellow Admiral Raeder. *Imprisonment for life.* He gulps hard, stands rooted for a full half-minute and droops away.

The most handsome man in the dock – and youngest – von Schirach, who, as leader of the Hitler Youth, taught the youth of Germany Nazism and militarism – *Twenty years' imprisonment.* He pales, strives to whisper a word, and races through the panel.

Sauckel, who always impressed on the Court he was only a working man, but who sent five million people to slave labour in Germany – *Death by hanging.* He makes a whining noise. His every utterance in court has been a whine. He goes out helplessly.

Jodl, the General who ordered soldiers to butcher civilians – *Death by hanging.* He frowns as if a lance-corporal has cheeked him, glares, marches out.

Seyss-Inquart, the Austrian traitor who helped to put Austria under the German heel and then crushed Holland for his German masters – *Death by hanging.* He looks round the court anxiously, as if to see the effect, bows, leaves with swing.

Speer, the genius architect who used slave labour cruelly – *Twenty years' imprisonment.* He screws up his eyes and mumbles as if doing a sum in his head. Then bows, and walks away.

Grey, aristocratic von Neurath, one of the worst oppressors of occupied countries – *Fifteen years.* He puts the earphones down gently like a good butler, and almost tiptoes out.

And now sentence on an empty dock. As missing Martin Bormann is sentenced to death, spectators begin to trek to the doors.

Execution of Nazi War Criminals, Nuremberg, 16 October 1946 KINGSBURY SMITH

The author was the pool representative of the American press.

Hermann Wilhelm Göring cheated the gallows of Allied justice by committing suicide in his prison cell shortly before the ten other condemned Nazi leaders were hanged in Nuremberg gaol. He swallowed cyanide he had concealed in a copper cartridge shell, while lying on a cot in his cell.

The one-time Number Two man in the Nazi hierarchy was dead two hours before he was scheduled to have been dropped through the trapdoor of a gallows erected in a small, brightly lighted gymnasium in the gaol yard, thirty-five yards from the cell block where he spent his last days of ignominy.

Joachim von Ribbentrop, foreign minister in the ill-starred regime of Adolf Hitler, took Göring's place as first to the scaffold.

Last to depart this life in a total span of just about two hours was Arthur Seyss-Inquart, former Gauleiter of Holland and Austria.

In between these two once-powerful leaders, the gallows claimed, in the order named, Field Marshal Wilhelm Keitel; Ernst Kaltenbrunner, once head of the Nazis' security police; Alfred Rosenberg, arch-priest of Nazi culture in foreign lands; Hans Frank, Gauleiter of Poland; Wilhelm Frick, Nazi Minister of the Interior; Fritz Sauckel, boss of slave labour; Colonel General Alfred Jodl; and Julius Streicher, who bossed the anti-Semitism drive of the Hitler Reich.

As they went to the gallows, most of the ten endeavoured to show bravery. Some were defiant and some were resigned and some begged the Almighty for mercy.

All except Rosenberg made brief, last-minute statements on the scaffold. But the only one to make any reference to Hitler or the Nazi ideology in his final moments was Julius Streicher.

Three black-painted wooden scaffolds stood inside the gymnasium, a room approximately thirty-three feet wide by eighty feet long with plaster walls in which cracks showed. The gymnasium had been used only three days before by the American security guards for a basketball game. Two gallows were used alternatively. The third was a spare for use if needed. The men were hanged one at a time, but to get the executions over quickly, the military police would bring in a man while the prisoner who preceded him still was dangling at the end of the rope.

The ten once great men in Hitler's Reich that was to have lasted for a thousand years walked up thirteen wooden steps to a platform eight feet high which also was eight feet square.

Ropes were suspended from a crossbeam supported on two posts. A new one was used for each man.

When the trap was sprung, the victim dropped from sight in the interior of the scaffolding. The bottom of it was boarded up with wood on three sides and shielded by a dark canvas curtain on the fourth, so that no one saw the death struggles of the men dangling with broken necks.

Von Ribbentrop entered the execution chamber at 1.11 a.m. Nuremberg time. He was stopped immediately inside the door by two Army sergeants who closed in on each side of him and held his arms, while another sergeant who had followed him in removed manacles from his hands and replaced them with a leather strap.

It was planned originally to permit the condemned men to walk from their cells to the execution chamber with their hands free, but all were manacled immediately following Göring's suicide.

Von Ribbentrop was able to maintain his apparent stoicism to the last. He walked steadily towards the scaffold between his two guards, but he did not answer at first when an officer standing at the foot of the gallows went through the formality of asking his name. When the query was repeated he almost shouted, 'Joachim von Ribbentrop!' and then mounted the steps without any signs of hesitation.

When he was turned around on the platform to face the witnesses, he seemed to clench his teeth and raise his head with the old arrogance. When asked whether he had any final message he said, 'God protect Germany,' in German, and then added, 'May I say something else?'

The interpreter nodded and the former diplomatic wizard of Nazidom spoke his last words in loud, firm tones: 'My last wish is that Germany realize its entity and that an understanding be reached between the East and the West. I wish peace to the world.'

As the black hood was placed in position on his head, von Ribbentrop looked straight ahead.

Then the hangman adjusted the rope, pulled the lever, and von Ribbentrop slipped away to his fate.

Field Marshal Keitel, who was immediately behind von Ribbentop in the order of executions, was the first military leader to be executed under the new concept of international law – the principle that professional soldiers cannot escape punishment for waging aggressive wars and permitting crimes against humanity with the claim they were dutifully carrying out orders of superiors.

Keitel entered the chamber two minutes after the trap had dropped beneath von Ribbentrop, while the latter still was at the end of his rope. But von Ribbentrop's body was concealed inside the first scaffold; all that could be seen was the taut rope.

Keitel did not appear as tense as von Ribbentrop. He held his head high while his hands were being tied and walked erect towards the gallows with a military bearing. When asked his name he responded loudly and mounted the gallows as he might have mounted a reviewing stand to take a salute from German armies.

He certainly did not appear to need the help of guards who walked alongside, holding his arms. When he turned around atop the platform he looked over the crowd with the iron-jawed haughtiness of a proud Prussian officer. His last words, uttered in a full, clear voice, were translated as 'I call on God Almighty to have mercy on the German people. More than two million German soldiers went to their death for the fatherland before me. I follow now my sons – all for Germany.'

After his black-booted, uniformed body plunged through the trap, witnesses agreed Keitel had showed more courage on the scaffold than in the courtroom, where he had tried to shift his guilt upon the ghost of Hitler, claiming that all was the Führer's fault and that he merely carried out orders and had no responsibility.

With both von Ribbentrop and Keitel hanging at the end of their ropes there was a pause in the proceeding. The American colonel directing the executions asked the American general representing the United States on the Allied Control Commission if those present could smoke. An affirmative answer brought cigarettes into the hands of almost every one of the thirty-odd persons present. Officers and GIs walked around nervously or spoke a few words to one another in hushed voices while Allied correspondents scribbled furiously their notes on this historic though ghastly event.

In a few minutes an American Army doctor accompanied by a Russian Army doctor and both carrying stethoscopes walked to the first scaffold, lifted the curtain and disappeared within.

They emerged at 1.30 a.m. and spoke to an American colonel. The colonel swung around and facing official witnesses snapped to attention to say, 'The man is dead.'

Two GIs quickly appeared with a stretcher which was carried up and lifted into the interior of the scaffold. The hangman mounted the gallows steps, took a large commando-type knife out of a sheath strapped to his side and cut the rope.

Von Ribbentrop's limp body with the black hood still over his head was removed to the far end of the room and placed behind a black canvas curtain. This all had taken less than ten minutes.

The directing colonel turned to the witnesses and said, 'Cigarettes out, please gentlemen.' Another colonel went out the door and over to the condemned block to fetch the next man. This was Ernst Kaltenbrunner. He entered the execution chamber at 1.36 a.m., wearing a sweater beneath his blue double-breasted coat. With his lean haggard face furrowed by old duelling scars, this terrible successor to Reinhard Heydrich had a frightening look as he glanced around the room.

He wet his lips apparently in nervousness as he turned to mount the gallows, but he walked steadily. He answered his name in a calm, low voice. When he turned around on the gallows platform he first faced a United States Army Roman Catholic chaplain wearing a Franciscan habit. When Kaltenbrunner was invited to make a last statement, he said, 'I have loved my German people and my fatherland with a warm heart. I have done my duty by the laws of my people and I am sorry my people were led this time by men who were not soldiers and that crimes were committed of which I had no knowledge.'

This was the man, one of whose agents – a man named Rudolf Hess – confessed at a trial that under Kaltenbrunner's orders he gassed three million human beings at the Auschwitz concentration camp!

As the black hood was raised over his head Kaltenbrunner, still speaking in a low voice, used a German phrase which translated means, 'Germany, good luck.'

His trap was sprung at 1.39 a.m.

Field Marshal Keitel was pronounced dead at 1.44 a.m. and three minutes later guards had removed his body. The scaffold was made ready for Alfred Rosenberg.

Rosenberg was dull and sunken-cheeked as he looked around the court. His complexion was pasty-brown, but he did not appear nervous and walked with a steady step to and up the gallows.

Apart from giving his name and replying 'no' to a question as to whether he had anything to say, he did not utter a word. Despite his avowed atheism he was accompanied by a Protestant chaplain who followed him to the gallows and stood beside him praying.

Rosenberg looked at the chaplain once, expressionless. Ninety seconds after he was swinging from the end of a hangman's rope. His was the swiftest execution of the ten.

There was a brief lull in the proceedings until Kaltenbrunner was pronounced dead at 1.52 a.m.

Hans Frank was next in the parade of death. He was the only one of the condemned to enter the chamber with a smile on his countenance.

Although nervous and swallowing frequently, this man, who was converted to Roman Catholicism after his arrest, gave the appearance of being relieved at the prospect of atoning for his evil deeds.

He answered to his name quietly and when asked for any last statement, he replied in a low voice that was almost a whisper, 'I am thankful for the kind treatment during my captivity and I ask God to accept me with mercy.'

Frank closed his eyes and swallowed as the black hood went over his head.

The sixth man to leave his prison cell and walk with handcuffed wrists to the death house was sixty-nine-year-old Wilhelm Frick. He entered the execution chamber at 2.05 a.m., six minutes after Rosenberg had been pronounced dead. He seemed the least steady of any so far and stumbled on the thirteenth step of the gallows. His only words were, 'Long live eternal Germany,' before he was hooded and dropped through the trap.

Julius Streicher made his melodramatic appearance at 2.12 a.m.

While his manacles were being removed and his hands bound, this ugly, dwarfish little man, wearing a threadbare suit and a well-worn bluish shirt buttoned to the neck but without a tie (he was notorious during his days of power for his flashy dress), glanced at the three wooden scaffolds rising up menacingly in front of him. Then he glared around the room, his eyes resting momentarily upon the small group of witnesses. By this time, his hands were tied securely behind his back. Two guards, one on each arm, directed him to Number One gallows on the left of the entrance. He walked steadily the six feet to the first wooden step but his face was twitching.

As the guards stopped him at the bottom of the steps for identification formality he uttered his piercing scream: 'Heil Hitler!'

The shriek sent a shiver down my back.

As its echo died away an American colonel standing by the steps said sharply, 'Ask the man his name.' In response to the interpreter's query Streicher shouted, 'You know my name well.'

The interpreter repeated his request and the condemned man yelled, 'Julius Streicher.'

As he reached the platform, Streicher cried out, 'Now it goes to God.' He was pushed the last two steps to the mortal spot beneath the hangman's rope. The rope was being held back against a wooden rail by the hangman.

Streicher was swung around to face the witnesses and glared at them. Suddenly he screamed, 'Purim Fest 1946.' (Purim is a Jewish holiday celebrated in the spring, commemorating the execution of Haman, ancient persecutor of the Jews described in the Old Testament.)

The American officer standing at the scaffold said, 'Ask the man if he has any last words.'

When the interpreter had translated, Streicher shouted, 'The Bolsheviks will hang you one day.'

When the black hood was raised over his head, Streicher said, 'I am with God.'

As it was being adjusted, Streicher's muffled voice could be heard to say, 'Adele, my dear wife.'

At that instant the trap opened with a loud bang. He went down kicking. When the rope snapped taut with the body swinging wildly, groans could be heard from within the concealed interior of the scaffold. Finally, the hangman, who had descended from the gallows platform, lifted the black canvas curtain and went inside. Something happened that put a stop to the groans and brought the rope to a standstill. After it was over I was not in a mood to ask what he did, but I assume that he grabbed the swinging body and pulled down on it. We were all of the opinion that Streicher had strangled.

Then, following removal of the corpse of Frick, who had been pronounced dead at 2.20 a.m., Fritz Sauckel was brought face to face with his doom.

Wearing a sweater with no coat and looking wild-eyed, Sauckel proved to be the most defiant of any except Streicher.

Here was the man who put millions into bondage on a scale unknown since the pre-Christmas era. Gazing around the room from the gallows platform he suddenly screamed, 'I am dying innocent. The sentence is wrong. God protect Germany and make Germany great again. Long live Germany! God protect my family.'

The trap was sprung at 2.26 a.m. and, as in the case of Streicher, there was a loud groan from the gallows pit as the noose snapped tightly under the weight of his body.

Ninth in the procession of death was Alfred Jodl. With the black coat-collar of his *Wehrmacht* uniform half turned up at the back as though hurriedly put on, Jodl entered the dismal death house with obvious signs of nervousness. He wet his lips constantly and his features were drawn and haggard as he walked, not nearly so steady as Keitel, up the gallows steps. Yet his voice was calm when he uttered his last six words on earth: 'My greetings to you, my Germany.'

At 2.34 a.m. Jodl plunged into the black hole of the scaffold. He and Sauckel hung together until the latter was pronounced dead six minutes later and removed.

The Czechoslovak-born Seyss-Inquart, whom Hitler had made ruler of Holland and Austria, was the last actor to make his appearance in this unparalleled scene. He entered the chamber at 2.38 a.m., wearing glasses which made his face an easily remembered caricature.

He looked around with noticeable signs of unsteadiness as he limped on his left clubfoot to the gallows. He mounted the steps slowly, with guards helping him.

When he spoke his last words his voice was low but intense. He said, 'I hope that this execution is the last act of the tragedy of the Second World War and that the lesson taken from this world war will be that peace and understanding should exist between peoples. I believe in Germany.'

He dropped to death at 2.45 a.m.

With the bodies of Jodl and Seyss-Inquart still hanging, awaiting formal pronouncement of death, the gymnasium doors opened again and guards entered carrying Göring's body on a stretcher.

He had succeeded in wrecking plans of the Allied Control Council to have him lead the parade of condemned Nazi chieftains to their death. But the council's representatives were determined that Göring at least would take his place as a dead man beneath the shadow of the scaffold.

The guards carrying the stretcher set it down between the first and second gallows. Göring's big bare feet stuck out from under the bottom end of a khaki-coloured United States Army blanket. One blue-silk-clad arm was hanging over the side.

The colonel in charge of the proceedings ordered the blanket removed so that witnesses and Allied correspondents could see for themselves that Göring was definitely dead. The Army did not want any legend to develop that Göring had managed to escape.

As the blanket came off it revealed Göring clad in black silk pyjamas with a blue jacket shirt over them, and this was soaking wet, apparently the result of efforts by prison doctors to revive him.

The face of this twentieth-century freebooting political racketeer was still contorted with the pain of his last agonizing moments and his final gesture of defiance.

They covered him up quickly and this Nazi warlord, who like a character out of the days of the Borgias, had wallowed in blood and beauty, passed behind a canvas curtain into the black pages of history.

Appendix:
Estimated Number of Jews Killed in the Final Solution

Country	Estimated pre-final solution population	Estimated Jewish population annihilated	Per cent
Poland	3,300,000	3,000,000	90
Baltic countries	253,000	228,000	90
Germany/Austria	240,000	210,000	90
Protectorate	90,000	80,000	89
Slovakia	90,000	75,000	83
Greece	70,000	54,000	77
The Netherlands	140,000	105,000	75
Hungary	650,000	450,000	70
SSR White Russia	375,000	245,000	65
SSR Ukraine*	1,500,000	900,000	60
Yugoslavia	43,000	26,000	60
Belgium	65,000	40,000	60
Rumania	600,000	300,000	50
Norway	1,800	900	50
France	350,000	90,000	26
Bulgaria	64,000	14,000	22
Italy	40,000	8,000	20
Luxembourg	5,000	1,000	20

Russia (RSFSR)*	975,000	107,000	11
Finland	2,000	— —	— —
Denmark	8,000	— —	— —
TOTAL	8,861,800	5,933,900	67

* The Germans did not occupy all the territory of this republic.

BIBLIOGRAPHY

Anatoli, A., *Babi Yar* (Farrar, Straus & Giroux, 1970).

Anonymous, *Holocaust Historical Documents*, n.d.

Abraham-Podietz, Eva and Anne Fox, *Ten Thousand Children: True Stories Told by Children Who Escaped the Holocaust on the Kindertransport* (Behrman House, 1998).

Arendt, Hannah, *The Origins of Totalitarianism* (George Allen & Unwin, 1958).

Berr, Hélène, *Journal* (MacLehose/Quercus, 2008).

Browning, Christopher R., *The Path to Genocide: Essays on Launching the Final Solution* (Cambridge University Press, 1995).

Bullock, Alan, *Hitler: A Study in Tyranny* (Penguin, 1962).

Cowles, Virginia, *Looking For Trouble* (Harper, 1941).

Dafni, Reuven and Yehudit Kleiman (eds), *Final Letters from the YadVashem Archive* (YadVashem, 1991).

Dawidowicz, Lucy S., *The War Against the Jews* (Penguin, 1977).

_____ (ed.), *A Holocaust Reader* (Behrman House, 1976).

Dwork, D., *Children with a Star: Jewish Youth in Nazi Europe* (1991).

Edelheit, A. J. and H. Edelheit, *History of the Holocaust : A Handbook and Dictionary* (Westview Press, 1994).

Eisenbach, Artur, *Operation Reinhard: Mass Extermination of the Jewish Population in Poland* (Instytut Zachodni, 1962).

Fest, Joachim C., *The Face of the Third Reich: Portraits of the Nazi Leadership* (Pantheon, 1970).

Frank, Anne, *Anne Frank: The Diary of a Young Girl*, Otto H. Frank and Mirjam Pressler (eds) (Penguin, 1998).

Gilbert, Martin, *The Holocaust: The Jewish Tragedy* (HarperCollins, 1987).

_____, *The Boys* (Weidenfeld & Nicolson, 1996).

_____, *The Righteous* (Doubleday, 2002).

_____, *Kristallnacht: Prelude to Destruction* (HarperCollins, 2006).

Goldhagen, Daniel Jonathan, *Hitler's Willing Executioners: Ordinary Germans and the Holocaust* (Little, Brown & Company, 1996).

Grynberg, Michal (ed.), *Words to Outlive Us* (Metropolitan Books, 2002).

Harris, Mark Jonathan and Deborah Oppenheimer, *Into the Arms of Strangers: Stories of the Kindertransport* (Bloomsbury, 2000).

Hilberg, Raul, *The Destruction of the European Jews* (Holmes and Meier, 1966).

Hitler, Adolf, *Mein Kampf* (Houghton Mifflin, 1943).

Hoess, Rudolf and Constantine Fitzgibbon, *Commandant of Auschwitz* (Weidenfeld & Nicolson, 1959).

International Military Tribunal, *Trial of the Major War Criminals Before the International Military Tribunal: Official Text*, 42 vols, Nuremberg, 1947–9.

Kershaw, Alex, *To Save a People* (2010).

Kershaw, Ian, *Hitler, the Germans and the Final Solution* (Yale, 2008).

Kinnaird, Clark (ed.), *It Happened in 1946* (Duell, Sloan and Pearce, 1947).

Klemperer, Victor, *I Will Bear Witness 1933–1941: A Diary of the War Years* (Weidenfeld & Nicolson, 1998).

Kluger, Ruth, *Landscapes of Memory* (Bloomsbury, 2004).

Landau, Felix, *Love Letters of a Nazi Murderer in Lemberg and Drohobycz* (Yad Vashem, 1987).

Langbein, H., *Against All Hope: Resistance in the Nazi Concentration Camps, 1938–1945* (Constable, 1994).

Laquer, W., *The Holocaust Encyclopedia* (Yale University Press, 2001).

Levi, Primo, *Survival in Auschwitz* (Scribner, 1959).

Lifton, Robert J., *The Nazi Doctors: Medical Killing and the Psychology of Genocide* (Basic Books 1988).

Mendelsohn, John (ed.), *The Holocaust: Selected Documents in Eighteen Volumes* (Garland Publishing Co., 1982).

Milton, Edith, *The Tiger in the Attic: Memories of the Kindertransport and Growing Up English* (University of Chicago Press, 2005).

Müller, Filip, *Eyewitness Auschwitz* (Routledge & Kegan Paul, 1979).

Nyiszli, Miklos, *Auschwitz: A Doctor's Eyewitness Account* (Little, Brown, 1993).

Read, Anthony and David Fisher, *Kristallnacht: The Nazi Night of Terror* (Michael Joseph, 1989).

Rees, Laurence, *Auschwitz: The Nazis and the 'Final Solution'* (BBC Books, 2005).

Robinson, Jacob, *The Holocaust and After: Sources and Literature in English* (Israel Universities Press, 1973).

Schellenberg, Walter, *The Schellenberg Memoirs* (Andre Deutsch, 1956).

Sereny, Gitta, *Into that Darkness: From Mercy Killing to Mass Murder* (Andre Deutsch, 1991).

Sierakowiak, Dawid, edited by Alan Adelson, *The Diary of Dawid Sierakowiak* (Oxford University Press, 1996).

Smith, Lyn, *Forgotten Voices of the Holocaust* (Ebury Press, 2005).

BIBLIOGRAPHY

Smith, Michael, *Foley: The Spy Who Saved 10,000 Jews* (Hodder & Stoughton, 1999).

Tedeschi, Giuliana, *There is a Place on Earth* (Lime Tree, 1993).

Thalmann, Rita and Emmanuel Feinermann, *Crystal Night* (Thames & Hudson, 1974).

Turner, Barry, *... And the Policeman Smiled: 10,000 Children Escape from Nazi Europe* (Bloomsbury, 1990).

Von Hassell, Ulrich, *The Von Hassell Diaries* (Hamish Hamilton, 1948).

Weidenfeld, George, *Remembering My Good Friends* (HarperCollins, 1994).

Wiesel, Elie, *Night* (MacGibbon and Kee, 1960).

Zsolt, Béla, *Nine Suitcases* (Pimlico, 2005).

SOURCES AND ACKNOWLEDGEMENTS

In order to reprint material in this volume the editor has made every reasonable effort to secure permission from relevant copyright holders. Any errors or omissions should be notified to him c/o Constable & Robinson.

Anonymous, 'Expulsion of Polish Jews from Germany', reprinted from the *Guardian*, 31 October 1938. Copyright © 1938 Guardian Media

Anonymous, 'Kindertransport: A Girl Arrives in Britain', reprinted from Milton, *The Tiger in the Attic*. Copyright © 2005 Edith Milton/University of Chicago Press

Anonymous, 'Kristallnacht: A Planned Action', The Wiener Library (http://wienerlibrary.co.uk)

Anonymous, 'Kristallnacht: A Jew is Taken to Oranienburg Concentration Camp', The Wiener Library (http://wienerlibrary.co.uk)

Anonymous, 'Life Inside the Warsaw Ghetto', reprinted from Grynberg (ed.), *Words to Outlive Us*. Copyright © 1998 and 1993 Panstowe Wysawnictwo Naukowe. Translation copyright © 2002 Metropolitan Books

Anonymous, 'Song of the Bialystok Ghetto', reprinted from Dawidowicz (ed.), *A Holocaust Reader*

Anonymous, 'Tell our brothers we went to our death in full consciousness and with pride', quoted in Gilbert, *The Holocaust*

Anonymous, 'There are still Jews!', quoted in Gilbert, *The Holocaust*

Szlamek Bajler, 'I tried to get closer to the corpses', quoted in Gilbert, *The Holocaust*

Aharon Beilin, 'Portrait of a Muselmann', quoted in Gilbert, *The Holocaust*

Anna Bergman, 'A Performance of Verdi's *Requiem*', Imperial War Museum Sound Archive

Hélène Berr, 'To Wear the Yellow Star or Not?', reprinted from Berr, *Journal*, Quercus, 2008. Translation © Quercus 2008

SOURCES AND ACKNOWLEDGEMENTS

Leo Bretholz, 'Escape From a Train Bound for the Camps', quoted in Gilbert, *The Holocaust*

Franz Blaha, 'Medical Experiments at Dachau', reprinted from the International Military Tribunal 1974-9, *Trial of the Major War Criminals: Official Text*

David H. Buffum, 'Kristallnacht: The Confidential Report of the American Consul in Leipzig', reprinted from Thalmann and Feinermann, *Crystal Night*. Translation © 1974 Thames & Hudson

Virginia Cowles, 'Hitler Speaks', reprinted from *Looking for Trouble*, Hamish Hamilton, 1942. Copyright © 1942 Virginia Cowles

D. Sefton Delmer, 'The Reichstag is Set Alight', *Daily Express*, 27 February 1933

Zdenka Ehrlich, 'The Angel of Death: Dr Mengele on the Ramp at Auschwitz', quoted in Smith, *Forgotten Voices of the Holocaust*

Adolf Eichmann, 'Minutes of the Wannsee Conference', reprinted from Mendelsohn (ed.), *The Holocaust*, vol. 11

Michael Etkind, 'People were being hanged for nothing', quoted in Smith, *Forgotten Voices of the Holocaust*

Maurice Fagence, 'Sentence Day in the Great Trial at Nuremberg', *Daily Herald*, 2 October 1946

John Fink, 'The Death March from Auschwitz', Imperial War Museum Sound Archive

The Führer (Adolf Hitler) et al., 'Law for the Protection of German Blood and Honour', from Dawidowicz (ed.), *A Holocaust Reader*

_____, 'First Decree to the Reich Citizenship Law', ibid.

Anne Frank, 'Diary of a Dutch Girl in Hiding', from Frank and Pressler (eds), *Anne Frank: The Diary of a Young Girl*. Copyright © The Anne Frank-Fonds, Basle, 1991. English translation copyright © Doubleday, 1995

August Frank, 'Spectacles and eyeglasses of every kind ...', reprinted from *Holocaust Historical Documents*, n.d.

Lukianovska Friedhof, 'It is impossible to live with this knowledge', reprinted from http://www.holocaustresearchproject.org/einsatz/babiyar.html

Kurt Gerstein, 'Like basalt pillars the dead stand inside...', http://www.deathcamps.org/belzec/gerstein.html

Gisa, Kristallnacht: 'everything devastated and destroyed', The Wiener Library (http://wienerlibrary.co.uk)

P. Gordon Walker, 'A BBC Reporter Visits Belsen', http://www.bbc.co.uk/archive/holocaust

Hermann Graebe, 'SS Execution Squad in Action', reprinted from witness statement, November 1945, International Military Tribunal, document PS-2992

Hugo Gryn, 'Arrival at Auschwitz', Imperial War Museum Sound Archive, quoted in Smith, *Forgotten Voices of the Holocaust*

Berta Grynszpan, 'A Postcard from Zbąszyń', reprinted from Thalmann and Feinermann, *Crystal Night*. Translation copyright © 1974 Thames & Hudson

Guardian Correspondent, 'Kristallnacht: Shopwreckers in Berlin', the *Guardian*, 10 November 1938. Copyright © Guardian Media 1938

Sebastian Haffner, 'The Brown Shirts Throw Out Jewish Judges', reprinted from Haffner, *Defying Hitler*, Weidenfeld & Nicolson, 2002. Copyright © 2000 Sarah Haffner and Oliver Pretzel. Copyright © 2000 Deutsche Verlags-Anstalt GmbH. Translation copyright © 2002 Oliver Pretzel

Abel J. Herzberg, 'A Day in the Life of a Prisoner' and 'Deaths, deaths, deaths', reprinted from Herzberg, *Between Two Streams*, IB Tauris, 1997. Copyright © 1989 Estate of Abel J. Herzberg

Reinhard Heydrich, 'All Necessary Measures', reprinted from Dawidowicz (ed.), *A Holocaust Reader*

Heinrich Himmler, 'A page of glory never mentioned and never to be mentioned', reprinted from http://www.holocaust-history.org/himmler-poznan/speech-text.shtmland *Holocaust Historical Documents*, n.d.

Hermann Hoefle, 'The Hoefle Telegram', reprinted from *Holocaust Historical Documents*, n.d.

Rudolf Hoess, 'A Konzentrationslager is Built at Oświęcim', 'The Commandant of Auschwitzis Ordered to Construct a Mass Extermination Facility' and 'The Gas Trial' reprinted from Hoess and Fitzgibbon, *Commandant of Auschwitz*. Copyright © 1951 WysawnictwoPrawnicze. English translation copyright © 1959 Weidenfeld& Nicolson

Karl Jager, 'Field Report', http://www.jewishvirtuallibrary.org/jsource/Holocaust/jager.html

Jewish Combat Organization, 'For Your Freedom and Ours', reprinted from Dawidowicz (ed.), *A Holocaust Reader*

Jewish Society for Social Welfare, 'Life Inside the Warsaw Ghetto', III, reprinted from Dawidowicz (ed.), *A Holocaust Reader*

Raya Kagan, 'Mala Zimetbaum', *The Eichmann Trial Transcripts*, http://www.nizkor.org/hweb/people/e/eichmann-adolf/transcripts/

Fritz Katzmann, 'The Jews tried to avoid evacuation by all possible means', http://www1.yadvashem.org/about_holocaust/documents/part2/doc159.html

Gerda Weissman Klein, 'Liberation: A Jewess Meets a GI', http://www.ushmm.org/museum/exhibit/online/phistories/phi_individuals_kurt_gerda_klein_uu.htm

Ruth Kluger, 'A Jewish Girl Risks a Visit to the Cinema' and 'Theresienstadt: The Children's Quarters', reprinted from Kluger, *Landscapes of Memory*. Copyright © 2001 Ruth Kluger

Felix Landau, 'Diary of an SS Executioner', reprinted from Landau, *Love Letters of a Nazi Murderer in Lemberg and Drohobycz*, Inst. of Documentation in Israel for the Investigation of Nazi War Crimes, 1987

Primo Levi, 'The Great Selection in Auschwitz', reprinted from Levi, *Survival in Auschwitz*. Copyright © 2007 Primo Levi

Filip Müller, 'Inside the Crematorium at Auschwitz', reprinted from Müller, *Eyewitness Auschwitz*. Copyright © Filip Müller. Translation copyright © Routledge and Kegan Paul Ltd

Miklos Nyiszli, 'A Girl Is Found Alive in the Gas-chamber', reprinted from Nyiszli, *Auschwitz: A Doctor's Eyewitness Account*, Seaver, 1986

Peretz Opocznski, 'Smuggling in the Warsaw Ghetto', reprinted from Dawidowicz (ed.), *A Holocaust Reader*

Chaim Prinzenthal, 'On the Run', reprinted from Dafni and Kleiman (eds), *Final Letters from the Yad Vashem Archive*, Weidenfeld & Nicolson, 1991. Copyright © 1991 Weidenfeld & Nicolson

Dina Pronicheva, 'Escape from BabiYar', reprinted from A. Anatoli (Kuznetsov), *Babi Yar*, Farrar Straus Giroux, 1970

Otto Rasch, 'Operational Situation Report from Einsatzgruppe C', reprinted from Dawidowicz (ed.), *A Holocaust Reader*

Rudolf Reder, 'Now you're going to the bath house', quoted in Gilbert, *The Holocaust*

Reuters Correspondent, 'Kristallnacht: Synagogues Fired', *Guardian*, 11 November 1938. Copyright © 1938 Guardian Media

John Richards, 'Kindertransport: 'A Boy Leaves Vienna', Imperial War Museum Sound Archive, quoted in Smith, *Forgotten Voices of the Holocaust*

Charles Salt, 'The Arrest of Irma Grese', Imperial War Museum Sound Archive

Ryvka Salt, 'Parents Ordered to Give Up Their Children', Imperial War Museum Sound Archive

Moshe Shklarek, 'Deportation, Plock', quoted in Gilbert, *Holocaust*

Dawid Sierakowiak, 'Mass Arrests in Łódź', reprinted from *The Diary of Dawid Sierakowiak*, trans. Kamil Turowski. Copyright © 1998 Oxford University Press

John Silberman, 'It was bullying all down the line' and 'A Boy Leaves Berlin', Imperial War Museum Sound Archive

Leah Hammerstein Silverstein, 'Pretending to be Aryan', reprinted from http://www.ushmm.org/museum/exhibit/online/phistories/

Kingsbury Smith, 'Execution of Nazi War Criminals', reprinted from Kinnaird (ed.), *It Happened in 1946*

Jurgen Stroop, 'The Destruction of the Warsaw Ghetto', reprinted from Dawidowicz (ed.), *A Holocaust Reader*

Giuliana Tedeschi, 'Punishment … and Kindness' and 'The Death March from Auschwitz', II, reprinted from Tedeschi, *There Is a Place on Earth*. Copyright © 1992 Random House Inc.

Rudolf Vrba and Alfred Wetzler, 'Auschwitz Observed', reprinted from Dawidowicz (ed.), *A Holocaust Reader*

David Wdowinski, 'They [three German officers]', reprinted from Gilbert, *The Holocaust*

George Weidenfeld, 'Litigious politics entered the classroom' and 'Departure: A Young Student Leaves Vienna', from Weidenfeld, *Remembering My Good Friends*. Copyright © 1995 George Weidenfeld. Reprinted by permission of HarperCollins

Rabbi Wilde, 'A Rabbi is Incarcerated in Buchenwald', reprinted from Thalmann and Feinermann, *Crystal Night*. Translation copyright © 1974 Thames and Hudson

Elie Wiesel, 'Train Journey to Auschwitz' and 'The Liberation of Buchenwald: The Prisoner's View', reprinted from Wiesel, *Night*. Copyright © 1958 Elie Wiesel

Andrzej Wojcik, 'The cries and screams of the children could be heard', http://www.deathcamps.org/occupation/krepiec.html

Karl Wolff, 'Himmler Watches a Demonstration Shooting of Jews', quoted in Gilbert, *The Holocaust*

Franciszek Zabecki, 'The Deputy Commandant Kicks a Baby to Death', quoted in Gilbert, *The Holocaust*

Natan Zelichower, 'Life Inside the Warsaw Ghetto', II, reprinted from Grynberg (ed.), *Words to Outlive Us*. Copyright © 1998 and 1993 Panstowe Wysawnictwo Naukowe. Translation copyright © 2002 Metropolitan Books

Josef Zelkowicz, 'Blood flows in the streets', reprinted from Davidowicz, *A Holocaust Reader*

Samuel Zylbersztejn, 'The Warsaw Ghetto Uprising', reprinted from Grynberg, *Words to Outlive Us*. Translation copyright © 2002 Metropolitan Books

INDEX